Words for the Wild

The Sierra Club Totebooks®

Words for the Wild

The Sierra Club Trailside Reader

edited by
Ann Ronald

Sierra Club Books
San Francisco

The Sierra Club, founded in 1892 by John Muir, has devoted itself to the study and protection of the earth's scenic and ecological resources—mountains, wetlands, woodlands, wild shores and rivers, deserts and plains. The publishing program of the Sierra Club offers books to the public as a nonprofit educational service in the hope that they may enlarge the public's understanding of the club's basic concerns. The point of view expressed in each book, however, does not necessarily represent that of the club. The Sierra Club has some sixty chapters coast to coast, in Canada, Hawaii, and Alaska. For information about how you may participate in its program to preserve wilderness and the quality of life, please address inquiries to Sierra Club, 730 Polk Street, San Francisco, CA 94109.

Copyright © 1987 by Ann Ronald

Library of Congress Cataloging-in-Publication Data

Ronald, Ann, 1939–
    Words for the wild.

    (A Sierra Club totebook)
    Bibliography: p. 359
    1. Nature. I. Sierra Club. II. Title. III. Series.
QH81.R734   1987   508.7   86–22097
ISBN 0-87156-709-1

Cover design by Bonnie Smetts

Cover photo by Willard Clay

Book design by Nancy Warner

Printed in the United States of America

10 9 8 7 6 5 4 3 2 1

Special thanks to all my hiking friends, past and present; this book is for you.

Contents

PART III

More Recent Sojourners
in the Natural World...161

Introduction

I can't imagine going backpacking without a book along for company. Even a day hike seems happier with something to read close at hand. I must confess, in fact, that often I characterize a trip by the book I happened to be carrying at the time. Sometimes the accompanying volume was just right; other combinations were downright laughable. My short-lived "intellectual phase" was one such fiasco, two somewhat unpleasant weeks of August wind and snow in Wyoming's Wind River Range, highlighted by Nietzsche's *Thus Spake Zarathustra*. Not only were the contents inappropriate, but I had to spend so much time cowering in my tent that I read every page at least three times. I might add, though, that I remember both the book and the hike very well.

I guess I've always been a compulsive reader. Without a book in the wilderness, I know I would find myself scanning the washing instructions inside my clothes or lingering over the cooking directions on my food packets. My tastes are uncategorizable, a wholly eclectic mixture of nonfiction, fiction, and poetry. As a matter of fact, I can't even predict my choice in advance (although I can affirm that Nietzsche is no longer on my list). Often I'll drive to the trailhead with half a dozen options in the car, then make a whimsical last-minute decision. Last summer I spent the day before a ten-day trek sprawled beside a stream, reading the first three chapters of each of four novels. The result? *The White Clouds of Idaho* punctuated by seven hundred and fifty pages of Mormon polygamy. But that turned out to be a wonderful selection, a bit too heavy in the backpack but just right for all the hours I had to spend while the fisherman hooked the perfect trout.

My overweight novel is just one of the many delights I've toted with me over the years. I'm a sucker for any kind of historical fiction, the longer the better, although I've discovered that white knights and damsels in distress are out of place in a wilderness setting. (Rugged cowboys and damsels in distress are much more apropos.) Three times I've tried biographies, but I don't remember getting to the end of any of the lives. While poetry books have served me a little better, like the slim edition of modern poets I took cross country around Mount Robson in British Columbia or the thicker volume I hauled for miles along the old Cascade Crest Trail, even poems haven't been entirely satisfactory. The real joy, indeed, has been the kind of reading found here in *Words for the Wild.*

Every time I've carried a book of essays about the natural world, the trip has been a good one. Maybe that's just luck, but more likely it's because I try to match the author to the locale. Mary Austin's *Land of Little Rain* went with me on a desert climb in Nevada. In my pack, the first time I wandered down a slickrock canyon, was Edward Abbey's *Desert Solitaire;* later Arizona trips have been highlighted by Joseph Wood Krutch's *Voice of the Desert* and Colin Fletcher's *Man Who Walked Through Time.* Nearly a decade ago, Annie Dillard's *Pilgrim at Tinker Creek* kept me company beside a series of trout streams and lakes in the high

Sierras. And I remember reading John Muir's ascent of Ritter while camped by Lake Ediza at that mountain's very base. Just as he made the climb in the late fall, with winter snows threatening, so I hiked into Ediza one October weekend, when a brush of white already touched the shady places and ice thinly appeared along the shore.

Sometimes, though, I wanted more essays than my pack would carry. Holding John Muir's *Mountains of California*, I would think of his contemporaries who described the same scenes—Joseph LeConte in Tuolumne Meadows or Clarence King near Mount Whitney—and I would imagine the fun of comparing their views to Muir's. Or, sunning beside a stagnant desert pool, I would daydream about checking David Muench's photographs and Edward Abbey's words against the tiny barrel cactus growing near my hand. But *Desert Images*, Muench and Abbey's priceless look at the Southwest, is a hardcover book that must weigh at least two or three pounds. Not even the most masochistic hiker wants to carry a knapsack filled with paperbacks or hardcover picture books.

The solution? I couldn't find one. Although two or three collections of American nature writing do exist, they are anthologies designed for the college classroom, not for the mountain meadow. One is too heavy, another too stuffy. Moreover, a textbook focus doesn't suit me when I'm sprawled in the shade on a lazy afternoon. History, science, politics—each sounds a slightly discordant note when juxtaposed with the trill of a meadowlark or a pika's sharp whistle. Instead, I want my wilderness music played against words that, more than anything else, emphasize the beauties of the natural scene. This is not to say that I disdain history or science or politics (witness my youthful enthusiasm for Nietzsche or the way I earn my living), but rather that out-of-doors I like essays to echo my spiritual needs. Because I'm basically a romantic at heart, I want to share fresh visual descriptions of the wilderness, and I want to share some deep-felt rejuvenation. In short, I want *Words for the Wild*.

Some words of Joseph Wood Krutch define more precisely the viewpoint of what I like best. On the first page of a collection of his own best nature essays, Krutch indicates what he believes is the proper subject for nature writing—"an account of the writer's *experience with* the natural world." The italics are Krutch's own, and they underscore the importance he places on the sound of a human voice interacting with the surrounding environment. Nature writing is neither scientific writing, where knowledge about natural phenomena is key and cold objectivity is symptomatic, nor is it polemical, so that arguments and arm-twisting become its essence. Rather, nature writing is just what Krutch says, the narration and description of a writer's firsthand experience in the environment. The most effective pieces, I think, are those in which an author speaks directly to a reader about a landscape that is important to him.

John Burroughs would have agreed, for despite his scientific proclivities, he insisted on an emotional relationship with the environment as well. "The literary naturalist does not take liberties with facts, facts are the flora upon which he lives. . . . I can do nothing without them," he avowed, "but *I must give them my own flavor*" (italics mine). Then he added, "To interpret nature is not to improve upon her: it is to draw her out; it is to have an emotional intercourse with her, absorb her, and reproduce her tinged with the colors of the spirit"—the spirit, that is, of the individual author.

Perhaps my favorite John Muir passage, although any one of a hundred such paragraphs would do as well, exemplifies how an author reproduces nature "tinged with the colors of the spirit." In this particular excerpt, Muir offers a unique perspective on Yosemite Falls. While it's not a view I would choose for myself, the experience is exactly the kind I enjoy secondhand. "I was eager to reach the extreme verge" of the falls, Muir begins, "to see how it behaved in flying so far through the air." He warns, though, that "after enjoying this view and getting safely away I have never advised anyone to follow my steps." Yet, as readers, we can do just that. Cautious, exhilarated, we can inch out over the precipice and peer vicariously with Muir into the depths below.

The last incline down which the stream journeys so gracefully is so steep and smooth one must slip cautiously forward on hands and feet alongside the rushing water, which so near one's head is very exciting. But to gain a perfect view one must go yet farther, over a curving brow to a slight shelf on the extreme brink. This shelf, formed by the flaking off of a fold of granite, is about three inches wide, just wide enough for a safe rest for one's heels. To me it seemed nerve-trying to slip to this narrow foothold and poise on the edge of such a precipice so close to the whirl of the waters; and after casting long glances over the shining brow of the fall and listening to its sublime psalm, I concluded not to attempt to go nearer, but, nevertheless, against reasonable judgment, I did. Noticing some tufts of artemisia in a cleft of rock, I filled my mouth with the leaves, hoping their bitter taste might help to keep caution keen and prevent giddiness. In spite of myself I reached the little ledge, got my heels well set, and worked sidewise twenty or thirty feet to a point close to the out-plunging current. Here the view is perfectly free down into the heart of the bright irised throng of comet-like streamers into which the whole ponderous volume of the fall separates, two or

three hundred feet below the brow. So glorious a display
of pure wildness, acting at close range while cut off from
all the world beside, is terribly impressive.

Since today's Park Service would take a dim view of anyone crawling to the edge of Yosemite Falls, the only viable
way to share Muir's adventure is to read his nature essay about
the experience. Closing my eyes, I can sense my toes tightening
in my boots, can taste the acrid artemisia, can feel the mist
dampening my hair. I can also appreciate Muir's caution
thrown to the winds of the falls, for his stuttering syntax
exactly echoes his state of mind (and mine)—deciding "not
to go nearer, but, nevertheless, against reasonable judgment," doing just that. Once I actually mustered the courage
to imitate Muir's recklessness in miniature. Although my
Sierra waterfall was only twenty feet high and my narrow
ledge perhaps two feet wide, Muir's inspiration made me feel
as though I were braving a torrential cascade. The mist
dampening my hair was real, the toe-tightening produced a
genuinely cramped foot. I even saw "comet-like streamers"
—brief ones, to be sure, but "bright irised" nonetheless—
dancing below my perch. In that precipitous moment above
my Piute Creek whitewater, an author's words—"so glorious
a display of pure wildness"—came to life for me.

This is what nature writing, to my way of thinking, is
all about. *Words for the Wild* take me places I might not
otherwise visit, or they introduce me to new friends. Sometimes they join me with old ones, or they show me new per-
spectives of things I've seen a dozen times. On occasion, they
even send me in directions I would not have dared before,
challenging me to attempt the inconceivable or persuading
me to try the impossible. More often, though, they just tan-
talize my brain. But whatever they do, they suggest new ways

of thinking about and responding to the world in which I live.

Words for the Wild is an eclectic compilation. No two pieces are exactly the same, for no two authors experience any environment in like fashion. This particular collection reflects the enthusiasms of more than a century of readers along with my own somewhat catholic tastes. These are essays that have been loved and respected in the past, that should be admired now and in the future as well—a blend of philosophic contemplations, naturalistic descriptions, environmental pleas, idealistic speculations, and downright feisty arguments. There ought to be ingredients here to suit everyone who cares about the natural world.

Some readers, of course, may complain about editorial license. While I admit that the contents of *Words for the Wild* could be a little skewed, I insist that the distortion was done with the best of intentions. Because I'm a college professor, I chose contemplation over adventure. Because I'm a westerner, I preferred landscapes that lie beyond the hundredth meridian. Because I live in a desert environment near the Sierras, I naturally read more desert and Sierra essays than pieces about the Everglades and Adirondacks. Because I care about conservation and preservation, I especially honored any writer who respects the land. Any time, any place will do—but I acknowledge the fact that certain times and places interest me more than others. Nonetheless, I think most readers will find themselves just as intrigued by the Muirs and McPhees, by the Birds and Broomes, by the somewhat random range of authors whose prose found a way onto my bookshelves first, and then into these pages.

This Totebook should be read under a tree somewhere, or in the midst of a field of gentians, or beside a big red rock.

Even as I write these words, my mind ranges back to locales where I wish I'd carried such a book along. I see a mountain meadow tinged with tiny lavender flowers, a gray-white glacier hanging against the skyline, a flock of British Columbia mosquitos jabbing at my Cutters-covered jeans, a damp drizzle permeating my clothes. Romance and realism together—I see a place where *Words for the Wild* would have suited me fine.

PART 1
The Nineteenth-Century Transcendentalists

My favorite definition of transcendentalism is a single word: *incomprehensibilityosityivityalityationment-nessism*. Succinctly, it captures the essence of an almost un-definable movement that intrigued New Englanders during the mid-nineteenth century and that continues to influence nature essayists today. More than any other *ism* of American intellectual thought, this one has wended its abstract way out of the college classroom and into the pathless wilderness.

A concise definition cannot be set down in twenty-five words or less. "I should have told them at once that I was a transcendentalist," Thoreau noted in 1853. "That would have been the shortest way of telling them that they would not understand my explanations." But I believe a set of characteristically transcendental elements can be isolated, elements that can be found again and again in essays written fifty, a hundred, a hundred and fifty years after the actual movement abstracted itself out of literary fashion.

Basically, transcendentalism is a mode of perception. Its first literary proponent was Ralph Waldo Emerson, who perceived a oneness in man, nature, and God that transcended the individual nature of each separate part. He reached that conclusion through intuition, a heightened awareness that reached beyond mere understanding and transported his thoughts to a loftier plateau of pure reason. While gazing at a star, for example, Emerson could intuitively comprehend man's relation to the universe, to all the elements within it, and to God. The same instantaneous epiphany might occur when he strolled across a field, or when he eyed a single flower, or whenever anyone took the time to see (both literally and figuratively).

Thoreau understood his friend's ideas as well as anyone could. He agreed that something happened to man's perceptions when he took the time to be close to nature, and he realized that to express those heightened observations in clear, insightful prose ought to be his life's work, too. Inspired by Emerson's 1836 piece, *Nature*, Thoreau began spending more days away from the cities and towns, more hours with a pencil in his hand. The resulting essays, one of which is excerpted in these pages, are more nearly like what we read in the twentieth century, with their romanticized descriptions of treks into the wilderness. By contrast, the words of his mentor sound the colder and more neoclassic tones of an earlier age.

Substantively, of course, both men are meditating about man's relationship with his spiritual and physical environment, yet there is a difference in where that process begins. For Emerson, the focus of his perceptions is man himself, while for Thoreau the center is always nature. That is, Thoreau keeps his eye on the world before him, on the owls, the squirrels, the rocks, the water, the ice. He touches them, too. Then, after describing what he has touched and seen, he generalizes about the greater implications. In contrast, Emerson more often reverses the procedure, using deductive rather than inductive logic.

When Emerson discusses beauty, for example, he begins by broadly asserting that "the simple perception of natural forms is a delight." Then he specifies, "To the body and mind which have been cramped by noxious work or company, nature is medicinal and restores their tone. The tradesman, the attorney comes out of the din and craft of the street and sees the sky and the woods, and is a man again. In their eternal calm, he finds himself." Even Emerson's details sound abstract. "I see the spectacle of morning from the hilltop over against my house, from daybreak to sunrise, with emotions which an angel might share," he observes. "I seem to partake its rapid transformations; the active enchantment reaches my dust, and I dilate and conspire with the morning wind."

Meanwhile, Thoreau is getting dust in his nostrils, rubbing his hands in the dirt before he extrapolates from his experiences. At Walden Pond he not only builds his own cabin, but he plants his own beanfield, bakes his own bread, and catches his own fish. A description of night-fishing, "anchored in forty feet of water, and twenty or thirty rods from the shore, surrounded sometimes by thousands of small perch and shiners, dimpling the surface with their tails in the moonlight," shows exactly how Thoreau's body and his mind function quite unlike Emerson's. "Serenaded by owls and foxes," he sits quietly, "communicating by a long flaxen line with mysterious nocturnal fishes which had their dwelling forty feet below, or sometimes dragging sixty feet of line about the pond as I drifted in the gentle night breeze."

Animal sounds, measured distances, and a real edible fish

then lead to transcendence. "At length you slowly raise, pulling hand over hand, some horned pout squeaking and squirming to the upper air." Thoreau reels the reader in as well. "It was very queer, especially in dark nights, when your thoughts had wandered to vast and cosmogonal themes in other spheres, to feel this faint jerk, which came to interrupt your dreams and line you to Nature again. It seemed as if I might cast my line upward into the air, as well as downward into this element which was scarcely more dense. Thus I caught two fishes as it were with one hook." And Thoreau's hand physically pulls in what Emerson's eye only envisions metaphorically.

Despite their cognitive and physical differences, though, the two authors' thoughts show some striking similarities. For one thing, each adopted a strong narrative voice, a solitary persona who guides the reader on walks and explorations even as he disclaims the need for any other human company. For another, each reveals a remarkable need to lecture. Emerson sermonizes more about man and god and philosophical abstractions, while Thoreau spends more time ruminating about his direct observations of nature itself, but each takes every opportunity to inform the reader of the metaphysical education available through the natural world. And each does so by means of a conversational tone that invites the reader to join with the author's meditative process.

More significantly, the two essayists rely heavily on analogies to express their thoughts. Each saw correspondences in all living things and in God, too. While most twentieth-century thinkers would scoff at Emerson's statement that the structure of the universe is echoed in the shape of a drop of water, they would probably agree that his notion of symbolic correspondences makes good sense. So, from Emerson's argument that the design of every living thing is repeated in the design of every other living thing, Thoreau was able to arrive at a series of profound metaphors about man's intellectual and emotional correspondences with the natural world. Sounding the depths of Walden Pond, then, becomes a process of plumbing the depths of the writer's own soul. And watching the tiny lake's ice break up when winter turns to spring becomes analogous with Thoreau's own artistic fruition after a year spent with the seasons.

Many of these characteristics of Emerson and Thoreau's transcendentalism—the trust in organic form, the notion of correspondences between elements of the natural world, the concern with man's relationship to his environment, the intuitions of a solitary and often curmudgeonly voice—should sound familiar. "Sons and daughters of Thoreau abound in contemporary American writing," the author of *Abbey's Road* laughs, listing eight and alluding to numerous others. Eliot Porter and the Sierra Club crafted a best-selling book of photography, *In Wildness Is the Preservation,* with words borrowed from Henry David Thoreau. Others—like Rachel Carson, Edwin Way Teale, Harvey Broome—drop his name with surprising frequency. And in spite of his bemused pronouncements, Abbey's own 1982 collection of essays, *Down the River*, was subtitled "with Henry David Thoreau."

I remember studying transcendentalism when I was in college. I don't think I really understood the meaning or even the significance of the word in those days. Walt Whitman's "barbaric yawp" rasped incoherently across the rooftop of my immediate world, while Ralph Waldo Emerson's lines echoed something other than the enthusiasms of a twenty-year-old. I guess I lacked the necessary intuition. Henry David Thoreau's observations, however, were another matter. "Civil Disobedience" sounded exactly right to a coed who began the sixties in a sorority house with a one-o'clock curfew and ended the decade on another campus where tear gas and fixed bayonets were the order of the day. Even more appealing was *Walden*, with its plea that we go back to basics, its clear love for the land, and its firm belief in the tonic of wildness. It was with genuine excitement, then, that I set out to see the famous pond for myself a few years later.

During the ten- or fifteen-minute drive from Boston to Concord, I let my imagination play over the landscape. Because of so much time spent in the Pacific Northwest wilds and because of my romanticized reading of *Walden*, I had a pretty fair mental picture of Thoreau's famous homesite. Or so I thought. The pond would be as he described, "a clear and deep green well, half a mile long and mile and three quarters in circumference, . . . a perennial spring in the midst of pine and oak woods." I would see exactly what he saw, "a perfect forest mirror, set round with stones as precious to my eye as if fewer or rarer. Nothing so fair, so pure, and at the same time so large, as a lake, perchance, lies on the surface of the earth. Sky water. It needs no fence. Nations come and go without defiling it. . . . A field of water betrays the spirit that is in the air."

I realized my naivete, and what betrayal and defilement really mean, as soon as we turned into the parking lot—acres of blacktop and neatly striped white lines—room for thousands of cars. The white bathhouse jarred too, as did the little bubbles that so carefully kept the beginning swimmers from the advanced. No one was in the water, for the hour was close to sundown, and the parking lot was almost deserted. But I still felt the press of bodies and heard imagined shouts and laughter in this place that should be a shrine to silence and dreams.

The walk to Thoreau's cabin site was a little more agreeable, although the paved pathway grated on tennis shoes more used to deer trails through high flowered meadows. The cabin itself was, of course, not there. Only pieces of fireplace, a Park Service outline, and a metal sign to proclaim "No Fishing" marked the place where Thoreau wrote so many of his remarkable observations about the wilderness. When the nearby railroad's whistle echoed through the trees, I was even more disappointed because my response was the reverse of Thoreau's. I heard a very nonromantic cry.

I should have known the reality would differ from my fancy, I guess. A score of years have taught me that man's sweep reaches everywhere and that I rarely will find a spot wholly undamaged. But the shocking discrepancy between Thoreau's Walden and that pond a century later remains with me to this day. The schism is not one easily forgotten.

Actually, it's the inverse of transcendentalism. Instead of perceiving man's oneness with the universe and with God, I saw the sharp disjunction between man's essence and the rest of the natural world, between man's desires and the rights of everything that gets in his way. And now we're back to intuition, which is, after all, the element of transcendentalism most untransformed today. It's the way Emerson looked at nature and found man and God replicated there; it's the way Thoreau looked at nature and found where he belonged in the universal scheme. It's also the element of transcendentalism most difficult to describe to anyone who hasn't felt epiphany after epiphany—instantaneous moments of profound understanding—in the natural world.

To me it's a blue gentian in a high mountain meadow, the chill carried by a loon's sharp cry, the press of humility a summer thunderstorm can bring to an exposed peak in the middle of nowhere, the northern lights at midnight. "Am I not partly leaves and vegetable mold myself?"

RALPH WALDO EMERSON

(1803–1882)

I doubt that many of us have hauled an entire volume of Ralph Waldo Emerson's writings into the wilderness, and perhaps we never will. Yet every time we enjoy the prose of John Burroughs, of Joseph Wood Krutch, of Annie Dillard, and of a good many other nature essayists past and present, we are vicariously enjoying the words of their mentor too.

Such a legacy would have been a surprise to the sage of Concord, for his notion of wilderness was more intellectual than absolute. Not only did Emerson prefer thinking, talking, and writing to experiencing, but he also held himself aloof from that which smacked of wildness. His descriptions detail farms instead of forests. He was content to look at the landscape close to home, to eye a sunrise from the hilltop by his house, to view a storm from behind a window glass, to speculate rather than to participate.

The true center of Emerson's world was man. Nature was valuable either as a vehicle whereby man, through transcendence, could perceive a oneness with God, or as a system whereby man could perceive ethical analogies. Thus nature was more significant for its mental than for its physical challenges. Such activities as peak bagging, river running, or even wandering through unexplored terrain were meaningless to Emerson, but an accompanying spiritual release was something he well understood. "The health of the eye seems to demand a horizon," he wrote in 1836. "We are never tired, so long as we can see far enough."

Beginning with these thoughts, Emerson penned a doctrine that sounds quite conventional in the 1980s but that was wholly new to his countrymen who perceived the natural world as a place to be tamed, an environment to be conquered. His tiny book, *Nature*, and his later collections of essays stirred a number of his contemporaries into fresh ways of thinking and writing about the American landscape. It was Emerson who first described the correspondences between man, nature, and God. It was Emerson who saw in nature signs analogous to human and spiritual facts. It was Emerson who preached so successfully the doctrine of intellectual and physical self-reliance. And it was Emerson who affirmed, "Nature is made to conspire with spirit to emancipate us." Of course it was Henry David Thoreau who attached these concepts to an actual way of life, but it was Emerson among the Transcendentalists who first saw the possibilities. Moreover, it was Emerson who brought the essay about nature into the American literary marketplace.

From *Nature* (1836)

To go into solitude, a man needs to retire as much from his chamber as from society. I am not solitary whilst I read and write, though nobody is with me. But if a man would be alone, let him look at the stars. The rays that come from those heavenly worlds will separate between him and what he touches. One might think the atmosphere was made transparent with this design, to give man, in the heavenly bodies, the perpetual presence of the sublime. Seen in the streets of cities, how great they are! If the stars should appear one night in a thousand years, how would men believe and adore; and preserve for many generations the remembrance of the city of God which had been shown! But every night come out these envoys of beauty, and light the universe with their admonishing smile.

The stars awaken a certain reverence, because though always present, they are inaccessible; but all natural objects make a kindred impression, when the mind is open to their influence. Nature never wears a mean appearance. Neither does the wisest man extort her secret, and lose his curiosity by finding out all her perfection. Nature never became a toy to a wise spirit. The flowers, the animals, the mountains, reflected the wisdom of his best hour, as much as they had delighted the simplicity of his childhood.

When we speak of nature in this manner, we have a distinct but most poetical sense in the mind. We mean the integrity of impression made by manifold natural objects. It is this which distinguishes the stick of timber of the wood-cutter from the tree of the poet. The charming landscape which I saw this morning is indubitably made up of some twenty or thirty farms. Miller owns this field, Locke that, and Manning the woodland beyond. But none of them owns the landscape. There is a property in the horizon which no man has but he whose eye can integrate all the parts, that is, the poet. This is the best part of these men's farms, yet to this their warranty-deeds give no title.

To speak truly, few adult persons can see nature. Most persons do not see the sun. At least they have a very superficial seeing. The sun illuminates only the eye of the man, but shines into the eye and the heart of the child. The lover of nature is he whose inward and outward senses are still truly adjusted to each other; who has retained the spirit of infancy even into the era of manhood. His intercourse with heaven and earth becomes part of his daily food. In the presence of nature a wild delight runs through the man, in spite of real sorrows. Nature says—he is my creature, and maugre all his impertinent griefs, he shall be glad with me. Not the sun or the summer alone, but every hour and season yields its tribute of delight; for every hour and change corresponds to and authorizes a different state of the mind, from breathless noon to grimmest midnight. Nature is a setting that fits equally well a comic or a mourning piece. In good health, the air is a cordial of incredible virtue. Crossing a bare common, in snow puddles, at twilight, under a clouded sky, without having in my thoughts any occurrence of special good fortune, I have enjoyed a perfect exhilaration. I am glad to the brink of fear. In the woods, too, a man casts off his years, as the snake his slough, and at what period soever of life is always a child. In the woods is perpetual youth. Within these plantations of God, a decorum and sanctity reign, a perennial festival is dressed, and the guest sees not how he should tire of them in a thousand years. In the woods, we return to reason and faith. There I feel that nothing can befall me in life,—no disgrace, no calamity (leaving me my eyes), which nature cannot repair. Standing on the bare ground,—my head bathed by the blithe air and uplifted into infinite space,—all mean egotism vanishes. I become a transparent eyeball; I am nothing; I see all; the currents of the Universal Being circulate through me; I am part or parcel of God. The name of the nearest friend sounds then foreign and accidental: to be brothers, to be acquaintances, master or servant, is then a trifle and a disturbance. I am the lover of uncontained and immortal beauty. In the wilderness, I find something more dear and connate than in streets or villages. In the tranquil landscape, and especially in the distant line of the horizon, man beholds somewhat as beautiful as his own nature.

The greatest delight which the fields and woods minister is the suggestion of an occult relation between man and the vegetable. I am not alone and unacknowledged. They nod to me, and I to them. The waving of the boughs in the storm is new to me and old. It takes me by surprise, and yet is not unknown. Its effect is like that of a higher thought or a better emotion coming over me, when I deemed I was thinking justly or doing right.

Yet it is certain that the power to produce this delight does not reside in nature, but in man, or in a harmony of both. It is necessary to use these pleasures with great temperance. For nature is not always tricked in holiday attire, but the same scene which yesterday breathed perfume and glittered as for the frolic of the nymphs is overspread with melancholy to-day. Nature always wears the colors of the spirit. To a man laboring under calamity, the heat of his own fire hath sadness in it. Then there is a kind of contempt of the landscape felt by him who has just lost by death a dear friend. The sky is less grand as it shuts down over less worth in the population.

From "Nature" in *Essays*
(Second Series)

There are days which occur in this climate, at almost any season of the year, wherein the world reaches its perfection; when the air, the heavenly bodies and the earth, make a harmony, as if nature would indulge her offspring; when, in these bleak upper sides of the planet, nothing is to desire that we have heard of the happiest latitudes, and we bask in the shining hours of Florida and Cuba; when everything that has life gives sign of satisfaction, and the cattle that lie on the ground seem to have great and tranquil thoughts. These halcyons may be looked for with a little more assurance in that pure October weather which we distinguish by the name of the Indian summer. The day, immeasurably long, sleeps over the broad hills and warm wide fields. To have lived through all its sunny hours, seems longevity enough. The solitary places do not seem quite lonely. At the gates of the forest, the surprised man of the world is forced to leave his city estimates of great and small, wise and foolish. The knapsack of custom falls off his back with the first step he takes into these precincts. Here is sanctity which shames our religions, and reality which discredits our heroes. Here we find Nature to be the circumstance which dwarfs every other circumstance, and judges like a god all men that come to her. We have crept out of our close and crowded houses into the night and morning, and we see what majestic beauties daily wrap us in their bosom. How willingly we would escape the barriers which render them comparatively impotent, escape the sophistication and second thought, and suffer nature to intrance us. The tempered light of the woods is like a perpetual morning, and is stimulating and heroic. The anciently-reported spells of these places creep on us. The stems of pines, hemlocks and oaks almost gleam like iron on the excited eye. The incommunicable trees begin to persuade us to live with them, and quit our life of solemn trifles. Here no history, or church, or state, is interpolated on the divine sky and the immortal year. How easily we might walk onward into the opening landscape, absorbed by new pictures and by thoughts fast succeeding each other, until by degrees the recollection of home was crowded out of the mind, all memory obliterated by the tyranny of the present, and we were led in triumph by nature.

These enchantments are medicinal, they sober and heal us. These are plain pleasures, kindly and native to us. We come to our own, and make friends with matter, which the ambitious chatter of the schools would persuade us to despise. We never can part with it; the mind loves its old home: as water to our thirst, so is the rock, the ground, to our eyes and hands and feet. It is firm water; it is cold flame; what health, what affinity! Ever an old friend, ever like a dear friend and brother when we chat affectedly with strangers, comes in this honest face, and takes a grave liberty with us, and shames us out of our nonsense. Cities give not the human senses room enough. We go out daily and nightly to feed the eyes on the horizon, and require so much scope, just as we need water for our bath. There are all degrees of natural influence, from these quarantine powers of nature, up to her dearest and gravest ministrations to the imagination and the soul. There is the bucket of cold water from the spring, the wood-fire to which the chilled traveller rushes for safety,—and there is the sublime moral of autumn and of noon. We nestle in nature, and draw our living as parasites from her roots and grains, and we receive glances from the heavenly bodies, which call us to solitude and foretell the remotest future. The blue zenith is the point in which romance and reality meet. I think if we should be rapt away into all that and dream of heaven, and should converse with Gabriel and Uriel, the upper sky would be all that would remain of our furniture.

It seems as if the day was not wholly profane in which we have given heed to some natural object. The fall of snowflakes in a still air, preserving to each crystal its perfect form; the blowing of sleet over a wide sheet of water, and over plains; the waving rye-field; the mimic waving of acres of houstonia, whose innumerable florets whiten and ripple before the eye; the reflections of trees and flowers in glassy lakes; the musical, steaming, odorous south wind, which converts all trees to wind-harps; the crackling and spurting of hemlock in the flames, or of pine logs, which yield glory to the walls and faces in the sitting-room,—these are the music and pictures of the most ancient religion. My house stands in low land, with limited outlook, and on the skirt of the village. But I go with my friend to the shore of our little river, and with one stroke of the paddle I leave the village politics and personalities, yes, and the world of villages and personalities, behind, and pass into a delicate realm of sunset and moonlight, too bright almost for spotted man to enter without novitiate and probation. We penetrate bodily this incredible beauty; we dip our hands in this painted element; our eyes are bathed in these lights and forms. A holiday, a *villeggiatura*, a royal revel, the proudest, most heart-rejoicing festival that valor and beauty, power and taste, ever decked and enjoyed, establishes itself on the instant. These sunset clouds, these delicately emerging stars, with their private and ineffable glances, signify it and proffer it. I am taught the poorness of our invention, the ugliness of towns and palaces. Art and luxury have early learned that they must work as enhancement and sequel to this original beauty. I am over-instructed for my return. Henceforth I shall be hard to please. I cannot go back to toys. . . .

Nature is loved by what is best in us. It is loved as the city of God, although, or rather because there is no citizen. The sunset is unlike anything that is underneath it: it wants men. And the beauty of nature must always seem unreal and mocking, until the landscape has human figures that are as good as itself. If there were good men, there would never be this rapture in nature. If the king is in the palace, nobody looks at the walls. It is when he is gone, and the house is filled with grooms and gazers, that we turn from the people to find relief in the majestic men that are suggested by the pictures and the architecture. The critics who complain of the sickly separation of the beauty of nature from the thing to be done, must consider that our hunting of the picturesque is inseparable from our protest against false society. Man is fallen; nature is erect, and serves as a differential thermometer, detecting the presence or absence of the divine sentiment in man. . . .

Nature is always consistent, though she reigns to contravene her own laws. She keeps her laws, and seems to transcend them. She arms and equips an animal to find its place and living in the earth, and at the same time she arms and equips another animal to destroy it. Space exists to divide creatures; but by clothing the sides of a bird with a few feathers she gives him a petty omnipresence. The direction is forever onward, but the artist still goes back for materials and begins again with the first elements on the most advanced stage: otherwise all goes to ruin. If we look at her work, we seem to catch a glance of a system in transition. Plants are the young of the world, vessels of health and vigor; but they grope ever upward towards consciousness; the trees are imperfect men, and seem to bemoan their imprisonment, rooted in the ground. The animal is the novice and probationer of a more advanced order. The men, though young, having tasted the first drop from the cup of thought, are already dissipated: the maples and ferns are still uncorrupt; yet no doubt when they come to consciousness they too will curse and swear. Flowers so strictly belong to youth that we adult men soon come to feel that their beautiful generations concern not us: we have had our day; now let the children have theirs. The flowers jilt us, and we are old bachelors with our ridiculous tenderness. . . .

Quite analogous to the deceits in life, there is, as might be expected, a similar effect on the eye from the face of external nature. There is in woods and waters a certain enticement and flattery, together with a failure to yield a present satisfaction. This disappointment is felt in every landscape. I have seen the softness and beauty of the summer clouds floating feathery overhead, enjoying, as it seemed, their height and privilege of motion, whilst yet they appeared not so much the drapery of this place and hour, as forelooking to some pavilions and gardens of festivity beyond. It is an odd jealousy, but the poet finds himself not near enough to his object. The pine-tree, the river, the bank of flowers before him does not seem to be nature. Nature is still elsewhere. This or this is but outskirt and a far-off reflection and echo of the triumph that has passed by and is now at its glancing splendor and heyday, perchance in the neighboring fields, or, if you stand in the field, then in the adjacent woods. The present object shall give you this sense of stillness that follows a pageant which has just gone by. What splendid distance, what recesses of ineffable pomp and loveliness in the sunset! But who can go where they are, or lay his hand or plant his foot thereon? Off they fall from the round world forever and ever. It is the same among the men and women as among the silent trees; always a referred existence, an absence, never a presence and satisfaction. Is it that beauty can never be grasped? in persons and in landscape is equally inaccessible? The accepted and betrothed lover has lost the wildest charm of his maiden in her acceptance of him. She was heaven whilst he pursued her as a star: she cannot be heaven if she stoops to such a one as he.

What shall we say of this omnipresent appearance of that first projectile impulse, of this flattery and balking of so many well-meaning creatures? Must we not suppose somewhere in the universe a slight treachery and derision? Are we not engaged to a serious resentment of this use that is made of us? Are we tickled trout, and fools of nature? One look at the face of heaven and earth lays all petulance at rest, and soothes us to wiser convictions. To the intelligent, nature converts itself into a vast promise, and will not be rashly explained. Her secret is untold. . . .

Nature is the incarnation of a thought, and turns to a thought again, as ice becomes water and gas. The world is mind precipitated, and the volatile essence is forever escaping again into the state of free thought. Hence the virtue and pungency of the influence on the mind of natural objects, whether inorganic or organized. Man imprisoned, man crystallized, man vegetative, speaks to man impersonated. That power which does not respect quantity, which makes the whole and the particle its equal channel, delegates its smile to the morning, and distils its essence into every drop of rain. Every moment instructs, and every object; for wisdom is infused into every form. It has been poured into us as blood; it convulsed us as pain; it slid into us as pleasure; it enveloped us in dull, melancholy days, or in days of cheerful labor; we did not guess its essence until after a long time.

HENRY DAVID THOREAU

(1817–1862)

⸺

"I went to the woods because I wished to live deliber-
ately," Henry David Thoreau announces in *Walden*,
"to front only the essential facts of life, and see if I could
not learn what it had to teach, and not, when I came to die,
discover that I had not lived." Thus Thoreau prescribes a
model lifestyle for countless men and women—some of us,
perhaps—who dream of a similar wilderness retreat where
the individual can explore a relationship with the natural
world. Those two years at Walden, compressed into a single
literary achievement, remain profoundly influential on anyone who either writes or reads "words for the wild."

Beside the tiny Massachusetts pond, Thoreau built his
own shelter (at a cost of $28.12½), cultivated about two-
and-a-half acres of beans and potatoes and corn (as the spirit

moved him), worked a little in town ($13.34 worth of labor), entertained only those visitors he chose (more animals than people, as I recall), and pursued his own digressions. Believing that "the mass of men lead lives of quiet desperation," he turned his back on convention and pursued instead an existence more in touch with what he deemed the "necessaries of life." The "necessaries" are whatever sustains "the vital heat in us," this sociable recluse firmly believed. Thus he wrote not only of food and shelter, but of watching ants, of fishing, of listening to the ice break up in spring, of sounding his pond to the depths.

When the experiment was finished, he left, for "it seemed to me that I had several more lives to live, and could not spare any more time for that one." Nonetheless, he had learned some valuable lessons about himself and about the natural world, and he had learned to express his findings well. His scientific contemporaries scrutinized and his transcendental friends philosophized, while Thoreau did both together. That conjunction of close observation and contemplative thoughtfulness, of scrutiny and speculation, is the pattern not only for Thoreau's prose but for generations of essays to follow.

It would be easy to fill an entire volume like *Words for the Wild* with excerpts from Thoreau's writing, or to fill this section with nothing but passages from *Walden*. But copies of that famous 1854 book are readily available, and one can always carry it along another day. Thoreau wrote a great many other memorable pieces about man's relationship with the natural world, so I have left out the more familiar passages about the pond. Instead, I have chosen the less well-known climb of Maine's tallest peak, a spiritual as well as a physical journey that has always been one of my favorite wilderness selections. . . .

From "Ktaadn" in *The Maine Woods*

So, scanning the woody side of the mountain, which lay still at an indefinite distance, stretched out some seven or eight miles in length before us, we determined to steer directly for the base of the highest peak, leaving a large slide, by which, as I have since learned, some of our predecessors ascended, on our left. This course would lead us parallel to a dark seam in the forest, which marked the bed of a torrent, and over a slight spur, which extended southward from the main mountain, from whose bare summit we could get an outlook over the country, and climb directly up the peak, which would then be close at hand. Seen from this point, a bare ridge at the extremity of the open land, Ktaadn presented a different aspect from any mountain I have seen, there being a greater proportion of naked rock rising abruptly from the forest; and we looked up at this blue barrier as if it were some fragment of a wall which anciently bounded the earth in that direction. Setting the compass for a northeast course, which was the bearing of the southern base of the highest peak, we were soon buried in the woods.

We soon began to meet with traces of bears and moose, and those of rabbits were everywhere visible. The tracks of moose, more or less recent, to speak literally, covered every square rod on the sides of the mountain; and these animals are probably more numerous there now than ever before, being driven into this wilderness, from all sides, by the settlements. The track of a full-grown moose is like that of a cow, or larger, and of the young, like that of a calf. Sometimes we found ouselves traveling in faint paths, which they had made, like cowpaths in the woods, only far more indistinct, being rather openings, affording imperfect vistas through the dense underwood, than trodden paths; and everywhere the twigs had been browsed by them, clipped as smoothly as if by a knife. The bark of trees was stripped up by them to the height of eight or nine feet, in long, narrow strips, an inch wide, still showing the distinct marks of their teeth. We expected nothing less than to meet a herd of them every moment, and our Nimrod held his shooting-iron in readiness; but we did not go out of our way to look for them, and, though numerous, they are so wary that the unskilled hunter might range the forest a long time before he could get sight of one. They are sometimes dangerous to encounter, and will not turn out for the hunter, but furiously rush upon him and trample him to death, unless he is lucky enough to avoid them by dodging round a tree. The largest are nearly as large as a horse, and weigh sometimes one thousand pounds; and it is said that they can step over a five-foot gate in their ordinary walk. They are described as exceedingly awkward-looking animals, with their long legs and short bodies, making a ludicrous figure when in full run, but making great headway, nevertheless. It seemed a mystery to us how they could thread these woods, which it required all our suppleness to accomplish,—climbing, stooping, and winding, alternately. They are said to drop their long and branching horns, which usually spread five or six feet, on their backs, and make their way easily by the weight of their bodies. Our boatmen said, but I know not with how much truth, that their horns are apt to be gnawed away by vermin while they sleep. Their flesh, which is more like beef than venison, is common in Bangor market.

We had proceeded on thus seven or eight miles, till about noon, with frequent pauses to refresh the weary ones, crossing a considerable mountain stream, which we conjectured to be Murch Brook, at whose mouth we had camped, all the time in woods, without having once seen the summit, and rising very gradually, when the boatmen beginning to despair a little, and fearing that we were leaving the mountain on one side of us, for they had not entire faith in the compass, McCauslin climbed a tree, from the top of which he could see the peak, when it appeared that we had not swerved from a right line, the compass down below still ranging with his arm, which pointed to the summit. By the side of a cool mountain rill, amid the woods, where the water began to partake of the purity and transparency of the air, we stopped to cook some of our fishes, which we had brought thus far in order to save our hard bread and pork, in the use of which we had put ourselves on short allowance. We soon had a fire blazing, and stood around it, under the damp and sombre forest of firs and birches, each with a sharpened stick, three or four feet in length, upon which he had spitted his trout, or roach, previously well gashed and salted, our sticks radiating like the spokes of a wheel from one centre and each crowding his particular fish into the most desirable exposure, not with the truest regard always to his neighbor's rights. Thus we regaled ourselves, drinking meanwhile at the spring, till one man's pack, at least, was considerably lightened, when we again took up our line of march.

At length we reached an elevation sufficiently bare to afford a view of the summit, still distant and blue, almost as if retreating from us. A torrent, which proved to be the same we had crossed, was seen tumbling down in front, literally from out of the clouds. But this glimpse at our whereabouts was soon lost, and we were buried in the woods again. The wood was chiefly yellow birch, spruce, fir, mountain-ash, or round-wood, as the Maine people call it, and moose-wood. It was the worst kind of traveling; sometimes like the densest scrub-oak patches with us. The cornel, or bunch-berries, were very abundant, as well as Solomon's seal and

mooseberries. Blueberries were distributed along our whole
route; and in one place the bushes were drooping with the
weight of the fruit, still as fresh as ever. It was the 7th of
September. Such patches afforded a grateful repast, and
served to bait the tired party forward. When any lagged behind, the cry of "blueberries" was most effectual to bring
them up. Even at this elevation we passed through a moose-
yard, formed by a large flat rock, four or five rods square,
where they tread down the snow in winter. At length, fearing that if we held the direct course to the summit, we should
not find any water near our camping-ground, we gradually
swerved to the west, till, at four o'clock, we struck again
the torrent which I have mentioned, and here, in view of
the summit, the weary party decided to camp that night.

While my companions were seeking a suitable spot for
this purpose, I improved the little daylight that was left in
climbing the mountain alone. We were in a deep and narrow
ravine, sloping up to the clouds, at an angle of nearly forty-
five degrees, and hemmed in by walls of rock, which were
at first covered with low trees, then with impenetrable thickets of scraggy birches and spruce-trees, and with moss, but
at last bare of all vegetation but lichens, and almost continually draped in clouds. Following up the course of the torrent
which occupied this,—and I mean to lay some emphasis on
this word *up*,—pulling myself up by the side of perpendicular
falls of twenty or thirty feet, by the roots of firs and birches,
and then, perhaps, walking a level rod or two in the thin
stream, for it took up the whole road, ascending by huge
steps, as it were, a giant's stairway, down which a river
flowed, I had soon cleared the trees, and paused on the successive shelves, to look back over the country. The torrent
was from fifteen to thirty feet wide, without a tributary, and
seemingly not diminishing in breadth as I advanced; but still

it came rushing and roaring down, with a copious tide, over and amidst masses of bare rock, from the very clouds, as though a waterspout had just burst over the mountain. Leaving this at last, I began to work my way, scarcely less arduous than Satan's anciently through Chaos, up the nearest, though not the highest peak. At first scrambling on all fours over the tops of ancient black spruce-trees (*Abies nigra*), old as the flood, from two to ten or twelve feet in height, their tops flat and spreading, and their foliage blue, and nipped with cold, as if for centuries they had ceased growing upward against the bleak sky, the solid cold. I walked some good rods erect upon the tops of these trees, which were overgrown with moss and mountain-cranberries. It seemed that in the course of time they had filled up the intervals between the huge rocks, and the cold wind had uniformly leveled all over. Here the principle of vegetation was hard put to it. There was apparently a belt of this kind running quite around the mountain, though, perhaps, nowhere so remarkable as here. Once slumping through, I looked down ten feet, into a dark and cavernous region, and saw the stem of a spruce, on whose top I stood, as on a mass of coarse basket-work, fully nine inches in diameter at the ground. These holes were bears' dens, and the bears were even then at home. This was the sort of garden I made my way *over*, for an eighth of a mile, at the risk, it is true, of treading on some of the plants, not seeing any path *through* it,—certainly the most treacherous and porous country I ever traveled.

But nothing could exceed the toughness of the twigs,—not one snapped under my weight, for they had slowly grown. Having slumped, scrambled, rolled, bounced, and walked, by turns, over this scraggy country, I arrived upon a side-hill, or rather a side-mountain, where rocks, gray, silent

rocks, were the flocks and herds that pastured, chewing a
rocky cud at sunset. They looked at me with hard gray eyes,
without a bleat or a low. This brought me to the skirt of
a cloud, and bounded my walk that night. But I had already
seen that Maine country when I turned about, waving, flowing, rippling, down below.

When I returned to my companions, they had selected
a camping-ground on the torrent's edge, and were resting
on the ground; one was on the sick list, rolled in a blanket,
on a damp shelf of rock. It was a savage and dreary scenery
enough; so wildly rough, that they looked long to find a level
and open space for the tent. We could not well camp higher,
for want of fuel; and the trees here seemed so evergreen and
sappy, that we almost doubted if they would acknowledge
the influence of fire; but fire prevailed at last, and blazed
here, too, like a good citizen of the world. Even at this height
we met with frequent traces of moose, as well as of bears.
As here was no cedar, we made our bed of coarser feathered
spruce; but at any rate the feathers were plucked from the
live tree. It was, perhaps, even a more grand and desolate
place for a night's lodging than the summit would have been,
being in the neighborhood of those wild trees, and of the
torrent. Some more aerial and finer-spirited winds rushed
and roared through the ravine all night, from time to time
arousing our fire, and dispersing the embers about. It was
as if we lay in the very nest of a young whirlwind. At midnight, one of my bed-fellows, being startled in his dreams
by the sudden blazing up to its top of a fir-tree, whose green
boughs were dried by the heat, sprang up, with a cry, from
his bed, thinking the world on fire, and drew the whole camp
after him.

In the morning, after whetting our appetite on some raw
pork, a wafer of hard bread, and a dipper of condensed cloud

or waterspout, we all together began to make our way up the falls, which I have described; this time choosing the right hand, or highest peak, which was not the one I had approached before. But soon my companions were lost to my sight behind the mountain ridge in my rear, which still seemed ever retreating before me, and I climbed alone over huge rocks, loosely poised, a mile or more, still edging toward the clouds; for though the day was clear elsewhere, the summit was concealed by mist. The mountain seemed a vast aggregation of loose rocks, as if some time it had rained rocks, and they lay as they fell on the mountain sides, nowhere fairly at rest, but leaning on each other, all rocking-stones, with cavities between, but scarcely any soil or smoother shelf. They were the raw materials of a planet dropped from an unseen quarry, which the vast chemistry of nature would anon work up, or work down, into the smiling and verdant plains and valleys of earth. This was an undone extremity of the globe; as in lignite, we see coal in the process of formation.

At length I entered within the skirts of the cloud which seemed forever drifting over the summit, and yet would never be gone, but was generated out of that pure air as fast as it flowed away; and when, a quarter of a mile farther, I reached the summit of the ridge, which those who have seen in clearer weather say is about five miles long, and contains a thousand acres of table-land, I was deep within the hostile ranks of clouds, and all objects were obscured by them. Now the wind would blow me out a yard of clear sunlight, wherein I stood; then a gray, dawning light was all it could accomplish, the cloud-line ever rising and falling with the wind's intensity. Sometimes it seemed as if the summit would be cleared in a few moments, and smile in sunshine; but what was gained on one side was lost on another. It was like sitting in a chimney and waiting for the smoke to blow away. It was, in fact, a cloud factory,—these were the cloud-works, and the wind turned them off done from the cool, bare rocks. Occasionally, when the windy columns broke in to me, I caught sight of a dark, damp crag to the right or left; the mist driving ceaselessly between it and me. It reminded me of the creations of the old epic and dramatic poets, of Atlas, Vulcan, the Cyclops, and Prometheus. Such was Caucasus and the rock where Prometheus was bound. Aeschylus had no doubt visited such scenery as this. It was vast, Titanic, and such as man never inhabits. Some part of the beholder, even some vital part, seems to escape through the loose grating of his ribs as he ascends. He is more lone than you can imagine. There is less of substantial thought and fair understanding in him than in the plains where men inhabit. His reason is dispersed and shadowy, more thin and subtile, like the air. Vast, Titanic, inhuman Nature has got him at disadvantage, caught him alone, and pilfers him of some of his divine faculty. She does not smile on him as in the plains. She seems to say sternly, Why came ye here before your time. This ground is not prepared for you. Is it not enough that I smile in the valleys? I have never made this soil for thy feet, this air for thy breathing, these rocks for thy neighbors. I cannot pity nor fondle thee here, but forever relentlessly drive thee hence to where I *am* kind. Why seek me where I have not called thee, and then complain because you find me but a stepmother? Shouldst thou freeze or starve, or shudder thy life away, here is no shrine, nor altar, nor any access to my ear.

The tops of mountains are among the unfinished parts of the globe, whither it is a slight insult to the gods to climb and pry into their secrets, and try their effect on humanity. Only dar-

ing and insolent men, perchance, go there. Simple races, as
savages, do not climb mountains,—their tops are sacred and
mysterious tracts never visited by them. Pomola is always
angry with those who climb to the summit of Ktaadn.

According to Jackson, who, in his capacity of geological
surveyor of the State, has accurately measured it,—the altitude of Ktaadn is 5300 feet, or a little more than one mile
above the level of the sea,—and he adds, "It is then evidently
the highest point in the State of Maine, and is the most abrupt
granite mountain in New England." The peculiarities of that
spacious table-land on which I was standing, as well as the
remarkable semi-circular precipice or basin on the eastern
side, were all concealed by the mist. I had brought my whole
pack to the top, not knowing but I should have to make my
descent to the river, and possibly to the settled portion of
the State alone, and by some other route, and wishing to
have a complete outfit with me. But at length, fearing that
my companions would be anxious to reach the river before
night, and knowing that the clouds might rest on the mountain for days, I was compelled to descend. Occasionally, as
I came down, the wind would blow me a vista open, through
which I could see the country eastward, boundless forests,
and lakes, and streams, gleaming in the sun, some of them
emptying into the East Branch. There were also new mountains in sight in that direction. Now and then some small
bird of the sparrow family would flit away before me, unable
to command its course, like a fragment of the gray rock
blown off by the wind.

I found my companions where I had left them, on the
side of the peak, gathering the mountain-cranberries, which
filled every crevice between the rocks, together with blueberries, which had a spicier flavor the higher up they grew,
but were not the less agreeable to our palates. When the

country is settled, and roads are made, these cranberries will perhaps become an article of commerce. From this elevation, just on the skirts of the clouds, we could overlook the country, west and south, for a hundred miles. There it was, the State of Maine, which we had seen on the map, but not much like that,—immeasurable forest for the sun to shine on, that eastern *stuff* we hear of in Massachusetts. No clearing, no house. It did not look as if a solitary traveler had cut so much as a walking-stick there. Countless lakes,—Moosehead in the southwest, forty miles long by ten wide, like a gleaming silver platter at the end of the table; Chesuncook, eighteen long by three wide, without an island; Millinocket, on the south, with its hundred islands; and a hundred others without a name; and mountains, also, whose names, for the most part, are known only to the Indians. The forest looked like a firm grass sward, and the effect of these lakes in its midst has been well compared, by one who has since visited this same spot, to that of a "mirror broken into a thousand fragments, and wildly scattered over the grass, reflecting the full blaze of the sun." It was a large farm for somebody, when cleared. According to the Gazetteer, which was printed before the boundary question was settled, this single Penobscot county, in which we were, was larger than the whole State of Vermont, with its fourteen counties; and this was only a part of the wild lands of Maine. We are concerned now, however, about natural, not political limits. We were about eighty miles, as the bird flies, from Bangor, or one hundred and fifteen, as we had ridden, and walked, and paddled. We had to console ourselves with the reflection that this view was probably as good as that from the peak, as far as it went; and what were a mountain without its attendant clouds and mists? Like ourselves, neither Bailey nor Jackson had obtained a clear view from the summit.

Setting out on our return to the river, still at an early hour in the day, we decided to follow the course of the torrent, which we supposed to be Murch Brook, as long as it would not lead us too far out of our way. We thus traveled about four miles in the very torrent itself, continually crossing and recrossing it, leaping from rock to rock, and jumping with the stream down falls of seven or eight feet, or sometimes sliding down on our backs in a thin sheet of water. This ravine had been the scene of an extraordinary freshet in the spring, apparently accompanied by a slide from the mountain. It must have been filled with a stream of stones and water, at least twenty feet above the present level of the torrent. For a rod or two, on either side of its channel, the trees were barked and splintered up to their tops, the birches bent over, twisted, and sometimes finely split, like a stable-broom; some, a foot in diameter, snapped off, and whole clumps of trees bent over with the weight of rocks piled on them. In one place we noticed a rock, two or three feet in diameter, lodged nearly twenty feet high in the crotch of a tree. For the whole four miles, we saw but one rill emptying in, and the volume of water did not seem to be increased from the first. We traveled thus very rapidly with a downward impetus, and grew remarkably expert at leaping from rock to rock, for leap we must, and leap we did, whether there was any rock at the right distance or not. It was a pleasant picture when the foremost turned about and looked up the winding ravine, walled in with rocks and the green forest to see, at intervals of a rod or two, a red-shirted or green-jacketed mountaineer against the white torrent, leaping down the channel with his pack on his back, or pausing upon a convenient rock in the midst of the torrent to mend a rent in his clothes, or unstrap the dipper at his belt to take a draught of the water. At one place we were startled by seeing, on a little sandy shelf by the side of the stream, the fresh print of a man's foot, and for a moment realized how Robinson Crusoe felt in a similar case; but at last we remembered that we had struck this stream on our way up, though we could not have told where, and one had descended into the ravine for a drink. The cool air above and the continual bathing of our bodies in mountain water, alternate foot, sitz, douche, and plunge baths, made this walk exceedingly refreshing, and we had traveled only a mile or two, after leaving the torrent, before every thread of our clothes was as dry as usual, owing perhaps to a peculiar quality in the atmosphere.

After leaving the torrent, being in doubt about our course, Tom threw down his pack at the foot of the loftiest spruce-tree at hand, and shinned up the bare trunk some twenty feet, and then climbed through the green tower, lost to our sight, until he held the topmost spray in his hand. McCauslin, in his younger days, had marched through the wilderness with a body of troops, under General Somebody, and with one other man did all the scouting and spying service. The General's word was, "Throw down the top of that tree," and there was no tree in the Maine woods so high that it did not lose its top in such a case. I have heard a story of two men being lost once in these woods, nearer to the settlements than this, who climbed the loftiest pine they could find, some six feet in diameter at the ground, from whose top they discovered a solitary clearing and its smoke. When at this height, some two hundred feet from the ground, one of them became dizzy, and fainted in his companion's arms, and the latter had to accomplish the descent with him, alternately fainting and reviving, as best he could. To Tom we cried, Where away does the summit bear? where the burnt lands? The last he could only conjecture; he descried, how-ever, a little meadow and pond, lying probably in our course, which we concluded to steer for. On reaching this secluded meadow, we found fresh tracks of moose on the shore of the pond, and the water was still unsettled as if they had fled before us. A little farther, in a dense thicket, we seemed to be still on their trail. It was a small meadow, of a few acres, on the mountain side, concealed by the forest, and perhaps never seen by a white man before, where one would think that the moose might browse and bathe, and rest in peace. Pursuing this course, we soon reached the open land, which went sloping down some miles toward the Penobscot.

Perhaps I most fully realized that this was primeval, untamed, and forever untamable *Nature*, or whatever else men call it, while coming down this part of the mountain. We were passing over "Burnt Lands," burnt by lightning, perchance, though they showed no recent marks of fire, hardly so much as a charred stump, but looked rather like natural pasture for the moose and deer, exceedingly wild and desolate, with occasional strips of timber crossing them, and low poplars springing up, and patches of blueberries here and there. I found myself traversing them familiarly, like some pasture run to waste, or partially reclaimed by man; but when I reflected what man, what brother or sister or kinsman of our race made it and claimed it, I expected the proprietor to rise up and dispute my passage. It is difficult to conceive of a region uninhabited by man. We habitually presume his presence and influence everywhere. And yet we have not seen pure Nature, unless we have seen her thus vast and drear and inhuman, though in the midst of cities. Nature was here something savage and awful, though beautiful. I looked with awe at the ground I trod on, to see what the Powers had made there, the form and fashion and material of their work. This was that Earth of which we have heard, made out of Chaos and Old Night. Here was no man's

garden, but the unhandseled globe. It was not lawn, nor
pasture, nor mead, nor woodland, nor lea, nor arable, nor
waste land. It was the fresh and natural surface of the planet
Earth, as it was made forever and ever,—to be the dwelling
of man, we say,—so Nature made it, and man may use it
if he can. Man was not to be associated with it. It was Matter, vast, terrific,—not his Mother Earth that we have heard
of, not for him to tread on, or be buried in,—no, it were
being too familiar even to let his bones lie there,—the home,
this, of Necessity and Fate. There was clearly felt the presence
of a force not bound to be kind to man. It was a place for
heathenism and superstitious rites,—to be inhabited by men
nearer of kin to the rocks and to wild animals than we. We
walked over it with a certain awe, stopping, from time to
time, to pick the blueberries which grew there, and had a
smart and spicy taste. Perchance where *our* wild pines stand,
and leaves lie on their forest floor, in Concord, there were
once reapers, and husbandmen planted grain; but here not
even the surface had been scarred by man, but it was specimen of what God saw fit to make this world. What is it to
be admitted to a museum, to see a myriad of particular
things, compared with being shown some star's surface, some
hard matter in its home! I stand in awe of my body, this
matter to which I am bound has become so strange to me.
I fear not spirits, ghosts, of which I am one,—*that* my body
might,—but I fear bodies, I tremble to meet them. What
is this Titan that has possesssion of me? Talk of mysteries!
Think of our life in nature,—daily to be shown matter, to
come in contact with it,—rocks, trees wind on our cheeks!
the *solid* earth! the *actual* world! the *common sense! Contact! Contact! Who* are we? *where* are we?

PART 2
Other Early Naturalists and Essayists

W hen I began planning *Words for the Wild*, the sections fell naturally into place. I envisioned the nineteenth century separated from the twentieth, with towering figures like Emerson, Thoreau, and Muir as the keystones. Their prose would define their peers', and I would use their words to define the major patterns of thought. The more I read, however, the more I discovered that what I learned years ago about Romantics and Victorians holds true for American nature writers, too. No one's essays contain the pure characteristics of a single age, no one's ideas can be isolated from the others', and, for the most part, no one's life span fits tidily into the parameters of this decade or that.

It turned out that a good many writers had a foot in every world I could think of. Both John Muir and John Burroughs, for example, read *Walden* and were admittedly enthralled by the tenets of transcendentalism. Both, on meeting Ralph

Waldo Emerson, were visibly impressed. Both were explorers, one of the distant high Sierras, the other of local pastures and fields. Yet both joined forces on Harriman's 1899 expedition north and enjoyed equally the unfolding Alaskan scenery. Both were admiring friends of Theodore Roosevelt; one hunted with him, the other did not. Both lived on into the twentieth century, the one leading a growing crusade for the conservation of our natural resources, the other retiring quietly to his farm in upstate New York. Both were born in covered-wagon days and died in an age that saw planes flying overhead. Both, along with about a dozen other men and women, comprise the reasons why I have found it impossible to draw a line through the year 1900 and declare it inviolate. Time frames and ideologies simply won't stay put.

Yet, to give some sort of structure to *Words for the Wild*, I need to make time and ideas do just that. Somehow I need to separate this section from the next. I feel like I'm walking a log, not a very big one, balanced across a bushy ravine. It's slippery, and I have to keep lifting my boots over the branches and snags. Sometimes I teeter left, sometimes right. If I fall I probably won't kill myself, but extricating my arms and legs from the tangle below would be a nightmare of welts and scratches. Since I have no intention of turning back, I'll just hang onto two walking sticks—one called chronology and the other thematic repetition—for balance.

By the time transcendentalism caught the public's attention, other sorts of nature writing already were in existence. The Bartrams, father and son, set the early standards. A native American botanist, John Bartram described the flora and fauna of early eighteenth-century Pennsylvania. The more artistic William followed in his parent's footsteps, producing a 1791 book called *Travels Through North and South Carolina, Georgia, East and West Florida, the Cherokee*

Country, the Extensive Territories of the Muscogules, or Creek Confederacy, and the Country of the Chactaws. While the Bartrams' works languish on dusty library shelves today, their conceptions of nature writing are significant because they point the way to the nineteenth century. The one cherished scientific observation; the other, exploration and literary description. So, too, did men of the next few generations focus their thoughts primarily on science and travel.

The first to do so in the nineteenth century were Meriwether Lewis and William Clark. Sent by President Jefferson to explore the boundaries of the 1803 Louisiana Purchase, they took two long years to traverse the country from the Mississippi River up the Missouri, across to the Columbia, down it to the Pacific Ocean, and back again. Each man kept a journal, documenting the highlights and low points of the trip. Charming prose—marked by idiosyncratic spelling, unintelligible punctuation, and apparent understatement about the hardships involved—tells the story of their adventures. Students often laugh at the oddities of Lewis and Clark's writing, but the journals rank with the very best pre–Civil War exploration narratives.

While these two men were defining the role of explorer-scientists, others chose to be scientist-explorers. Lewis and Clark knew that the primary object of their mission was exploration and that scientific discovery was just a bonus. Other early nineteenth-century investigators, like ornithologists Alexander Wilson and John James Audubon, placed scientific observation first. Going somewhere new was always inviting, but their chief goal was to find and to describe. Different objectives meant different prose styles. Explorer-scientists tended to write narratives; scientist-explorers, descriptions. Both groups, however, produced vigorous and attractive writing.

Alexander Wilson's four-volume masterpiece, *American Ornithology*, contains fabulous drawings of birds and hundreds of pages of realistic observations. Each description begins by outlining the general behavior of a bird, including its nesting and mating habits, then concludes with a host of scientific details gathered by measurement and dissection. The hummingbird "suspends himself on wing, for the space of two or three seconds, so steadily, that his wings become invisible, or only like a mist; and you can plainly distinguish the pupil of his eye looking round with great quickness and circumspection; the glossy golden green of his back, and the fire of his throat, dazzling in the sun, form altogether a most interesting appearance."

Certain elements of such typical early nineteenth-century American nature writing are characteristic of later writing, too. First and foremost these authors were observant. Translating the details of their surroundings with painstaking care and resisting the temptation to hyperbolize, they all sought pictorial accuracy. Furthermore, these men were excited about what they were doing. Every minute spent in the natural world was a privilege and a thrill. Like nature writers everywhere in every circumstance, they loved their work. "I felt my heart expand with joy at the novelties which surrounded me; I listened with pleasure to the whistling of the red bird on the banks as I passed, and contemplated the forest scenery, as it receded, with increasing delight." The lines are Wilson's, but they could just as easily be Lewis's, Clark's, Audubon's, or Henry David Thoreau's.

There is a difference, however, between the pieces written by explorers and scientists in the early nineteenth century and the transcendental essays of studied authors like Thoreau or Ralph Waldo Emerson. Immersed in the process of discovery, Lewis and Clark concerned themselves with survival,

Wilson and Audubon with classification. Man's philosophic relationship to nature played little part in their thinking because their eyes were turned outward, not inward. Discovery urged them forth. For the most part, then, their journals and books sounded the notes of historical immediacy and lacked the tones of contemplative leisure. Never, to my knowledge, did they discuss experiences of a directly transcendental nature.

Explorers and scientists of the second half of the nineteenth century had advantages unavailable to their predecessors. Most significantly, they were writers who used their authorial talents in tandem with their professional interests. Some worked for the government and wrote federal reports, others penned more popular versions of their travels, others even transformed their adventures into something more like fiction than fact. But not a one was solely an explorer, a scientist, a traveller. Rather, they were embryonic nature essayists whose writing, as often as not, displayed literary characteristics. Some of their names are familiar; others, though popular in their time, are almost unknown today. What they had in common though—the Parkmans and the Fremonts, the Powells and the Kings—was the desire to describe their adventures in publishable form.

Increasingly they combined the Lewis and Clark technique of narrative gusto with the ornithologists' close attention to sensory detail. From John Charles Fremont's winter attack on the Sierras to John Muir's summer thrills a few miles away, an incredible amount of spirit and sensitivity enlivens genuinely hair-raising adventures. A zest, a tremendous enthusiasm, a curiosity, a *joie de vivre* propelled these men toward the unknown, and that same attitude of mind strongly shaped their prose. The writing sounds energetic, driving, vigorous. Filled with strong verbs, the sentences move dynamically. The dominant mode is active, not static or effete.

Many such writers were so-called Renaissance men. Unlike today's scientists, who live in a world of fast-moving technology and cannot take precious time to read widely in other fields, these author-explorer-scientists could and did learn other things. They knew the classics, spoke other languages, appreciated the arts, and read poetry. Rhetorical training, for example, shows in the graceful syntax of a John Wesley Powell sentence. "The landscape everywhere, away from the river, is of rock—cliffs of rock, tables of rock, plateaus of rock, terraces of rock, crags of rock—ten thousand strangely carved forms; rocks everywhere, and no vegetation, no soil, no sand." Elsewhere, literary allusions appear with increasing frequency, as the post–Civil War authors revealed a working knowledge of Romantic predecessors. The California writers especially—Brewer, King, LeConte, Muir—showed a love for Wordsworthian terrain.

Perhaps the most significant quality of all, though, was thematic in nature. "I believe that fellow had rather sit on a peak all day, and stare at those snow-mountains, than find a fossil in the metamorphic Sierra," chides the senior paleontologist of the California Geological Survey. Clarence King's response was self-deprecating and ironic. "Can it be? I asked myself; has a student of geology so far forgotten his devotion to science? Am I really fallen to the level of a mere naturelover?" Obviously King was making fun of the dewy-eyed type, but he also was recognizing what happened to a man who spent a lot of contemplative time in the wilderness. He began to love the natural world, and he began to say so.

A passage describing a glacial moraine on Mount Whitney's flank reveals what actually was going on in his head. "I can never enter one of these great hollow mountain chambers without a pause," King confesses. "There is a grandeur and spaciousness which expand and fit the mind for yet larger sensations when you shall stand on the height above.'' So the erstwhile scientist found himself increasingly captivated by his surroundings and by his personal feelings, somewhat less enchanted by hunting, collecting, counting, or digging. He was thinking like a nature essayist, taking his reader along on a literary excursion in order to reveal personal experiences along the way. In so doing, he was expressing that ''proper'' subject for nature writing, ''an account of the writer's *experience* with the natural world.''

I suppose any of us who appreciate words for the wild can describe instances when we and the land came together in some meaningful way. When I think of canoeing in Wisconsin, for example, I see a long-legged skinny bird, pinkish and silhouetted against the early morning sun, intently watching us glide through a riffle. When I think of canyon country, I picture my first private Anasazi ruin, high up a vertical wall, dark and protected, its floor sprinkled with tiny corn cobs and pieces of a broken pot. ''A drop of dew reveals the rainbow tints as well as the myriad drops of the summer shower,'' noted Burroughs in his transcendental fashion. So, too, a mountain or a mound, a canyon or a crevice, a torrent or a trickle may trigger some personal epiphany with the natural world. Watching a forest fire crown up a Washington hillside leaves little doubt about human potency. Nor does wading across a glacial river, chest deep, and slipping. And once when I was young, a cougar on its way to the lake for a drink stolled past the foot of my sleeping bag.

Similar epiphanies—each one personal in nature—recurred with increasing frequency for the nineteenth-century essayists as their relationships with the land grew more intimate. Powell's ''unknown distance yet to run, an unknown river to explore'' left little time for studied contemplation, yet the evenings and layover days led to numerous philosophical insights. Muir easily could turn a mountain climb into a pantheistic journey to the stars, and then a Mary Austin came along. So, by the end of the 1800s, the contemplative spirit of the transcendentalists had married the energy of the pioneers, metaphorically speaking, and the two together were giving birth to a host of twentieth-century progeny.

JOSEPH LeCONTE

(1823–1901)

In the summer of 1870 a party of ten men circled from Oakland to the California Big Trees, Yosemite Valley, and Tuolumne Meadows, across the Sierras to Mono Lake and Lake Tahoe, then back to San Francisco. Covering nearly 600 miles on horseback, they visited most of the spots still beloved by tourists today. Their accommodations were rough, to be sure, their food tiresome, and their route at times difficult to follow, but they relished the mountain vistas and the challenges of the trip itself.

The oldest participant was Joseph LeConte, a forty-six-year-old professor who had come west the preceding year to help organize the University of California. A native of Georgia with wide-ranging scientific interests, LeConte not only possessed a medical degree but had studied with Agassiz at Harvard, then had taught chemistry and geology at the

University of Georgia and at South Carolina College. The year 1870 marked his first extended visit to the high Sierras, although he returned many, many times to continue his studies of their origin and structure. Indeed, he died there thirty years later, in Yosemite Valley where he was preparing to go on the Sierra Club's first large group outing.

Joseph LeConte kept records of all his scientific expeditions and explorations. His diary of the 1870 tour, reprinted as *A Journal of Ramblings Through the High Sierra of California*, reports one man's responses to a wilderness in its early stages of human discovery. Trampled by thousands of sheep rather than by millions of travellers, it already was changing.

The highlights of the journey were many. Part of the way John Muir accompanied the group, bringing a provocative sprightliness to the evening campfire discussions. He also guided the men safely along some steep and rather difficult trails near Yosemite. The rest of the time LeConte and his young friends were on their own, scrambling up precipitous cliffs, dropping into valleys overgrown with thick underbrush, worrying constantly about footsore horses that "shrink and limp and groan at every step."

What seems most remarkable, though, is the already apparent contrast between the scenic wilderness itself and the encroachments made by civilizations. It is hard to imagine that, just twenty-five years after the Donner Party tragedy, the mountains near Tahoe had been invaded quite thoroughly. There LeConte saw "sad evidences of the effects of the speculative spirit—and evidences of time and money and energies wasted. Deserted houses and deserted mines in every direction." By contrast, Yosemite Valley far exceeded LeConte's expectations. "I can truly say I have never imagined the grandeur of the reality," he reported, gazing down at Mirror Lake from a sunrise perch on Glacier Point, although even then he noted that the hotel and the orchards peripherally diminished the view.

From *A Journal of Ramblings Through the High Sierra of California*

Our trail this morning has been up the Tenaya Cañon, over the divide, and into the Tuolumne Valley. There is abundant evidence of an immense former glacier, coming from Mt. Dana and Mt. Lyell group, filling the Tuolumne Valley, over-running the divide, and sending a branch down the Tenaya Cañon. The rocks in and about Tenaya Cañon are everywhere scored and polished. We had to dismount and lead over some of these polished surfaces. The horses' feet slipped and sprawled in every direction, but none fell. A conspicuous feature of the scenery on Lake Tenaya is a granite knob, eight hundred feet high, at the upper end of the lake and in the middle of the cañon. This knob is bare, destitute of vegetation, round and polished to the very top. It has evidently been enveloped in the icy mass, and its shape has been determined by it. We observed similar scorings and polishings on the sides of the cañon, to an equal and much greater height. Splendid view of the double peaks of the Cathedral, from the Tenaya Lake and from the trail. Looking back from the trail soon after leaving the lake, we saw a conspicuous and very picturesque peak, with a vast amphitheater, with precipitous sides, to the north, filled with a grand mass of snow, evidently the fountain of an ancient tributary of the Tenaya Glacier. We call this *Coliseum Peak*. So let it be called hereafter, to the end of time.

The Tuolumne Meadow is a beautiful grassy plain of great

extent, thickly enameled with flowers, and surrounded with the most magnificent scenery. Conspicuous amongst the hundreds of peaks visible are Mt. Dana, with its grand symmetrical outline and purplish red color; Mt. Gibbs, of gray granite; Mt. Lyell and its group of peaks, upon which great masses of snow still lie; and the wonderfully picturesque group of sharp, inaccessible peaks (viz., Unicorn Peak, Cathedral Peaks, etc.), forming the Cathedral group.

Sode Springs is situated on the northern margin of the Tuolumne Meadow. It consists of several springs of ice-cold water, bubbling up from the top of a low reddish mound. Each spring itself issues from the top of a small subordinate mound. The mound consists of carbonate of lime, colored with iron deposited from the water. The water contains principally carbonates of lime and iron, dissolved in excess of carbonic acid, which escapes in large quantities, in bubbles. It possibly, also, contains carbonate of soda. It is very pungent, and delightful to the taste. Before dinner we took a swim in the ice-cold water of the Tuolumne River.

About 3 P.M. commenced saddling up, intending to go on to Mt. Dana. Heavy clouds have been gathering for some time past. Low mutterings of thunder have also been heard. But we had already been so accustomed to the same, without rain, in the Yosemite, that we thought nothing of it. We had already saddled, and some had mounted, when the storm burst upon us. "Our provisions—sugar, tea, salt, flour— must be kept dry!" shouted Hawkins. We hastily dismounted, constructed a sort of shed of blankets and india-rubber cloths, and threw our provisions under it. Now commenced peal after peal of thunder in an almost continuous roar, and floods of rain. We all crept under the temporary shed, but not before we had gotten pretty well soaked. So much delayed that we were now debating—after the rain—whether we had not better remain here overnight. Some were urgent for pushing on, others equally so for staying. Just at this juncture, when the debate ran high, a shout, "Hurrah!" turned all eyes in the same direction. Hawkins and Mr. Muir had scraped up the dry leaves underneath a huge prostrate tree, set fire and piled on fuel, and already, see!—a glorious blaze! This incident decided the question at once. With a shout, we ran for fuel, and piled on log after log, until the blaze rose twenty feet high. Before, shivering, crouching, and miserable; now joyous and gloriously happy.

The storm did not last more than an hour. After it, the sun came out and flooded all the landscape with liquid gold. I sat alone at some distance from the camp and watched the successive changes of the scene—first, the blazing sunlight flooding meadow and mountain; then the golden light on mountain peaks; and then the lengthening shadows on the valley; then a roseate bloom diffused over sky and air, over mountain and meadow. Oh, how exquisite! I never saw the like before. Last, the creeping shadow of night, descending and enveloping all. . . .

August 13.—Cold last night. We had to sleep near the fire, and keep it up during the night. Considerable frost this morning, for we are in the midst of the snows. We got up early, feeling bright and joyous, and enjoyed our breakfast as only mountaineers can. Over Mono Pass, and down Bloody Cañon today. I really dread it, for my horse's sake. Even well-shod horses get their feet and legs cut and bleeding in going down this cañon. My horse, since leaving Yosemite, has lost three shoes, and has already become very tender-footed. Got off by 6 A.M. Sorry, very sorry, to leave our delightful camp here. In commemoration of the delightful time we have spent here, we name it "Camp Dana."

The trail to the summit is a very gentle ascent, the whole way along the margin of a stream. Distance, three or four miles. Saw a deer, but Cobb was not on hand. On the very summit, 10,700 feet high, there is a marshy meadow, from which a stream runs each way: one east, into the Tuolumne, along which we ascended; the other west, down Bloody Cañon into Mono Lake, along which we expect to descend. Right on the summit, and in Bloody Cañon, we found great masses of snow. The trail passes by their edges and over their surfaces. The trail down Bloody Cañon is rough and precipitous beyond conception. It is the terror of all drovers and packers across the mountains. It descends four thousand feet in two or three miles, and is a mere mass of loose fragments of sharp slate. Our horses' legs were all cut and bleeding before we got down. I really felt pity for my horse, with his tender feet. We all dismounted and led them down with the greatest care. In going down we met a large party of Indians, some on horseback, and some on foot, coming up. We saluted them. In return they invariably whined, "Gie me towaca," "Gie me towaca." They were evidently incredulous when told that none of the party chewed.

The scenery of Bloody Cañon is really magnificent, and, in a scientific point of view, this is the most interesting locality I have yet seen. Conceive a narrow, winding gorge, with black slaty precipices of every conceivable form, fifteen hundred to two thousand feet high on either side. As the gorge descends precipitously, and winds from side to side, we often look from above down into the most glorious amphitheater of cliffs, and from time to time beyond, upon the glistening surface of Lake Mono, and the boundless plains, studded with volcanic cones. About one-third way down, in the center of the grandest of these amphitheaters, see! a deep, splendidly clear emerald-green lake, three or four times the size of Mirror Lake. It looks like an artificial basin, for its shores are everywhere hard, smooth, polished rock; especially the rim at the lower side is highly polished and finely striated. There can be no doubt that this lake basin has been scooped out by a glacier which once descended this cañon. In fact, glacial action is seen on every side around this lake, and all the way down the cañon and far into the plains below.

The cliffs on each side are scored and polished to the height of one thousand feet or more; projecting knobs in the bottom of the cañon are rounded and scored and polished in a similar manner.

After we had descended the steep slope, and had fairly escaped from the high rocky walls of Bloody Cañon proper; after we had reached the level plain and had prepared ourselves for an extensive view, we found ourselves still confined between two huge parallel ridges of débris five hundred feet high and only half a mile apart, and extending five or six miles out on the plain.

There are the *lateral moraines* of a glacier which once descended far into the plain toward Mono Lake. A little below the commencement of these moraines, in descending, we found a large and beautiful lake filling the whole cañon. Below this lake the lateral moraines on either side send each a branch which meet each other, forming a crescentic cross-ridge through which the stream breaks. This is evidently a *terminal* moraine, and the lake has been formed by the damming up of the water of the stream by this moraine border.

Below this, or still farther on the plain, I observed several other terminal moraines, formed in a similar way, by curving branches from the lateral moraines. Behind these are no lakes, but only marshes and meadows. These meadows are evidently formed in the same way as the lake; in fact, were lakes, subsequently filled up by deposit.

After getting from these lateral moraines fairly out on the plains, the most conspicuous objects which strike the eye are the extinct volcanoes. There are, I should think, at least twenty of them, with cones and craters as perfect as if they erupted yesterday. Even at this distance, I see that their snow-white, bare sides are composed of loose volcanic ashes and sand, above which projects a distinct rocky crater-rim, some of dark rock, but most of them of light-colored, probably pumice rock. Magnificent views of these cones and of Mono Lake are gotten from time to time, while descending Bloody Cañon. The cones are of all heights, from two hundred to twenty-seven hundred feet above the plain, and the plain itself about five thousand feet above sea-level.

We stopped for lunch at a cabin and meadow—a cattle ranch—about five miles from the lake. While our horses grazed, we cooked our dinner as usual, and then proceeded three miles and camped in a fine meadow on the banks of a beautiful stream—Rush Creek.

In riding down to our camp, I observed the terraces of Lake Mono, former water-levels, very distinctly marked, four or five in number. The whole region about Lake Mono, on this side, is covered with volcanic ashes and sand. It is the only soil except in the meadows. Even these seem to have the same soil, only more damp, and therefore more fertile. Scattered about, larger masses of pumice and obsidian are visible. Except in the meadows and along streams, the only growth is the sagebrush. Just before reaching camp, Mr. Muir and myself examined a fine section, made by Rush Creek, of lake and river deposit, beautifully stratified. It consists below of volcanic ashes, carried as sediment and deposited in the lake, and is therefore a true lake deposit, and beautifully stratified. Above this is a drift pebble deposit; the pebbles consisting of granite and slate from the Sierra.

Above this again, are volcanic ashes and sand, *unstratified*, probably blown ashes and sand, or else ejected since the drift. We have therefore certain evidence of eruptions before the drift, and possibly, also, after.

In the picture of the view from Mono Lake, I have yet said nothing about the Sierra. The general view of the range from this, the Mono, side is far finer than from the other side. The Sierra rises gradually on the western side for fifty or sixty miles. On the Mono, or eastern, side it is precipitous, the very summit of the range running close to the valley. From this side, therefore, the mountains present a sheer elevation of six or seven thousand feet above the plain. The sunset view of the Sierra, from an eminence near our camp, this evening, was, it seems to me, by far the finest mountain view I have ever in my life seen. The immense height of the chain above the plain, the abruptness of the declivity, the infinitely diversified forms, and the wonderful sharpness and ruggedness of the peaks, such as I have seen nowhere but in the Sierra, and all this strongly relieved against the brilliant sunset sky, formed a picture of indescribable grandeur. As I turn around in the opposite direction, the regular forms of the volcanoes, the placid surface of Lake Mono, with its picturesque islands, and far away in the distance the scarcely visible outlines of the White Mountains, pass in succession before the eye. I enjoyed this magnificent panoramic view until it faded away in the darkness.

From this feast I went immediately to another, consisting of excellent bread and such delicious mutton chops! If any restaurant in San Francisco could furnish such, I am sure it would quickly make a fortune. Some sentimentalists seem to think that these two feasts are incompatible; that the enjoyment of the beautiful is inconsistent with voracious appetite for mutton. I do not find it so.

After supper I again went out to enjoy the scene by night. As I gazed upon the abrupt slope of the Sierra, rising like a wall before me, I tried to picture to myself the condition of things during the glacial epoch. The long western slope of the Sierra is now occupied by long, complicated valleys, broad and full of meadows, while the eastern slope is deeply graven with short, narrow, steep ravines. During glacial times, therefore, it is evident that the western slope was occupied by long, complicated glaciers, with comparatively sluggish current; while on the east, short, simple parallel ice-streams ran down the steep slope and far out on the level plain. On each side of these protruded icy tongues: the débris brought down from the rocky ravines was droped as parallel moraines. Down the track of one of these glaciers, and between the outstretched *moraine arms*, our path lay this morning.

August 14 (Sunday).—I have not before suffered so much from cold as last night; yet yesterday the sun was very hot. No grand forests to protect us from wind and furnish us with logs for camp-fire; only sagebrush on the plains and small willows on the stream-banks. The winds blow furiously from the Sierra down the cañons upon the plains. Got up at 4 A.M.; couldn't sleep any more. After breakfast, went to visit the volcanic cones in the vicinity. The one we visited was one of the most perfect, and at the same time one of the most accessible. It was not more than one hundred and fifty or two hundred feet above the level of the sandy plain on which it stands.

I was very greatly interested in this volcano. It seems to me that its structure clearly reveals some points of its history. It consists of two very perfect cones and craters, one within the other. The outer cone, which rises directly from the level plain to a height of two hundred feet, is composed wholly of volcanic sand, and is about one mile in diameter. From the bottom and center of its crater rises another and much smaller cone of lava to a little greater height. We rode up the outer sand cone, then around on the rim of its crater, then down its inner slope to the bottom; tied our horses to sagebrush at the base of the inner lava cone, and scrambled on foot into its crater. Standing on the rim of this inner crater, the outer rises like a rampart on every side.

I believe we have here a beautiful example of cone-and-rampart structure, so common in volcanoes elsewhere; the rampart, or outer cone, being the result of an older and much greater eruption, within the wide yawning crater, of which by subsequent lesser eruption the smaller cone was built.

Mr. Muir is disposed to explain it differently. He thinks that this was once a much higher single cone, lava at top and sand on the slopes, like most of the larger cones in this vicinity; and that after its last eruption it suffered *engulf-ment*—i.e., its upper rocky portion has dropped down into its lower sandy portion.

The lava of this volcano is mostly pumice and obsidian, sometimes approaching trachyte. It was of all shades of color, from black to white, sometimes beautifully veined, like slags of an iron furnace; and of all physical conditions sometimes vesicular, sometimes glassy, sometimes stony. Wrinkled fusion-surfaces were also abundant. Again, I believe I can fix the date of the last eruption of this volcano. I found on the outer cone (or ash cone) several unmistakable drift *pebbles of granite*. At first I thought they might be the result of accidental deposit; but I found, also, several within the *lava crater*. These were reddened and semi-fused by heat. There can be no doubt, therefore, that the last eruption of this volcano was since the drift; it broke through a layer of drift deposit, and threw out the drift pebbles. Some fell back into the crater.

Mr. Muir took leave of us within the crater of this volcano. He goes today to visit some of the loftier cones. I would gladly accompany him, but my burnt hand has today become inflamed, and is very painful. The climb of twenty-seven hundred feet, over loose, very loose sand, will be very fatiguing, and the sun is very hot. In spite of all this, I had determined to go; but the party are impatient of delays.

I was really sorry to lose Mr. Muir from our party. I have formed a very high opinion of, and even a strong attachment for, him. He promises to write me if he observes any additional facts of importance.

ISABELLA BIRD

(1831–1904)

Isabella Bird fascinates me. Suffering from poor health all her life, this intrepid Englishwoman sought challenge and adventure around the globe. She embarked first when she was just past her teens, following that cruise with several more voyages to Canada, to the United States, to the Mediterranean, and to the United States again. In 1872, still suffering from spinal complications, she ventured alone to Australia, New Zealand, Hawaii, and back to the west coast of California.

The last months of that trip, completed in 1873, spurred the letters to her sister that were published in 1879 as *A Lady's Life in the Rocky Mountains*. They trace her train ride from San Francisco to Colorado, with a stop in Truckee so she could see Lake Tahoe, unescorted and on horseback. The bulk of the correspondence tells of time spent in the Rockies, again unescorted and on horseback, riding the length of the front range, exploring the wilds of Estes Park and points south.

Surprisingly, these sallies left Ms. Bird's thirst for adventure unquenched. The year 1878 found her in Japan and, later, on the Malay Peninsula. During the next decade and a half she saw India, Tibet, China, Korea, Persia, Kudistan, Canada, and the United States again. In her mid-sixties she was still exploring the unknown, on a trip that covered more than 8,000 miles of China and the Far East.

The results of her travels are diverse. Not only did she keep records of what she saw—each journey inspired at least one book—but she involved herself in philanthropical work as well, founding hospitals and church missions wherever possible in the non–English-speaking world. In short, she was woman of multiple talents and inexhaustible energy who impressed her contemporaries enormously. A century later, I remain in awe of her curiosity and courage.

Enjoying the pain as well as the pleasure of wilderness travel, Isabella Bird never gave up. She met challenge with as much self-reliance and fortitude as any male explorer and, equally, she was touched by the land. "Estes Park is mine . . . mine by right of love, appropriation, and appreciation; by the seizure of its peerless sunrises and sunsets, its glorious afterglow, its blazing noons, its hurricanes sharp and furious, its wild auroras, its glories of mountain and forest, of canyon, lake, and river, and the stereotyping them all in my memory." *A Lady's Life in the Rocky Mountains* iterates no stereotypes, however; instead, it offers a distinctive portrait of a most remarkable woman.

From *A Lady's Life in the Rocky Mountains*

ESTES PARK, COLORADO
October

As this account of the ascent of Long's Peak could not be
written at the time, I am much disinclined to write it, especially as no sort of description within my powers could enable
another to realize the glorious sublimity, the majestic solitude, and the unspeakable awfulness and fascination of the
scenes in which I spent Monday, Tuesday, and Wednesday.

Longs's Peak, 14,700 feet high, blocks up one end of
Estes Park, and dwarfs all the surrounding mountains. From
it on this side rise, snow-born, the bright St. Vrain, and the
Big and Little Thompson. By sunlight or moonlight its
splintered grey crest is the one object which, in spite of
wapiti and bighorn, skunk and grizzly, unfailingly arrests
the eyes. From it come all storms of snow and wind, and
the forked lightnings play round its head like a glory. It is
one of the noblest of mountains, but in one's imagination
it grows to be much more than a mountain. It becomes in-
vested with a personality. In its caverns and abysses one
comes to fancy that it generates and chains the strong winds,
to let them loose in its fury. The thunder becomes its voice,
and the lightnings do it homage. Other summits blush under
the morning kiss of the sun, and turn pale the next moment;
but it detains the first sunlight and holds it round its head
for an hour at least, till it pleases to change from rosy red
to deep blue; and the sunset, as if spell-bound, lingers latest
on its crest. The soft winds which hardly rustle the pine
needles down here are raging rudely up there round its mo-

tionless summit. The mark of fire is upon it; and though it has passed into a grim repose, it tells of fire and upheaval as truly, though not as eloquently, as the living volcanoes of Hawaii. Here under its shadow one learns how naturally nature worship, and the propitiation of the forces of nature, arose in minds which had no better light.

Longs's Peak, "the American Matterhorn," as some call it, was ascended five years ago for the first time. I thought I should like to attempt it, but up to Monday, when Evans left for Denver, cold water was thrown upon the project. It was late in the season, the winds were likely to be strong, etc.; but just before leaving, Evans said that the weather was looking more settled, and if I did not get farther than the timber line it would be worth going. Soon after he left, "Mountain Jim" came in, and said he would go up as guide, and the two youths who rode here with me from Longmount and I caught at the proposal. Mrs. Edwards at once baked bread for three days, steaks were cut from the steer which hangs up conveniently, and tea, sugar, and butter were benevolently added. Our picnic was not to be a luxurious or "well-found" one, for, in order to avoid the expense of a pack mule, we limited our luggage to what our saddle horses could carry. Behind my saddle I carried three pair of camping blankets and a quilt, which reached to my shoulders. My own boots were so much worn that it was painful to walk, even about the park, in them, so Evans had lent me a pair of his hunting boots, which hung to the horn of my saddle. . . . The ride was one series of glories and surprises of "park" and glade, of lake and stream, of mountains on mountains, culminating in the rent pinnacles of Long's Peak, which looked yet grander and ghastlier as we crossed an attendant mountain 11,000 feet high. The slanting sun added fresh beauty every hour. There were dark pines against a lemon

sky, grey peaks reddening and etherealizing, gorges of deep
and infinite blue, floods of golden glory pouring through
canyons of enormous depth, an atmosphere of absolute
purity, an occasional foreground of cottonwood, and aspen
flaunting in red and gold to intensify the blue gloom of the
pines, the trickle and murmur of streams fringed with icicles,
the strange *sough* of gusts moving among the pine tops—
sights and sounds not of the lower earth, but of the solitary,
beast-haunted, frozen upper altitudes. From the dry, buff
grass of Estes Park we turned off up a trail on the side of
a pine-hung gorge, up a steep pine-clothed hill, down to a
small valley, rich in fine, sun-cured hay about eighteen inches
high, and enclosed by high mountains whose deepest hollow
contains a lily-covered lake, fitly named "The Lake of the
Lilies." Ah, how magical its beauty was, as it slept in silence,
while *there* the dark pines were mirrored motionless in its
pale gold, and *here* the great white lily cups and dark green
leaves rested on amethyst-colored water!

From this we ascended into the purple gloom of great
pine forests which clothe the skirts of the mountains up to
a height of about 11,000 feet, and from their chill and solitary
depths we had glimpses of golden atmosphere and rose-lit
summits, not of "the land very far off," but of the land
nearer now in all its grandeur, gaining in sublimity by nearness—glimpses, too, through a broken vista of purple gorges,
of the illimitable Plains lying idealized in the late sunlight,
their baked, brown expanse transfigured into the likeness
of a sunset sea rolling infinitely in waves of misty gold.

We rode upwards through the gloom on a steep trail
blazed through the forest, all my intellect concentrated on
avoiding being dragged off my horse by impending branches,
or having the blankets badly torn, as those of my companions were, by sharp dead limbs, between which there was

hardly room to pass—the horses breathless, and requiring to stop every few yards, though their riders, except myself, were afoot. The gloom of the dense, ancient, silent forest is to me awe inspiring. On such an evening it is soundless, except for the branches creaking in the soft wind, the frequent snap of decayed timber, and a murmur in the pine tops as of a not distant waterfall, all tending to produce *eeriness* and sadness "hardly akin to pain." There no lumberer's axe has ever rung. The trees die when they have attained their prime, and stand there, dead and bare, till the fierce mountain winds lay them prostrate. The pines grew smaller and more sparse as we ascended, and the last stragglers wore a tortured, warring look. The timber line was passed, but yet a little higher a slope of mountain meadow dipped to the south-west towards a bright stream trickling under ice and icicles, and there a grove of the beautiful silver spruce marked our camping ground. The trees were in miniature, but so exquisitely arranged that one might well ask what artist's hand had planted them, scattering them here, clumping them there, and training their slim spires towards heaven. Hereafter, when I call up memories of the glorious, the view from this camping ground will come up. Looking east, gorges opened to the distant Plains, then fading into purple grey. Mountains with pine-clothed skirts rose in ranges, or, solitary, uplifted their grey summits, while close behind, but nearly 3,000 feet above us, towered the bald white crest of Long's Peak, its huge precipices red with the light of a sun long lost to our eyes. Close to us, in the caverned side of the Peak, was snow that, owing to its position, is eternal. Soon the afterglow came on, and before it faded a big half-moon hung out of the heavens, shining through the silver blue foliage of the pines on the frigid background of snow, and turning the whole into fairyland. . . .

Day dawned long before the sun rose, pure and lemon colored. The rest were looking after the horses, when one of the students came running to tell me that I must come farther down the slope, for "Jim" said he had never seen such a sunrise. From the chill, grey Peak above, from the everlasting snows, from the silvered pines, down through mountain ranges with their depths of Tyrian purple, we looked to where the Plains lay cold, in blue-grey, like a morning sea against a far horizon. Suddenly, as a dazzling streak at first, but enlarging rapidly into a dazzling sphere, the sun wheeled above the grey line, a light and glory as when it was first created. "Jim" involuntarily and reverently uncovered his head, and exclaimed, "I believe there is a God!" I felt as if, Parsee-like, I must worship. The grey of the Plains changed to purple, the sky was all one rose-red flush, on which vermilion cloud-streaks rested; the ghastly peaks gleamed like rubies, the earth and heavens were new created. Surely "the Most High dwelleth not in temples made with hands!" For a full hour those Plains simulated the ocean, down to whose limitless expanse of purple, cliff, rocks, and promontories swept down.

By seven we had finished breakfast, and passed into the ghastlier solitudes above, I riding as far as what, rightly or wrongly, are called the "Lava Beds," an expanse of large and small boulders, with snow in their crevices. It was very cold; some water which we crossed was frozen hard enough to bear the horse. "Jim" had advised me against taking any wraps, and my thin Hawaiian riding dress, only fit for the tropics, was penetrated by the keen air. The rarefied atmosphere soon began to oppress our breathing, and I found that Evans's boots were so large that I had no foothold. Fortunately, before the real difficulty of the ascent began, we found, under a rock, a pair of small overshoes, probably left by the Hayden exploring expedition, which just lasted for the day. As we were leaping from rock to rock, "Jim" said, "I was thinking in the night about your traveling alone, and wondering where you carried your Derringer, for I could see no signs of it." On my telling him that I traveled unarmed, he could hardly believe it, and adjured me to get a revolver at once.

On arriving at the "Notch" (a literal gate of rock), we found ourselves absolutely on the knifelike ridge or backbone of Long's Peak, only a few feet wide, covered with colossal boulders and fragments, and on the other side shelving in one precipitous, snow-patched sweep of 3,000 feet to a picturesque hollow, containing a lake of pure green water. Other lakes, hidden among dense pine woods, were farther off, while close above us rose the Peak, which, for about 500 feet, is a smooth, gaunt, inaccessible-looking pile of granite. Passing through the "Notch," we looked along the nearly inaccessible side of the Peak, composed of boulders and *débris* of all shapes and sizes, through which appeared broad, smooth ribs of reddish-colored granite, looking as if they upheld the towering rock mass above. I usually dislike bird's-eye and panoramic views, but, though from a mountain, this was not one. Serrated ridges, not much lower than that on which we stood, rose, one beyond another, far as that pure atmosphere could carry the vision, broken into awful chasms deep with ice and snow, rising into pinnacles piercing the heavenly blue with their cold, barren, grey, on, on for ever, till the most distant range upbore unsullied snow alone. There were fair lakes mirroring the dark pine woods, canyons dark and blue-black with unbroken expanses of pines, snow-slashed pinnacles, wintry heights frowning upon lovely parks, watered and wooded, lying in the lap of summer; North Park floating off into the blue distance, Middle Park closed till another season, the sunny slopes of Estes Park, and winding down among the mountains the snowy ridge of the Divide, whose bright waters seek both the Atlantic and Pacific Oceans. There, far below, links of diamonds showed where the Grand River takes its rise to seek the mysterious Colorado, with its still unsolved enigma, and lose itself in the waters of the Pacific; and nearer the snow-born Thompson bursts forth from the ice to begin its journey to the Gulf of Mexico. Nature, rioting in her grandest mood, exclaimed with voices of grandeur, solitude, sublimity, beauty, and infinity, "Lord, what is man, that Thou art mindful of him? or the son of man, that Thou visitest him?" Never-to-be-forgotten glories they were, burnt in upon my memory by six succeeding hours of terror.

You know I have no head and no ankles, and never ought to dream of mountaineering; and had I known that the ascent was a real mountaineering feat I should not have felt the slightest ambition to perform it. As it is, I am only humiliated by my success, for "Jim" dragged me up, like a bale of goods, by sheer force of muscle. At the "Notch" the real business of the ascent began. Two thousand feet of solid rock towered above us, four thousand feet of broken rock shelved precipitously below; smooth granite ribs, with barely foothold, stood out here and there; melted snow refrozen several times, presented a more serious obstacle; many of the rocks were loose, and tumbled down when touched. To me it was a time of extreme terror. I was roped to "Jim," but it was of no use; my feet were paralyzed and slipped on the bare rock, and he said it was useless to try to go that way, and we retraced our steps. I wanted to return to the "Notch," knowing that my incompetence would detain the party, and one of the young men said almost plainly that a woman was a dangerous encumbrance, but the trapper replied shortly that if it were not to take a lady up he would not go up at all. He went on to explore, and reported that further progress on the correct line of ascent was blocked by ice; and then for two hours we descended, lowering ourselves by our hands from rock to rock along a boulder-strewn sweep of 4,000 feet, patched with ice and snow, and perilous from rolling stones. My fatigue, giddiness, and pain from bruised ankles, and arms half pulled out of their sockets, were so great that I should never have gone halfway had not "Jim," *nolens volens*, dragged me along with a patience and skill, and withal a determination that I should ascend the Peak, which never failed. After descending about 2,000 feet to avoid the ice, we got into a deep ravine with inaccessible sides, partly filled with ice and snow and partly with large and small fragments of rock, which were constantly giving away, rendering the footing very insecure. That part to me was two hours of painful and unwilling submission to the inevitable; of trembling, slipping, straining, of smooth ice appearing when it was least expected, and of weak entreaties to be left behind while the others went on. "Jim" always said that there was no danger, that there was only a short bad bit ahead, and that I should go up even if he carried me!

Slipping, faltering, gasping from exhausting toil in the rarefied air, with throbbing hearts and panting lungs, we reached the top of the gorge and squeezed ourselves between two gigantic fragments of rock by a passage called the "Dog's Lift," when I climbed on the shoulders of one man and then was hauled up. This introduced us by an abrupt turn round the south-west angle of the Peak to a narrow shelf of considerable length, rugged, uneven, and so overhung by the cliff in some places that it is necessary to crouch to pass at all. Above, the Peak looks nearly vertical for 400 feet; and below, the most tremendous precipice I have ever seen descends in one unbroken fall. This is usually considered the most dangerous part of the ascent, but it does not seem so to me, for such foothold as there is is secure, and one fancies that it is possible to hold on with the hands. But there, and on the final, and, to my thinking, the worst part of the climb, one slip, and a breathing, thinking, human being would lie 3,000 feet below, a shapeless, bloody heap! ''Ring'' [Jim's hunting dog] refused to traverse the Ledge, and remained at the ''Lift'' howling piteously.

From thence the view is more magnificent even than that from the ''Notch.'' At the foot of the precipice below us lay a lovely lake, wood embosomed, from or near which the bright St. Vrain and other streams take their rise. I thought how their clear cold waters, growing turbid in the affluent flats, would heat under the tropic sun, and eventually form part of that great ocean river which renders our far-off islands habitable by impinging on their shores. Snowy ranges, one behind the other, extended to the distant horizon, folding in their wintry embrace the beauties of Middle Park. Pike's Peak, more than one hundred miles off, lifted that vast but shapeless summit which is the landmark of southern Colorado. There were snow patches, snow slashes, snow abysses, snow forlorn and soiled looking, snow pure and dazzling, snow glistening above the purple robe of pine worn by all the mountains; while away to the east, in limitless breadth, stretched the green-grey of the endless Plains. Giants everywhere reared their splintered crests. From thence, with a single sweep, the eye takes in a distance of 300 miles—that distance to the west, north, and south being made up of mountains ten, eleven, twelve, and thirteen thousand feet in height, dominated by Long's Peak, Gray's Peak, and Pike's Peak, all nearly the height of Mont Blanc! On the Plains we traced the rivers by their fringe of cottonwoods to the distant Platte, and between us and them lay glories of mountain, canyon, and lake, sleeping in depths of blue and purple most ravishing to the eye.

As we crept from the ledge round a horn of rock I beheld what made me perfectly sick and dizzy to look at—the terminal Peak itself—a smooth, cracked face or wall of pink granite, as nearly perpendicular as anything could well be up which it was possible to climb, well deserving the name of the "American Matterhorn."

Scaling, not climbing, is the correct term for this last ascent. It took one hour to accomplish 500 feet, pausing for breath every minute or two. The only foothold was in narrow cracks or on minute projections on the granite. To get a toe in these cracks, or here and there on a scarcely obvious projection, while crawling on hands and knees, all the while tortured with thirst and gasping and struggling for breath, this was the climb; but at last the Peak was won. A grand, well-defined mountain top it is, a nearly level acre of boulders, with precipitous sides all round, the one we came up being the only accessible one.

It was not possible to remain long. One of the young men was seriously alarmed by bleeding from the lungs, and the intense dryness of the day and the rarefication of the air, at a height of nearly 15,000 feet, made respiration very painful. There is always water on the Peak, but it was frozen as hard as rock, and the sucking of ice and snow increases thirst. We all suffered severely from the want of water, and the gasping for breath made our mouths and tongues so dry that articulation was difficult, and the speech of all unnatural.

From the summit were seen in unrivalled combination all the views which had rejoiced our eyes during the ascent. It was something at last to stand upon the storm-rent crown of this lonely sentinel of the Rocky Range, on one of the mightiest of the vertebrae of the backbone of the North American continent, and to see the waters start for both oceans. Uplifted above love and hate and storms of passion, calm amidst the eternal silences, fanned by zephyrs and bathed in living blue, peace rested for that one bright day on the Peak, as if it were some region

> *Where falls not rain, or hail, or any snow,*
> *Or ever wind blows loudly.*

We placed our names, with the date of ascent, in a tin within a crevice, and descended to the Ledge, sitting on the smooth granite, getting our feet into cracks and against projections, and letting ourselves down by our hands, "Jim" going before me, so that I might steady my feet against his powerful shoulders. I was no longer giddy, and faced the precipice of 3,500 feet without a shiver. Repassing the Ledge and Lift, we accomplished the descent through 1,500 feet of ice and snow, with many falls and bruises, but no worse mishap, and there separated, the young men taking the steepest but most direct way to the "Notch," with the intention of getting ready for the march home, and "Jim" and I taking what he thought the safer route for me—a descent over boulders for 2,000 feet, and then a tremendous ascent to the "Notch." I had various falls, and once hung by my frock, which caught on a rock, and "Jim" severed it with his hunting knife, upon which I fell into a crevice full of soft snow. We were driven lower down the mountains than he had intended by impassable tracts of ice, and the ascent was tremendous. For the last 200 feet the boulders were of enormous size, and the steepness fearful. Sometimes I drew myself up on hands and knees, sometimes crawled; sometimes "Jim" pulled me up by my arms or a lariat, and sometimes I stood on his shoulders, or he made steps for me of his feet and hands, but at six we stood on the "Notch" in the splendor of the sinking sun, all color deepening, all peaks glorifying, all shadows purpling, all peril past.

JOHN WESLEY POWELL

(1834–1902)

May 24, 1985.—Sitting safely at my desk, I think about John Wesley Powell and his nine companions pushing off into an unknown river cut between overhanging walls of red. One hundred and sixteen years ago today, they spun away from shore (oddly enough, I chose this morning to write about Powell without remembering that it marks the anniversary of his departure). In four wooden boats, they planned to descend the Green River to the Colorado, then drop through its cliffs and rapids all the way to the mouth of the Grand Canyon. The distance, although they didn't know it at the time, would be 900 miles; the journey would take a hundred nerve-racking days; not everyone would survive.

Fortunately Powell did, and so did his journal, a series of long and narrow strips of brown paper bound in sole leather. This remarkable piece of writing gives a daily account of the whitewater, the whirlpools, the marble walls, the side canyons, and the unbelievable adventures along the treacherous way. I've tried a lot of things in the wilderness, but river running isn't one of them. Nor will it ever be. So I'm particularly impressed by the courage of Powell and his crew as they braved absolutely unknown, unmapped territory. "And so we hold, and let go, and pull, and lift, and ward— among rocks, around rocks, and over rocks. And now we go on through this solemn, mysterious way. The river is very deep, the canyon very narrow, . . . the waters reel and roll and boil, and we are scarcely able to determine where we can go." I can scarcely conceive of the enormous curiosity and personal bravado that compelled these men to seek what lay beyond. Their feat, I think, is far more impressive than Lewis and Clark's.

Twenty-six years after his first trip down the Colorado, Powell revised and enlarged his journal, wrote more about prior and subsequent explorations, added several descriptive chapters, and published the whole as a book called *Canyons of the Colorado*. The text remains one of the best descriptions of canyon country ever written (some would say it *is* the best). Not only are the adventures themselves told with an understated flair that captures the imagination, but the scenery is pictured in such a way that one sees exactly the wonders that opened before Powell's eyes:

> When thinking of these rocks one must not conceive
> of piles of boulders or heaps of fragments, but of a
> whole land of naked rock, with giant forms carved on it:
> cathedral-shaped buttes, towering hundreds of thousands
> of feet, cliffs that cannot be scaled, and canyon walls
> that shrink the river into insignificance, with vast, hol-
> low domes and tall pinnacles and shafts set on the verge
> overhead; and all highly colored—buff, gray, red,

brown, and chocolate—never lichened, never moss-
covered, but bare, and often polished.

Reading these words I feel like I'm alongside him, gazing
at the stretch between Labyrinth Canyon and Bonita Bend.
If I didn't have to ride in a raft, I'd like to be there now.

From *Canyons of the Colorado*

June 8.—We enter the canyon, and until noon find a succession of rapids, over which our boats have to be taken.

Here I must explain our method of proceeding at such
places. The "Emma Dean" goes in advance; the other boats
follow, in obedience to signals. When we approach a rapid,
or what on other rivers would often be called a fall, I stand
on deck to examine it, while the oarsmen back water, and
we drift on as slowly as possible. If I can see a clear chute
between the rocks, away we go; but if the channel is beset
entirely across, we signal the other boats, pull to land, and
I walk along the shore for closer examination. If this reveals
no clear channel, hard work begins. We drop the boats to
the very head of the dangerous place and let them over by
lines or make a portage, frequently carrying both boats and
cargoes over the rocks.

The waves caused by such falls in a river differ much from
the waves of the sea. The water of an ocean wave merely
rises and falls; the form only passes on, and form chases
form unceasingly. A body floating on such waves merely rises
and sinks—does not progress unless impelled by wind or
some other power. But here the water of the wave passes
on while the form remains. The waters plunge down ten or
twenty feet to the foot of a fall, spring up again in a great

wave, then down and up in a series of billows that gradually disappear in the more quiet waters below; but these waves are always there, and one can stand above and count them.

A boat riding such billows leaps and plunges along with great velocity. Now, the difficulty in riding over these falls, when no rocks are in the way, is with the first wave at the foot. This will sometimes gather for a moment, heap up higher and higher, and then break back. If the boat strikes it the instant after it breaks, she cuts through, and the mad breaker dashes its spray over the boat and washes overboard all who do not cling tightly. If the boat, in going over the falls, chances to get caught in some side current and is turned from its course, so as to strike the wave "broadside on," and the wave breaks at the same instant, the boat is capsized; then we must cling to her, for the water-tight compartments act as buoys and she cannot sink; and so we go, dragged through the waves, until still waters are reached, when we right the boat and climb aboard. We have several such experiences to-day.

At night we camp on the right bank, on a little shelving rock between the river and the foot of the cliff; and with night comes gloom into these great depths. After supper we sit by our camp fire, made of driftwood caught by the rocks, and tell stories of wild life; for the men have seen such in the mountains or on the plains, and on the battlefields of the South. It is late before we spread our blankets on the beach.

Lying down, we look up through the canyon and see that only a little of the blue heaven appears overhead—a crescent of blue sky, with two or three constellations peering down upon us. I do not sleep for some time, as the excitement of the day has not worn off. Soon I see a bright star that appears to rest on the very verge of the cliff overhead to the east. Slowly it seems to float from its resting place on the rock over the canyon. At first it appears like a jewel set on the brink of the cliff, but as it moves out from the rock I almost wonder that it does not fall. In fact, it does seem to descend in a gentle curve, as though the bright sky in which the stars are set were spread across the canyon, resting on either wall, and swayed down by its own weight. The stars appear to be in the canyon. I soon discover that it is the bright star Vega; so it occurs to me to designate this part of the wall as the "Cliff of the Harp."

June 9.—One of the party suggests that we call this the Canyon of Lodore, and the name is adopted. Very slowly we make our way, often climbing on the rocks at the edge of the water for a few hundred yards to examine the channel before running it. During the afternoon we come to a place where it is necessary to make a portage. The little boat is landed and the others are signaled to come up.

When these rapids or broken falls occur usually the channel is suddenly narrowed by rocks which have been tumbled from the cliffs or have been washed in by lateral streams. Immediately above the narrow, rocky channel, on one or both sides, there is often a bay of quiet water, in which a landing can be made with ease. Sometimes the water descends with a smooth, unruffled surface from the broad quiet spread above into the narrow, angry channel below by a semi-circular sag. Great care must be taken not to pass over the brink into this deceptive pit, but above it we can row with safety. I walk along the bank to examine the ground, leaving one of my men with a flag to guide the other boats to the landing-place. I soon see one of the boats make shore all right, and feel no more concern; but a minute after, I hear a shout, and, looking around, see one of the boats shooting down the center of the sag. It is the "No Name," with Captain

Howland, his brother, and Goodman. I feel that its going
over is inevitable, and run to save the third boat. A minute
more, and she turns the point and heads for the shore. Then
I turn down stream again and scramble along to look for
the boat that has gone over. The first fall is not great, only
10 or 12 feet, and we often run such; but below, the river
tumbles down again for 40 or 50 feet, in a channel filled with
dangerous rocks that break the waves into whirlpools and
beat them into foam. I pass around a great crag just in time
to see the boat strike a rock and, rebounding from the shock,
careen and fill its open compartment with water. Two of
the men lose their oars; she swings around and is carried
down at a rapid rate, broadside on, for a few yards, when,
striking amidships on another rock with great force, she is
broken quite in two and the men are thrown into the river.
But the larger part of the boat floats buoyantly, and they
soon seize it, and down the river they drift, past the rocks
for a few hundred yards, to a second rapid filled with huge
boulders, where the boat strikes again and is dashed to pieces,
and the men and fragments are soon carried beyond my sight.
Running along, I turn a bend and see a man's head above
the water, washed about in a whirlpool below a great rock.
It is Frank Goodman, clinging to the rock with a grip upon
which life depends. Coming opposite, I see Howland trying
to go to his aid from an island on which he has been washed.
Soon he comes near enough to reach Frank with a pole,
which he extends toward him. The latter lets go the rock,
grasps the pole, and is pulled ashore. Seneca Howland is
washed farther down the island and is caught by some rocks,
and, though somewhat bruised, manages to get ashore in
safety. This seems a long time as I tell it, but it is quickly done.

   And now the three men are on an island, with a swift,
dangerous river on either side and a fall below. The "Em-

ma Dean'' is soon brought down, and Sumner, starting above as far as possible, pushes out. Right skillfully he plies the oars, and a few strokes set him on the island at the proper point. Then they all pull the boat up stream as far as they are able, until they stand in water up to their necks. One sits on a rock and holds the boat until the others are ready to pull, then gives the boat a push, clings to it with his hands, and climbs in as they pull for mainland, which they reach in safety. We are as glad to shake hands with them as though they had been on a voyage around the world and wrecked on a distant coast.

June 16.—Our first work this morning is to carry our cargoes to the foot of the falls. Then we commence letting down the boats. We take two of them down in safety, but not without great difficulty; for, where such a vast body of water, rolling down an inclined plane, is broken into eddies and cross-currents by rocks projecting from the cliffs and piles of boulders in the channel, it requires excessive labor and much care to prevent the boats from being dashed against the rocks or breaking away. Sometimes we are compelled to hold the boat against a rock above a chute until a second line, attached to the stem, is carried to some point below, and when all is ready the first line is detached and the boat given to the current, when she shoots down and the men below swing her into some eddy.

At such a place we are letting down the last boat, and as she is set free a wave turns her broadside down the stream, with the stem, to which the line is attached, from shore and a little up. They haul on the line to bring the boat in, but the power of the current, striking obliquely against her, shoots her out into the middle of the river. The men have their hands burned with the friction of the passing line; the boat breaks away and speeds with great velocity down the stream. The "Maid of the Canyon" is lost! So it seems; but she drifts some distance and swings into an eddy, in which she spins about until we arrive with the small boat and rescue her.

Soon we are on our way again, and stop at the mouth of a little brook on the right for a late dinner. This brook comes down from the distant mountains in a deep side canyon. We set out to explore it, but are soon cut off from farther progress up the gorge by a high rock, over which the brook glides in a smooth sheet. The rock is not quite vertical, and the water does not plunge over it in a fall.

Then we climb up to the left for an hour, and are 1,000 feet above the river and 600 above the brook. Just before us the canyon divides, a little stream coming down on the right and another on the left, and we can look away up either of these canyons, through an ascending vista, to cliffs and crags and towers a mile back and 2,000 feet overhead. To the right a dozen gleaming cascades are seen. Pines and firs stand on the rocks and aspens overhang the brooks. The rocks below are red and brown, set in deep shadows, but above they are buff and vermilion and stand in the sunshine. The light above, made more brilliant by the bright-tinted rocks, and the shadows below, more gloomy by reason of the somber hues of the brown walls, increase the apparent depths of the canyons, and it seems a long way up to the world of sunshine and open sky, and a long way down to the bottom of the canyon glooms. Never before have I received such an impression of the vast heights of these canyon walls, not even at the Cliff of the Harp, where the very heavens seemed to rest on their summits. We sit on some overhanging rocks and enjoy the scene for a time, listening to the music of the falling waters away up the canyon. We name this Rippling Brook.

June 21.—We float around the long rock and enter another canyon. The walls are high and vertical, the canyon is narrow, and the river fills the whole space below, so that there is no landing-place at the foot of the cliff. The Green is greatly increased by the Yampa, and we now have a much larger river. All this volume of water, confined, as it is, in a narrow channel and rushing with great velocity, is set eddying and spinning in whirlpools by projecting rocks and short curves, and the waters waltz their way through the canyon, making their own rippling, rushing, roaring music. The canyon is much narrower than any we have seen. We manage our boats with difficulty. They spin from side to side and we know not where we are going, and find it impossible to keep them headed down the stream. At first this causes us great alarm, but we soon find there is little danger, and that there is a general movement or progression down the river, to which this whirling is but an adjunct—that it is the merry mood of the river to dance through this deep, dark gorge, and right gaily do we join in the sport.

July 7.—We find quiet water to-day, the river sweeping in great and beautiful curves, the canyon walls steadily increasing in altitude. The escarpments formed by the cut edges of the rock are often vertical, sometimes terraced, and in some places the treads of the terraces are sloping. In these quiet curves vast amphitheaters are formed, now in vertical rocks, now in steps.

The salient point of rock within the curve is usually broken down in a steep slope, and we stop occasionally to climb up at such a place, where on looking down we can see the river sweeping the foot of the opposite cliff in a great, easy curve, with a perpendicular or terraced wall rising from the water's edge many hundreds of feet. One of these we find very symmetrical and name it Sumner's Amphitheater.

The cliffs are rarely broken by the entrance of side canyons, and we sweep around curve after curve with almost continuous walls for several miles.

Late in the afternoon we find the river very much rougher and come upon rapids, not dangerous, but still demanding close attention. We camp at night on the right bank, having made 26 miles.

July 8.—This morning Bradley and I go out to climb, and gain an altitude of more than 2,000 feet above the river, but still do not reach the summit of the wall.

After dinner we pass through a region of the wildest desolation. The canyon is very tortuous, the river very rapid, and many lateral canyons enter on either side. These usually have their branches, so that the region is cut into a wilderness of gray and brown cliffs. In several places these lateral canyons are separated from one another only by narrow walls, often hundreds of feet high,—so narrow in places that where softer rocks are found below they have crumbled away and left holes in the wall, forming passages from one canyon into another. These we often call natural bridges; but they were never intended to span streams. They would better, perhaps, be called side doors between canyon chambers. Piles of broken rock lie against these walls; crags and tower-shaped peaks are seen everywhere, and away above them, long lines of broken cliffs; and above and beyond the cliffs are pine forests, of which we obtain occasional glimpses as we look up through a vista of rocks. The walls are almost without vegetation; a few dwarf bushes are seen here and there clinging to the rocks, and cedars grow from the crevices—not like the cedars of a land refreshed with rains, great cones bedecked with spray, but ugly clumps, like war clubs beset with spines. We are minded to call this the Canyon of Desolation.

July 23.—On starting, we come at once to difficult rapids and falls, that in many places are more abrupt than in any of the canyons through which we have passed, and we decide to name this Cataract Canyon. From morning until noon the course of the river is to the west; the scenery is grand, with rapids and falls below, and walls above, beset with crags and pinnacles. Just at noon we wheel again to the south and go into camp for dinner.

While the cook is preparing it, Bradley, Captain Powell, and I go up into a side canyon that comes in at this point. We enter through a very narrow passage, having to wade along the course of a little stream until a cascade interrupts our progress. Then we climb to the right for a hundred feet until we reach a little shelf, along which we pass, walking with great care, for it is narrow; thus we pass around the fall. Here the gorge widens into a spacious, sky-roofed chamber. In the farther end is a beautiful grove of cotton-woods, and between us and the cottonwoods the little stream widens out into three clear lakelets with bottoms of smooth rock. Beyond the cottonwoods the brook tumbles in a series of white, shining cascades from heights that seem immeasurable. Turning around, we can look through the cleft through which we came and see the river with towering walls beyond. What a chamber for a restingplace is this! hewn from the solid rock, the heavens for a ceiling, cascade fountains within, a grove in the conservatory, clear lakelets for a refreshing bath, and an outlook through the doorway on a raging river, with cliffs and mountains beyond.

Our way after dinner is through a gorge, grand beyond description. The walls are nearly vertical, the river broad and swift, but free from rocks and falls. From the edge of the water to the brink of the cliffs it is 1,600 to 1,800 feet. At this great depth the river rolls in solemn majesty. The cliffs are reflected from the more quiet river, and we seem to be in the depths of the earth, and yet we can look down into waters that reflect a bottomless abyss. Early in the afternoon we arrive at the head of more rapids and falls, but, wearied with past work, we determine to rest, so go into camp, and the afternoon and evening are spent by the men in discussing the probabilities of successfully navigating the river below. The barometric records are examined to see what descent we have made since we left the mouth of the Grand, and what descent since we left the Pacific Railroad, and what fall there yet must be to the river ere we reach the end of the great canyons. The conclusion at which the men arrive seems to be about this: that there are great descents yet to be made, but if they are distributed in rapids and short falls, as they have been heretofore, we shall be able to overcome them; but may be we shall come to a fall in these canyons which we cannot pass, where the walls rise from the water's edge, so that we cannot land, and where the water is so swift that we cannot return. Such places have been found, except that the falls were not so great but that we could run them with safety. How will it be in the future? So they speculate over the serious probabilities in jesting mood.

August 1.—We drop down two miles this morning and go into camp again. There is a low, willow-covered strip of land along the walls on the east. Across this we walk, to explore an alcove which we see from the river. On entering, we find a little grove of box-elder and cottonwood trees, and turning to the right, we find ourselves in a vast chamber, carved out of the rock. At the upper end there is a clear, deep pool of water, bordered with verdure. Standing by the side of this, we can see the grove at the entrance. The chamber is more than 200 feet high, 500 feet long, and 200 feet wide. Through the ceiling, and on through the rocks for a thousand feet above, there is a narrow, winding skylight; and this is all carved out by a little stream which runs only during the few showers that fall now and then in this arid country. The waters from the bare rocks back of the canyon, gathering rapidly into a small channel, have eroded a deep side canyon, through which they run until they fall into the farther end of this chamber. The rock at the ceiling is hard, the rock below, very soft and friable; and having cut through the upper and harder portion down into the lower and softer, the stream has washed out these friable sandstones; and thus the chamber has been excavated. . . . Here we bring our camp. When "Old Shady" sings us a song at night, we are pleased to find that this hollow in the rock is filled with sweet sounds. It was doubtless made for an academy of music by its storm-born architect; so we name it Music Temple.

August 3.—Start early this morning. The features of this canyon are greatly diversified. Still vertical walls at times. These are usually found to stand above great curves. The river, sweeping around these bends, undermines the cliffs in places. Sometimes the rocks are overhanging; in other curves, curious, narrow glens are found. Through these we climb, by a rough stairway, perhaps several hundred feet, to where a spring bursts out from under an overhanging cliff, and where cottonwoods and willows stand, while along the curves of the brooklet oaks grow, and other rich vegetation is seen, in marked contrast to the general appearance of naked rock. We call these Oak Glens.

Other wonderful features are the many side canyons or gorges that we pass. Sometimes we stop to explore these for a short distance. In some places their walls are much nearer each other above than below, so that they look somewhat like caves or chambers in the rocks. Usually, in going up such a gorge, we find beautiful vegetation; but our way is often cut off by deep basins, or "potholes," as they are called.

On the walls, and back many miles into the country, numbers of monument-shaped buttes are observed. So we have a curious *ensemble* of wonderful features—carved walls, royal arches, glens, alcove gulches, mounds, and monuments. From which of these features shall we select a name? We decide to call it Glen Canyon.

August 4.—To-day the walls grow higher and the canyon much narrower. Monuments are still seen on either side; beautiful glens and alcoves and gorges and side canyons are yet found. After dinner we find the river making a sudden turn to the northwest and the whole character of the canyon changed. The walls are many hundreds of feet higher, and the rocks are chiefly variegated shales of beautiful colors—creamy orange above, then bright vermilion, and below, purple and chocolate beds, with green and yellow sands. We run four miles through this, in a direction a little to the west of north, wheel again to the west, and pass into a portion of the canyon where the characteristics are more like those above the bend. At night we stop at the mouth of a creek coming in from the right, and suppose it to be the Paria, which was described to me last year by a Mormon missionary. Here the canyon terminates abruptly in a line of cliffs, which stretches from either side across the river.

August 5.—With some feeling of anxiety we enter a new canyon this morning. We have learned to observe closely the texture of the rock. In softer strata we have a quiet river, in harder we find rapids and falls. Below us are the limestones and hard sandstones which we found in Cataract Canyon. This bodes toil and danger. Besides the texture of the rocks, there is another condition which affects the character of the channel, as we have found by experience. Where the strata are horizontal the river is often quiet and, even though it may be very swift in places, no great obstacles are found. Where the rocks incline in the direction traveled, the river usually sweeps with great velocity, but still has few rapids and falls. But where the rocks dip up stream and the river cuts obliquely across the upturned formations, harder strata above and softer below, we have rapids and falls. Into hard rocks and into rocks dipping up stream we pass this morning and start on a long, rocky, mad rapid. On the left there is a vertical rock, and down by this cliff and around to the left we glide, tossed just enough by the waves to appreciate the rate at which we are traveling.

The canyon is narrow, with vertical walls, which gradually grow higher. More rapids and falls are found. We come to one with a drop of sixteen feet, around which we make a portage, and then stop for dinner. Then a run of two miles, and another portage, long and difficult; then we camp for the night on a bank of sand.

August 9.—And now the scenery is on a grand scale. The walls of the canyon, 2,500 feet high, are of marble, of many beautiful colors, often polished below by the waves, and sometimes far up the sides, where showers have washed the sands over the cliffs. At one place I have a walk for more than a mile on a marble pavement, all polished and fretted with strange devices and embossed in a thousand fantastic patterns. Through a cleft in the wall the sun shines on this pavement and it gleams in iridescent beauty.

I pass up into the cleft. It is very narrow, with a succession of pools standing at higher levels as I go back. The water in these pools is clear and cool, coming down from springs. Then I return to the pavement, which is but a terrace or bench, over which the river runs at its flood, but left bare at present. Along the pavement in many places are basins of clear water, in strange contrast to the red mud of the river. At length I come to the end of this marble terrace and take again to the boat.

Riding down a short distance, a beautiful view is presented. The river turns sharply to the east and seems inclosed by a wall set with a million brilliant gems. What can it mean? Every eye is engaged, every one wonders. On coming nearer we find fountains bursting from the rock high overhead, and the spray in the sunshine forms the gems which bedeck the wall. The rocks below the fountain are covered with mosses and ferns and many beautiful flowering plants. We name it Vasey's Paradise, in honor of the botanist who traveled with us last year.

We pass many side canyons to-day that are dark, gloomy passages back into the heart of the rocks that form the plateau through which this canyon is cut. It rains again this afternoon. Scarcely do the first drops fall when little rills run down the walls. As the storm comes on, the little rills increase in size, until great streams are formed. Although the walls of the canyon are chiefly limestone, the adjacent country is of red sandstone; and now the waters, loaded with these sands, come down in rivers of bright red mud, leaping over the walls in innumerable cascades. It is plain now how these walls are polished in many places.

At last the storm ceases and we go on. We have cut through the sandstones and limestones met in the upper part of the canyon, and through one great bed of marble a thousand feet in thickness. In this, great numbers of caves are hollowed out, and carvings are seen which suggest architectural forms, though on a scale so grand that architectural terms belittle them. As this great bed forms a distinctive feature of the canyon, we call it Marble Canyon.

It is a peculiar feature of these walls that many projections are set out into the river, as if the wall was buttressed for support. The walls themselves are half a mile high, and these buttresses are on a corresponding scale, jutting into the river scores of feet. In the recesses between these projections there are quiet bays, except at the foot of a rapid, when there are dancing eddies or whirlpools. Sometimes these alcoves have caves at the back, giving them the appearance of great depth. Then other caves are seen above, forming vast dome-shaped chambers. The walls and buttresses and chambers are all of marble.

The river is now quiet; the canyon wider. Above, when the river is at its flood, the waters gorge up, so that the difference between high and low water mark is often 50 or even 70 feet, but here high-water mark is not more than 20 feet above the present stage of the river. Sometimes there is a narrow flood plain between the water and the wall. Here we first discover mesquite shrubs,—small trees with finely divided leaves and pods, somewhat like the locust.

August 13.—We are now ready to start on our way down the Great Unknown. Our boats, tied to a common stake, chafe each other as they are tossed by the fretful river. They ride high and buoyant, for their loads are lighter than we would desire. We have but a month's rations remaining. The flour has been resifted through the mosquito-net sieve; the spoiled bacon has been dried and the worst of it boiled; the few pounds of dried apples have been spread in the sun and reshrunken to their normal bulk. The sugar has all melted and gone on its way down the river. But we have a large sack of coffee. The lightening of the boats has this advantage: they will ride the waves better and we shall have but little to carry when we make a portage.

We are three quarters of a mile in the depths of the earth, and the great river shrinks into insignificance as it dashes its angry waves against the walls and cliffs that rise to the world above; the waves are but puny ripples, and we but pigmies, running up and down the sands or lost among the boulders.

We have an unknown distance yet to run, an unknown river to explore. What falls there are, we know not; what rocks beset the channel, we know not; what walls rise over the river, we know not. Ah, well! we may conjecture many things. The men talk as cheerfully as ever; jests are bandied about freely this morning; but to me the cheer is somber and the jests are ghastly.

With some eagerness and some anxiety and some misgiving we enter the canyon below and are carried along by the swift water through walls which rise from its very edge. They have the same structure that we noticed yesterday—tiers of irregular shelves below, and, above these, steep slopes to the foot of marble cliffs. We run six miles in a little more than half an hour and emerge into a more open portion of the canyon, where high hills and ledges of rock intervene between the river and the distant walls. Just at the head of this open place the river runs across a dike; that is, a fissure in the rocks, open to depths below, was filled with eruptive matter, and this on cooling was harder than the rocks through which the crevice was made, and when these were washed away the harder volcanic matter remained as a wall, and the river has cut a gateway through it several hundred feet high and as many wide. As it crosses the wall, there is a fall below and a bad rapid, filled with boulders of trap; so we stop to make a portage. Then on we go, gliding by hills and ledges, with distant walls in view; sweeping past sharp angles of rock; stopping at a few points to examine rapids, which we find can be run, until we have made another five miles, when we land for dinner.

Then we let down with lines over a long rapid and start again. Once more the walls close in, and we find ourselves in a narrow gorge, the water again filling the channel and being very swift. With great care and constant watchfulness we proceed, making about four miles this afternoon, and camp in a cave.

August 14.—At daybreak we walk down the bank of the river, on a little sandy beach, to take a view of a new feature in the canyon. Heretofore hard rocks have given us bad river; soft rocks, smooth water; and a series of rocks harder than any we have experienced sets in. The river enters the gneiss! We can see but a little way into the granite gorge, but it looks threatening.

After breakfast we enter on the waves. At the very introduction it inspires awe. The canyon is narrower than we have ever before seen it; the water is swifter; there are but few broken rocks in the channel; but the walls are set, on either side, with pinnacles and crags; and sharp, angular buttresses, bristling with wind- and wave-polished spires, extend far out into the river.

Ledges of rock jut into the stream, their tops sometimes just below the surface, sometimes rising a few or many feet above; and island ledges and island pinnacles and island towers break the swift course of the stream into chutes and eddies and whirlpools. We soon reach a place where a creek comes in from the left, and, just below, the channel is choked with boulders, which have washed down this lateral canyon and formed a dam, over which there is a fall of 30 or 40 feet; but on the boulders foothold can be had, and we make a portage. Three more such dams are found. Over one we make a portage; at the other two are chutes through which we can run.

As we proceed the granite rises higher, until nearly a thousand feet of the lower part of the walls are composed of this rock.

About eleven o'clock we hear a great roar ahead, and approach it very cautiously. The sound grows louder and louder as we run, and at last we find ourselves above a long, broken fall, with ledges and pinnacles of rock obstructing the river. There is a descent of perhaps 75 or 80 feet in a third of a mile, and the rushing waters break into great waves on the rocks, and lash themselves into a mad, white foam. We can land just above, but there is no foothold on either side by which we can make a portage. It is nearly a thousand feet to the top of the granite; so it will be impossible to carry our boats around, though we can climb to the summit up a side gulch and, passing along a mile or two, descend to the river. This we find on examination; but such a portage would be impracticable for us, and we must run the rapid or abandon the river. There is no hesitation. We step into our boats, push off, and away we go, first on smooth but swift water, then we strike a glassy wave and ride to its top, down again into the trough, up again on a higher wave, and down and up on waves higher and still higher until we strike one just as it curls back, and a breaker rolls over our little boat. Still on we speed, shooting past projecting rocks, till the little boat is caught in a whirlpool and spun around several times. At last we pull out again into the stream. And now the other boats have passed us. The open compartment of the "Emma

Dean'' is filled with water and every breaker rolls over us. Hurled back from a rock, now on this side, now on that, we are carried into an eddy, in which we struggle for a few minutes, and are then out again, the breakers still rolling over us. Our boat is unmanageable, but she cannot sink, and we drift down another hundred yards through breakers—how, we scarcely know. We find the other boats have turned into an eddy at the foot of the fall and are waiting to catch us as we come, for the men have seen that our boat is swamped. They push out as we come near and pull us in against the wall. Our boat bailed, on we go again.

The walls now are more than a mile in height—a vertical distance difficult to appreciate. Stand on the south steps of the Treasury building in Washington and look down Pennsylvania Avenue to the Capitol; measure this distance overhead, and imagine cliffs to extend to that altitude, and you will understand what is meant; or stand at Canal Street in New York and look up Broadway to Grace Church, and you have about the distance; or stand at Lake Street in Chicago and look down to the Central Depot, and you have it again.

A thousand feet of this is up through granite crags; then steep slopes and perpendicular cliffs rise one above another to the summit. The gorge is black and narrow below, red and gray and flaring above, with crags and angular projections on the walls, which, cut in many places by side canyons, seem to be a vast wilderness of rocks. Down in these grand, gloomy depths we glide, ever listening, for the mad waters keep up their roar; ever watching, ever peering ahead, for the narrow canyon is winding and the river is closed in so that we can see but a few hundred yards, and what there may be below we know not; so we listen for falls and watch for rocks, stopping now and then in the bay of a recess to admire the gigantic scenery; and ever as we go there is some new pinnacle or tower, some crag or peak, some distant view of the upper plateau, some strangely shaped rock, or some deep, narrow side canyon.

August 25.—We make 12 miles this morning, when we come to monuments of lava standing in the river,—low rocks mostly, but some of them shafts more than a hundred feet high. Going on down three or four miles, we find them increasing in number. Great quantities of cooled lava and many cinder cones are seen on either side; and then we come to an abrupt cataract. Just over the fall on the right wall a cinder cone, or extinct volcano, with a well-defined crater, stands on the very brink of the canyon. This, doubtless, is the one we saw two or three days ago. From this volcano vast floods of lava have been poured down into the river, and a stream of molten rock has run up the canyon three or four miles and down we know not how far. Just where it poured over the canyon wall is the fall. The whole north side as far as we can see is lined with the black basalt, and high up on the opposite wall are patches of the same material, resting on the benches and filling old alcoves and caves, giving the wall a spotted appearance. . . .

What a conflict of water and fire there must have been here! Just imagine a river of molten rock running down into a river of melted snow. What a seething and boiling of the waters; what clouds of steam rolled into the heavens!

Thirty-five miles to-day. Hurrah!

JOHN BURROUGHS

(1837–1921)

Quite simply, John Burroughs was the most popular naturalist of his generation. Even John Muir's accomplishments couldn't match Burroughs' list of twenty-five books published and a record million and a half volumes sold. A 1924 critical study, *The Development of the Natural History Essay in American Literature*, devotes fifty pages to Burroughs' career, less than six to Muir's. Since that time, though, Muir's reputation has grown year by year while Burroughs' has dwindled. His books are out of print, and even the most avid fans of nature writing may not recognize his name.

Three characteristics of Burroughs' essays may account for his relative neglect today. First of all, he introduced no innovations. He synthesized all the major trends of American nature writing, but he thought of nothing new. As a young

man he read Emerson and Thoreau with an "instant thrill";
as a young author he replicated most of their transcendental
ideas. Scientific observation interested him, too, with the
result that his essays also show signs of Audubon's influence
and, toward the end of the nineteenth century, Darwin's.
His contemporaries liked his books because they refined so
many popular issues and ideas, but readers today prefer
going to the original sources. So, paradoxically, what once
made Burroughs famous is the main reason for his present
obscurity.

He did his primary thinking on a New York farm and
in the woods nearby. With all its colloquial charm, that little
world was a rather circumscribed one. Sometimes the observations there, like *Locusts and Wild Honey*'s lengthy 1879
description of hornets and honeybees, were so domesticated
that they sound oddly out of place today. Modern audiences,
it would seem, prefer grizzlies to woodchucks, wild settings
to tame. Rejecting the plowed field for the pathless way, they
enjoy landscapes far less placid. But Burroughs agreed with
Thoreau—one "has only to stay at home and see the procession pass"—and penned his essays with this stricture in
mind.

Finally, Burroughs' old-fashioned point of view about
man's position in the universe sits oddly out of place in our
contemporary world. "Man can have but one interest in
nature," he professes, "namely, to see himself reflected or
interpreted there, and we quickly neglect both poet and phi-
losopher who fail to satisfy, in some measure, this feeling."
While such an anthropocentric thesis is interesting from an
historical perspective, especially when voiced by a Ralph
Waldo Emerson, it sounds exceedingly naive a hundred years
later.

I don't mean to give the impression, however, that John

Burroughs' prose is worthless. To the contrary, it has a certain antique charm that pulses healthy idealism, exuberance, nostalgia, and a genuine love for his chosen way of life. ''I am myself never so well pleased,'' he says, ''as when I can bring [my readers] a fresh bit of natural history, or give them a day in the fields and woods or along the murmuring streams.''

From ''Spring Jottings'' in *Riverby*

For ten or more years past I have been in the habit of jotting down, among other things in my note-book, observations upon the seasons as they passed,—the complexion of the day, the aspects of nature, the arrival of the birds, the opening of the flowers, or any characteristic feature of the passing moment or hour which the great open-air panorama presented.

. . . let me say a word or two in favor of the habit of keeping a journal of one's thoughts and days. To a countryman, especially of a meditative turn, who likes to preserve the flavor of the passing moment, or to a person of leisure anywhere, who wants to make the most of life, a journal will be found a great help. It is a sort of deposit account wherein one saves up bits and fragments of his life that would otherwise be lost to him.

What seemed so insignificant in the passing, or as it lay in embryo in his mind, becomes a valuable part of his experiences when it is fully unfolded and recorded in black and white. The process of writing develops it; the bud becomes the leaf or flower; the one is disentangled from the many and takes definite form and hue. I remember that Thoreau says in a letter to a friend, after his return from a climb to the top of Monadnock, that it is not till he gets home that he really goes over the mountain; that is, I suppose, sees what the climb meant to him when he comes to write an account of it to his friend. Every one's experience is probably much the same; when we try to tell what we saw and felt, even to our journals, we discover more and deeper meanings in things than we had suspected.

The pleasure and value of every walk or journey we take may be doubled to us by carefully noting down the impressions it makes upon us. How much of the flavor of Maine birch I should have missed had I not compelled that vague, unconscious being within me, who absorbs so much and says so little, to unbosom himself at the point of the pen! It was not till after I got home that I really went to Maine, or the the Adirondacks, or to Canada. Out of the chaotic and nebulous impressions which these expeditions gave me, I evolved the real experience. There is hardly anything that does not become much more in the telling than in the thinking or in the feeling.

I see the fishermen floating up and down the river above their nets, which are suspended far out of sight in the water beneath them. They do not know what fish they have got, if any, till after a while they lift the nets up and examine them. In all of us there is a region of sub-consciousness above which our ostensible lives go forward, and in which much comes to us, or is slowly developed, of which we are quite ignorant until we lift up our nets and inspect them.

Then the charm and significance of a day are so subtle and fleeting! Before we know it, it is gone past all recovery. I find that each spring, that each summer and fall and winter of my life, has a hue and quality of its own, given by some prevailing mood, a train of thought, an event, an experience,—a color or quality of which I am quite unconscious at the time, being too near to it, and too completely enveloped by it. But afterward some mood or circumstance, an odor, or fragment of a tune, brings it back as by a flash; for one brief second the adamantine door of the past swings open and gives me a glimpse of my former life. One's journal, dashed off without any secondary motive, may often preserve and renew the past for him in this way.

From "Is It Going to Rain?" in *Locusts and Wild Honey*

We were encamping in the primitive woods, by a little trout-lake which the mountain carried high on his hip, like a soldier's canteen. There were wives in the party, curious to know what the lure was that annually drew their husbands to the woods. That magical writing on a trout's back they would fain decipher, little heeding the warning that what is written here is not given to woman to know.

Our only tent or roof was the sheltering arms of the great birches and maples. What was sauce for the gander should be sauce for the goose, too, so the goose insisted.

A luxurious couch of boughs upon springing poles was prepared, and the night should be not less welcome than the day, which had been idyllic. (A trout dinner had been served by a little spring brook, upon an improvised table covered with moss and decked with ferns, with strawberries from a near clearing.)

At twilight there was an ominous rumble behind the

mountains. I was on the lake, and could see what was brewing there in the west.

As darkness came on, the rumbling increased, and the mountains and the woods and the still air were such good conductors of sound that the ear was vividly impressed. One seemed to feel the enormous convolutions of the clouds in the deep and jarring tones of the thunder. The coming of night in the woods is alone peculiarly impressive, and it is doubly so when out of the darkness comes such a voice as this. But we fed the fire the more industriously, and piled the logs high, and kept the gathering gloom at bay by as large a circle of light as we could command. The lake was a pool of ink and as still as if congealed; not a movement or a sound, save now and then a terrific volley from the cloud batteries now fast approaching. By nine o'clock little puffs of wind began to steal through the woods and tease and toy with our fire. Shortly after, an enormous electric bombshell exploded in the treetops over our heads, and the ball was fairly opened. Then followed three hours, with only two brief intermissions, of as lively elemental music and as copious an outpouring of rain as it was ever my lot to witness. It was a regular meteorological carnival, and the revelers were drunk with the wild sport. The apparent nearness of the clouds and the electric explosion was something remarkable. Every discharge seemed to be in the branches immediately overhead and made us involuntarily cower, as if the next moment the great limbs of the trees, or the trees themselves, would come crashing down. The mountain upon which we were encamped appeared to be the focus of three distinct but converging storms. The last two seemed to come into collision immediately over our camp-fire, and to contend for the right of way, until the heavens were ready to fall and both antagonists were literally spent. We stood in groups about the struggling fire, and when the cannonade became too terrible would withdraw into the cover of the darkness, as if to be a less conspicuous mark for the bolts; or did we fear the fire, with its currents, might attract the lightning? At any rate, some other spot than the one where we happened to be standing seemed desirable when those onsets of the contending elements were the most furious. Something that one could not catch in his hat was liable to drop almost anywhere any minute. The alarm and consternation of the wives communicated itself to the husbands, and they looked solemn and concerned. The air was filled with falling water. The sound upon the myriad leaves and branches was like the roar of a cataract. We put our backs up against the great trees, only to catch a brook on our shoulders or in the backs of our necks. Still the storm waxed. The fire was beaten down lower and lower. It surrendered one post after another, like a besieged city, and finally made only a feeble resistance from beneath a pile of charred logs and branches in the centre. Our garments yielded to the encroachments of the rain in about the same manner. I believe my necktie held out the longest, and carried a few dry threads safely through. Our cunningly devised and bedecked table, which the housekeepers had so doted on and which was ready spread for breakfast, was washed as by the hose of a fire-engine,— only the bare poles remained,—and the couch of springing boughs, that was to make Sleep jealous and o'er-fond, became a bed fit only for amphibians. Still the loosened floods came down; still the great cloud-mortars bellowed and exploded their missiles in the treetops above us. But all nervousness finally passed away, and we became dogged and resigned. Our minds became water-soaked; our thoughts were heavy and bedraggled. We were past the point of joking at one another's expense. The witticisms failed to kindle,—indeed, failed to go, like the matches in our pockets. About midnight the rain slackened, and by one o'clock ceased entirely. How the rest of the night was passed beneath the dripping trees and upon the saturated ground, I have only the dimmest remembrance. All is watery and opaque; the fog settles down and obscures the scene. But I suspect I tried the "wet pack" without being a convert to hydropathy. When the morning dawned, the wives begged to be taken home, convinced that the charms of camping-out were greatly overrated. We, who had tasted this cup before, knew they had read at least a part of the legend of the wary trout without knowing it.

JOHN MUIR

(1838–1914)

Since I assume that almost anyone who reads *Words for the Wild* will be familiar with John Muir's writing and reputation, I also assume that whatever introduction I give will be superfluous. His name is legend, his achievements renowned, his heritage revered. Cogently and forcefully, his words and his actions taught Americans a twentieth-century way of viewing their natural surroundings. Before Muir, we saw a land to be tested and explored; after him, we saw a land to be respected and embraced.

Initially he wrote a euphoric kind of words for the wild that brought out the beauties and pleasures inherent in the natural scene. Some of Muir's best essays were collected first in *The Mountains of California* and reprinted later in *The Yosemite*. They're the words I've chosen to include in this volume because, quite frankly, they're my favorites. Ebullient and enthusiastic, they display a kind of raw verbal power that echoes the energy of the man himself.

Once he wrote that "all Nature's wildness tells the same story—the shocks and outbursts of earthquakes, volcanoes, geysers, roaring, thundering waves and floods, the silent uprush of sap in plants, storms of every sort—each and all are the orderly beauty-making love-beats of Nature's heart." The same metaphor characterizes the rhythm of John Muir's prose. Whether he was lashing himself to a Douglas fir in order to know the sway of the wind, stepping behind a waterfall to feel the "fine, savage music sounding above, beneath, around," or climbing a dangerous alpine spire just because it was there, the man communicates an impassioned vision of the wilderness experience.

Today, nearly seventy-five years after his death, we regard him as the sage who foretold the entire American conservation movement. The heritage he left behind includes Yosemite National Park, some 148,000,000 acres of forest reserves, a glacier that bears his name, a list of titles proclaiming his reverence for the land, the Sierra Club itself, and a myriad of spiritual followers. Without John Muir, it is safe to say, America's wild spaces would have been curtailed drastically and a comprehension of her population's environmental needs arrested, perhaps irrevocably.

Others have shouted his battle cries with more effective results; others have articulated his pantheism more profoundly. But no one successfully has imitated his primal zest for the knowledge of self and surroundings engendered in the wilderness. John Muir, I think, stands alone.

From "A Near View of
the High Sierra" in
The Mountains of California

It was now about the middle of October, the springtime of
snow-flowers. The first winter-clouds had already bloomed,
and the peaks were strewn with fresh crystals, without, however, affecting the climbing to any dangerous extent. And
as the weather was still profoundly calm, and the distance
to the foot of the mountain only a little more than a day,
I felt that I was running no great risk of being storm-bound.

Mount Ritter is king of the mountains of the middle portion of the High Sierra, as Shasta of the north and Whitney
of the south sections. Moreover, as far as I know, it had
never been climbed. I had explored the adjacent wilderness
summer after summer, but my studies thus far had never
drawn me to the top of it. Its height above the sea-level is
about 13,300 feet, and it is fenced round by steeply inclined
glaciers, and cañons of tremendous depth and ruggedness,
which render it almost inaccessible. But difficulties of this
kind only exhilarate the mountaineer. . . .

My general plan was simply this: to scale the cañon wall,
cross over the the eastern flank of the range, and then make
my way southward to the northern spurs of Mount Ritter
in compliance with the intervening topography; for to push
on directly southward from camp through the innumerable
peaks and pinnacles that adorn this portion of the axis of
the range, however interesting, would take too much time,
besides being extremely difficult and dangerous at this time
of year.

All my first day was pure pleasure; simply mountaineering indulgence, crossing the dry pathways of the ancient

glaciers, tracing happy streams, and learning the habits of the birds and marmots in the groves and rocks. Before I had gone a mile from camp, I came to the foot of a white cascade that beats its way down a rugged gorge in the cañon wall, from a height of about nine hundred feet, and pours its throbbing waters into the Tuolumne. I was acquainted with its fountains, which, fortunately, lay in my course. What a fine traveling companion it proved to be, what songs it sang, and how passionately it told the mountain's own joy! Gladly I climbed along its dashing border, absorbing its divine music, and bathing from time to time in waftings of irised spray. Climbing higher, higher, new beauty came streaming on the sight: painted meadows, late-blooming gardens, peaks of rare architecture, lakes here and there, shining like silver, and glimpses of the forested middle region and the yellow lowlands far in the west. Beyond the range I saw the so-called Mono Desert, lying dreamily silent in thick purple light—a desert of heavy sun-glare beheld from a desert of ice-burnished granite. Here the waters divide, shouting in glorious enthusiasm, and falling eastward to vanish in the volcanic sands and dry sky of the Great Basin, or westward to the Great Valley of California, and thence through the Bay of San Francisco and the Golden Gate to the sea.

Passing a little way down over the summit until I had reached an elevation of about 10,000 feet, I pushed on southward toward a group of savage peaks that stand guard about Ritter on the north and west, groping my way, and dealing instinctively with every obstacle as it presented itself. Here a huge gorge would be found cutting across my path, along the dizzy edge of which I scrambled until some less precipitous point was discovered where I might safely venture to the bottom and then, selecting some feasible portion of the opposite wall, reascend with the same slow caution.

Massive, flat-topped spurs alternate with the gorges, plunging abruptly from the shoulders of the snowy peaks, and planting their feet in the warm desert. These were everywhere marked and adorned with characteristic sculptures of the ancient glaciers that swept over this entire region like one vast ice-wind, and the polished surfaces produced by the ponderous flood are still so perfectly preserved that in many places the sunlight reflected from them is about as trying to the eyes as sheets of snow.

God's glacial-mills grind slowly, but they have been kept in motion long enough in California to grind sufficient soil for a glorious abundance of life, though most of the grist has been carried to the lowlands, leaving these high regions comparatively lean and bare; while the post-glacial agents of erosion have not yet furnished sufficient available food over the general surface for more than a few tufts of the hardiest plants, chiefly carices and eriogonae. And it is interesting to learn in this connection that the sparseness and repressed character of the vegetation at this height is caused more by want of soil than by harshness of climate; for, here and there, in sheltered hollows (countersunk beneath the general surface) into which a few rods of well-ground moraine chips have been dumped, we find groves of spruce and pine thirty to forty feet high, trimmed around the edges with willow and huckleberry bushes, and oftentimes still further by an outer ring of tall grasses, bright with lupines, larkspurs, and showy columbines, suggesting a climate by no means repressingly severe. All the streams, too, and the pools at this elevation are furnished with little gardens wherever soil can be made to lie, which, though making scarce any show at a distance, constitute charming surprises to the appreciative observer. In these bits of leafiness a few birds find grateful homes. Having no acquaintance with man, they fear

no ill, and flock curiously about the stranger, almost allowing themselves to be taken in the hand. In so wild and so
beautiful a region was spent my first day, every sight and
sound inspiring, leading one far out of himself, yet feeding
and building up his individuality.

Now came the solemn, silent evening. Long, blue, spiky
shadows crept out across the snow-fields, while a rosy glow,
at first scarce discernible, gradually deepened and suffused
every mountain-top, flushing the glaciers and the harsh crags
above them. This was the alpenglow, to me one of the most
impressive of all the terrestrial manifestations of God. At
the touch of this divine light, the mountains seemed to kindle to a rapt, religious consciousness, and stood hushed and
waiting like devout worshipers. Just before the alpenglow
began to fade, two crimson clouds came streaming across
the summit like wings of flame, rendering the sublime scene
yet more impressive; then came darkness and the stars.

Icy Ritter was still miles away, but I could proceed no
farther that night. I found a good camp-ground on the rim
of a glacier basin about 11,000 feet above the sea. A small
lake nestles in the bottom of it from which I got water for
my tea, and a stormbeaten thicket near by furnished abundance of resiny fire-wood. Somber peaks, hacked and shattered, circled half-way around the horizon, wearing a savage
aspect in the gloaming, and a waterfall chanted solemnly
across the lake on its way down from the foot of a glacier.
The fall and the lake and the glacier were almost equally bare;
while the scraggy pines anchored in the rock-fissures were
so dwarfed and shorn by storm-winds that you might walk
over their tops. In tone and aspect the scene was one of the
most desolate I ever beheld. But the darkest scriptures of
the mountains are illumined with bright passages of love that
never fail to make themselves felt when one is alone.

I made my bed in a nook of the pine-thicket, where the branches were pressed and crinkled overhead like a roof, and bent down around the sides. These are the best bedchambers the high mountains afford—snug as squirrel-nests, well ventilated, full of spicy odors, and with plenty of wind-played needles to sing one asleep. I little expected company, but, creeping in through a low side-door, I found five or six birds nestling among the tassels. The night-wind began to blow soon after dark; at first only a gentle breathing, but increasing toward midnight to a rough gale that fell upon my leafy roof in ragged surges like a cascade, bearing wild sound from the crags overhead. The waterfall sang in chorus, filling the old ice-fountain with its solemn roar, and seeming to increase in power as the night advanced—fit voice for such a landscape. I had to creep out many times to the fire during the night, for it was biting cold and I had no blankets. Gladly I welcomed the morning star.

The dawn in the dry, wavering air of the desert was glorious. Everything encouraged my undertaking and betokened success. There was no cloud in the sky, no storm-tone in the wind. Breakfast of bread and tea was soon made. I fastened a hard, durable crust to my belt by way of provision, in case I should be compelled to pass a night on the mountain-top; then, securing the remainder of my little stock against wolves and wood-rats, I set forth free and hopeful.

How glorious a greeting the sun gives the mountains! To behold this alone is worth the pains of any excursion a thousand times over. The highest peaks burned like islands in a sea of liquid shade. Then the lower peaks and spires caught the glow, and long lances of light, streaming through many a notch and pass, fell thick on the frozen meadows. The majestic form of Ritter was full in sight, and I pushed rapidly on over rounded rock-bosses and pavements, my iron-shod shoes making a clanking sound, suddenly hushed now and then in rugs of bryanthus, and sedgy lake-margins soft as moss. Here, too, in this so-called "land of desolation," I met cassiope, growing in fringes among the battered rocks. Here blossoms had faded long ago, but they were still clinging with happy memories to the evergreen sprays, and still so beautiful as to thrill every fiber of one's being. Winter and summer, you may hear her voice, the low, sweet melody of her purple bells. No evangel among all the mountain plants speaks Nature's love more plainly than cassiope. Where she dwells, the redemption of the coldest solitude is complete. The very rocks and glaciers seem to feel her presence, and become imbued with her own fountain sweetness. All things were warming and awakening. Frozen rills began to flow, the marmots came out of their nests in boulder-piles and climbed sunny rocks to bask, and the dun-headed sparrows were flitting about seeking their breakfasts. The lakes seen from every ridge-top were brilliantly rippled and spangled, shimmering like the thickets of the low Dwarf Pines. The rocks, too, seemed responsive to the vital heat—rock-crystals and snow-crystals thrilling alike. I strode on exhilarated, as if never more to feel fatigue, limbs moving of themselves, every sense unfolding like the thawing flowers, to take part in the new day harmony.

All along my course thus far, excepting when down in the cañons, the landscapes were mostly open to me, and expansive, at least on one side. On the left were the purple plains of Mono, reposing dreamily and warm; on the right, the near peaks springing keenly into the thin sky with more and more impressive sublimity. But these larger views were at length lost. Rugged spurs, and moraines, and huge, projecting buttresses began to shut me in. Every feature became more rigidly alpine, without, however, producing any chilling effect; for going to the mountains is like going home. We always find that the strangest objects in these fountain wilds are in some degree familiar, and we look upon them with a vague sense of having seen them before.

On the southern shore of a frozen lake, I encountered an extensive field of hard, granular snow, up which I scampered in fine tone, intending to follow it to its head, and cross the rocky spur against which it leans, hoping thus to come direct upon the base of the main Ritter peak. The surface was pitted with oval hollows, made by stones and drifted pine-needles that had melted themselves into the mass by the radiation of absorbed sun-heat. These afforded good footholds, but the surface curved more and more steeply at the head, and the pits became shallower and less abundant, until I found myself in danger of being shed off like avalanching snow. I persisted, however, creeping on all fours, and shuffling up the smoothest places on my back, as I had often done on burnished granite, until, after slipping several times, I was compelled to retrace my course to the bottom, and make my way around the west end of the lake, and thence up to the summit of the divide between the head waters of Rush Creek and the northernmost tributaries of the San Joaquin.

Arriving on the summit of this dividing crest, one of the most exciting pieces of pure wilderness was disclosed that I ever discovered in all my mountaineering. There, immediately in front, loomed the majestic mass of Mount Ritter, with a glacier swooping down its face nearly to my feet, then curving westward and pouring its frozen flood into a dark blue lake, whose shores were bound with precipices of crystalline snow; while a deep chasm drawn between the divide and the glacier separated the massive picture from everything else. I could see only the one sublime mountain, the one glacier, the one lake; the whole veiled with one blue shadow —rock, ice, and water close together without a single leaf or sign of life. After gazing spellbound, I began instinctively to scrutinize every notch and gorge and weathered buttress of the mountain, with reference to making the ascent. The entire front above the glacier appeared as one tremendous precipice, slightly receding at the top, and bristling with spires and pinnacles set above one another in formidable array. Massive lichen-stained battlements stood forward here and there, hacked at the top with angular notches, and separated by frosty gullies and recesses that have been veiled in shadow ever since their creation; while to right and left, as far as I could see, were huge, crumbling buttresses, offering no hope to the climber. The head of the glacier sends up a few finger-like branches through narrow *couloirs*; but these seemed too steep and short to be available, especially as I had no ax with which to cut steps, and the numerous narrow-throated gullies down which stones and snow are avalanched seemed hopelessly steep, besides being interrupted by vertical cliffs; while the whole front was rendered still more terribly forbidding by the chill shadow and the gloomy blackness of the rocks.

Descending the divide in a hesitating mood, I picked my way across the yawning chasm at the foot, and climbed out upon the glacier. There were no meadows now to cheer with their brave colors, nor could I hear the dun-headed sparrows, whose cheery notes so often relieve the silence of our highest mountains. The only sounds were the gurgling of small rills down in the veins and crevasses of the glacier, and now and then the rattling report of falling stones, with the echoes they shot out into the crisp air.

I could not distinctly hope to reach the summit from this side, yet I moved on across the glacier as if driven by fate.

Contending with myself, the season is too far spent, I said, and even should I be successful, I might be storm-bound on the mountain; and in the cloud-darkness, with the cliffs and crevasses covered with snow, how could I escape? No; I must wait till next summer. I would only approach the mountain now, and inspect it, creep about its flanks, learn what I could of its history, holding myself ready to flee on the approach of the first storm-cloud. But we little know until tried how much of the uncontrollable there is in us, urging across glaciers and torrents, and up dangerous heights, let the judgment forbid as it may.

I succeeded in gaining the foot of the cliff on the eastern extremity of the glacier, and there discovered the mouth of a narrow avalanche gully, through which I began to climb, intending to follow it as far as possible, and at least obtain some fine wild views for my pains. Its general course is oblique to the plane of the mountain-face, and the metamorphic slates of which the mountain is built are cut by cleavage planes in such a way that they weather off in angular blocks, giving rise to irregular steps that greatly facilitate climbing on the sheer places. I thus made my way into a wilderness of crumbling spires and battlements, built together in bewildering combinations, and glazed in many places with a thin coating of ice, which I had to hammer off with stones. The situation was becoming gradually more perilous; but, having passed several dangerous spots, I dared not think of descending; for, so steep was the entire ascent, one would inevitably fall to the glacier in case a single misstep were made. Knowing, therefore, the tried danger beneath, I became all the more anxious concerning the developments to be made above, and began to be conscious of a vague foreboding of what actually befell; not that I was given to fear, but rather because my instincts, usually so positive and true, seemed vitiated in some way, and were leading me astray. At length, after attaining an elevation of about 12,800 feet, I found myself at the foot of a sheer drop in the bed of the avalanche channel I was tracing, which seemed absolutely to bar further progress. It was only about forty-five or fifty feet high, and somewhat roughened by fissures and projections; but these seemed so slight and insecure, as footholds, that I tried hard to avoid the precipice altogether, by scaling the wall of the channel on either side. But, though less steep, the walls were smoother than the obstructing rock, and repeated efforts only showed that I must either go right ahead or turn back. The tried dangers beneath seemed even greater than that of the cliff in front; therefore, after scanning its face again and again, I began to scale it, picking my holds with intense caution. After gaining a point about halfway to the top, I was suddenly brought to a dead stop, with arms outspread, clinging close to the face of the rock, unable to move hand or foot either up or down. My doom appeared fixed. I *must* fall. There would be a moment of bewilderment, and then a lifeless rumble down the one general precipice to the glacier below.

When this final danger flashed upon me, I became nerve-shaken for the first time since setting foot on the mountains, and my mind seemed to fill with a stifling smoke. But this terrible eclipse lasted only a moment, when life blazed forth again with preternatural clearness. I seemed suddenly to become possessed of a new sense. The other self, bygone experiences, Instinct, or Guardian Angel,—call it what you will,—came forward and assumed control. Then my trembling muscles became firm again, every rift and flaw in the rock was seen as through a microscope, and my limbs moved with a positiveness and precision with which I seemed to have nothing at all to do. Had I been borne aloft upon wings, my deliverance could not have been more complete.

Above this memorable spot, the face of the mountain is still more savagely hacked and torn. It is a maze of yawning chasms and gullies, in the angles of which rise beetling crags and piles of detached boulders that seem to have been gotten ready to be launched below. But the strange influx of strength I had received seemed inexhaustible. I found a way without effort, and soon stood upon the topmost crag in the blessed light.

How truly glorious the landscape circled around this noble summit!—giant mountains, valleys innumerable, glaciers and meadows, rivers and lakes, with the wide blue sky bent tenderly over them all. But in my first hour of freedom from that terrible shadow, the sunlight in which I was laving seemed all in all.

Looking southward along the axis of the range, the eye is first caught by a row of exceedingly sharp and slender spires, which rise openly to a height of about a thousand feet, above a series of short, residual glaciers that lean back against their bases; their fantastic sculpture and the unrelieved sharpness with which they spring out of the ice rendering them peculiarly wild and striking. These are "The Minarets." Beyond them you behold a sublime wilderness of mountains, their snowy summits towering together in crowded abundance, peak beyond peak, swelling higher, higher as they sweep on southward, until the culminating point of the range is reached on Mount Whitney, near the head of the Kern River, at an elevation of nearly 14,700 feet above the level of the sea.

Westward, the general flank of the range is seen flowing sublimely away from the sharp summits, in smooth undulations; a sea of huge gray granite waves dotted with lakes and meadows, and fluted with stupendous cañons that grow steadily deeper as they recede in the distance. Below this gray region lies the dark forest zone, broken here and there by upswelling ridges and domes; and yet beyond lies a yellow, hazy belt, marking the broad plain of the San Joaquin, bounded on its farther side by the blue mountains of the coast.

Turning now to the northward, there in the immediate foreground is the glorious Sierra Crown, with Cathedral Peak, a temple of marvelous architecture, a few degrees to the left of it; the gray, massive form of Mammoth Mountain to the right; while Mounts Ord, Gibbs, Dana, Conness, Tower Peak, Castle Peak, Silver Mountain, and a host of noble companions, as yet nameless, make a sublime show along the axis of the range.

Eastward, the whole region seems a land of desolation covered with beautiful light. The torrid volcanic basin of Mono, with its one bare lake fourteen miles long; Owen's Valley and the broad lava table-land at its head, dotted with craters, and the massive Inyo Range, rivaling even the Sierra in height; these are spread, map-like, beneath you, with countless ranges beyond, passing and overlapping one another and fading on the glowing horizon.

At a distance of less than 3,000 feet below the summit of Mount Ritter you may find tributaries of the San Joaquin and Owen's rivers, bursting forth from the ice and snow of the glaciers that load its flanks; while a little to the north of here are found the highest affluents of the Tuolumne and Merced. Thus, the fountains of four of the principal rivers of California are within a radius of four or five miles.

Lakes are seen gleaming in all sorts of places,—round, or oval, or square, like very mirrors; others narrow and sinuous, drawn close around the peaks like silver zones, the highest reflecting only rocks, snow, and the sky. But neither these nor the glaciers, nor the bits of brown meadow and moorland that occur here and there, are large enough to make any marked impression upon the mighty wilderness of mountains. The eye, rejoicing in its freedom, roves about the vast expanse, yet returns again and again to the fountain peaks. Perhaps some one of the multitude excites special attention, some gigantic castle with turret and battlement, or some Gothic cathedral more abundantly spired than Milan's. But, generally, when looking for the first time from an all-embracing standpoint like this, the inexperienced observer is oppressed by the incomprehensible grandeur, variety, and abundance of the mountains rising shoulder to shoulder beyond the reach of vision; and it is only after they have been studied one by one, long and lovingly, that their far-reaching harmonies become manifest. Then, penetrate the wilderness where you may, the main telling features, to which all the surrounding topography is subordinate, are quickly perceived, and the most complicated clusters of peaks stand revealed harmoniously correlated and fashioned like works of art— eloquent monuments of the ancient ice-rivers that brought them into relief from the general mass of the range. The cañons, too, some of them a mile deep, mazing wildly through the mighty host of mountains, however lawless and ungovernable at first sight they appear, are at length recognized as the necessary effects of causes which followed each other in harmonious sequence—Nature's poems carved on tables of stone—the simplest and most emphatic of her glacial compositions.

Could we have been here to observe during the glacial period, we should have overlooked a wrinkled ocean of ice as continuous as that now covering the landscapes of Greenland; filling every valley and cañon with only the tops of the fountain peaks rising darkly above the rock-encumbered ice-waves like islets in a stormy sea—those islets the only hints of the glorious landscapes now smiling in the sun. Standing here in the deep, brooding silence all the wilderness seems motionless, as if the work of creation were done. But in the midst of this outer steadfastness we know there is incessant motion and change. Ever and anon, avalanches are falling from yonder peaks. These cliff-bound glaciers, seemingly wedged and immovable, are flowing like water and grinding the rocks beneath them. The lakes are lapping their granite shores and wearing them away, and every one of these rills and young rivers is fretting the air into music, and carrying the mountains to the plains. Here are the roots of all the life of the valleys, and here more simply than elsewhere is the eternal flux of nature manifested. Ice changing to water, lakes to meadows, and mountains to plains. And while we thus contemplate Nature's methods of landscape creation, and, reading the records she has carved on the rocks, reconstruct, however imperfectly, the landscapes of the past, we also learn that as these we now behold have succeeded those of the pre-glacial age, so they in turn are withering and vanishing to be succeeded by others yet unborn.

But in the midst of these fine lessons and landscapes, I had to remember that the sun was wheeling far to the west, while a new way down the mountain had to be discovered to some point on the timber line where I could have a fire; for I had not even burdened myself with a coat. I first scanned the western spurs, hoping some way might appear through which I might reach the northern glacier, and cross its snout; or pass around the lake into which it flows, and thus strike my morning track. This route was soon sufficiently unfolded to show that, if practicable at all, it would require so much time that reaching camp that night would be out of the question. I therefore scrambled back eastward, descending the southern slopes obliquely at the same time. Here the crags seemed less formidable, and the head of a glacier that flows north-east came in sight, which I determined to follow as far as possible, hoping thus to make my way to the foot of the peak on the east side, and thence across the intervening cañons and ridges to camp.

The inclination of the glacier is quite moderate at the head, and, as the sun had softened the *névé*, I made safe and rapid progress, running and sliding, and keeping up a sharp outlook for crevasses. About half a mile from the head, there is an ice-cascade, where the glacier pours over a sharp declivity and is shattered into massive blocks separated by deep, blue fissures. To thread my way through the slippery mazes of this crevassed portion seemed impossible, and I endeavored to avoid it by climbing off to the shoulder of the mountain. But the slopes rapidly steepened and at length fell away in sheer precipices, compelling a return to the ice. Fortunately, the day had been warm enough to loosen the ice-crystals so as to admit of hollows being dug in the rotten portions of the blocks, thus enabling me to pick my way with far less difficulty than I had anticipated. Continuing down over the snout, and along the left lateral moraine, was only a confident saunter, showing that the ascent of the mountain by way of this glacier is easy, provided one is armed with an ax to cut steps here and there.

The lower end of the glacier was beautifully waved and barred by the outcropping edges of the bedded ice-layers which represent the annual snowfalls, and to some extent the irregularities of structure caused by the weathering of the walls of crevasses, and by separate snowfalls which have been followed by rain, hail, thawing and freezing, etc. Small rills were gliding and swirling over the melting surface with a smooth, oily appearance, in channels of pure ice—their quick, compliant movements contrasting most impressively with the rigid, invisible flow of the glacier itself, on whose back they all were riding.

Night drew near before I reached the eastern base of the mountain, and my camp lay many a rugged mile to the north; but ultimate success was assured. It was now only a matter of endurance and ordinary mountain-craft. The sunset was, if possible, yet more beautiful than that of the day before. The Mono landscape seemed to be fairly saturated with warm, purple light. The peaks marshaled along the summit were in shadow, but through every notch and pass streamed vivid sun-fire, soothing and irradiating their rough, black angles, while companies of small, luminous clouds hovered above them like very angels of light.

Darkness came on, but I found my way by the trends of the cañons and the peaks projected against the sky. All excitement died with the light, and then I was weary. But the joyful sound of the waterfall across the lake was heard at last, and soon the stars were seen reflected in the lake itself. Taking my bearings from these, I discovered the little pine thicket in which my nest was, and then I had a rest such as only a tired mountaineer may enjoy.

From "A Wind-Storm in the Forests" in *The Mountains of California*

One of the most beautiful and exhilarating storms I ever enjoyed in the Sierra occurred in December, 1874, when I happened to be exploring one of the tributary valleys of the Yuba River. The sky and the ground and the trees had been thoroughly rain-washed and were dry again. The day was intensely pure, one of those incomparable bits of California winter, warm and balmy and full of white sparkling sunshine, redolent of all the purest influences of the spring, and at the same time enlivened with one of the most bracing wind-storms conceivable. Instead of camping out, as I usually do, I then chanced to be stopping at the house of a friend. But when the storm began to sound, I lost no time in pushing out into the woods to enjoy it. For on such occasions Nature has always something rare to show us, and the danger to life and limb is hardly greater than one would experience crouching deprecatingly beneath a roof. . . .

Toward midday, after a long, tingling scramble through copses of hazel and ceanothus, I gained the summit of the highest ridge in the neighborhood; and then it occurred to me that it would be a fine thing to climb one of the trees to obtain a wider outlook and get my ear close to the Aeolian music of its topmost needles. But under the circumstances the choice of a tree was a serious matter. One whose instep was not very strong seemed in danger of being blown down, or of being struck by others in case they should fall; another was branchless to a considerable height above the ground, and at the same time too large to be grasped with arms and legs in climbing; while others were not favorably situated for clear views. After cautiously casting about, I made choice of the tallest of a group of Douglas Spruces that were grow-ing close together like a tuft of grass, no one of which seemed likely to fall unless all the rest fell with it. Though compara-tively young, they were about 100 feet high, and their lithe, brushy tops were rocking and swirling in wild ecstasy. Being accustomed to climb trees in making botanical studies, I ex-perienced no difficulty in reaching the top of this one, and never before did I enjoy so noble an exhilaration of motion. The slender tops fairly flapped and swished in the passionate torrent, bending and swirling backward and forward, round and round, tracing indescribable combinations of vertical and horizontal curves, while I clung with muscles firm braced, like a bobolink on a reed.

In its widest sweeps my tree-top described an arc of from twenty to thirty degrees, but I felt sure of its elastic temper, having seen others of the same species still more severely tried—bent almost to the ground indeed, in heavy snows—without breaking a fiber. I was therefore safe, and free to take the wind into my pulses and enjoy the excited forest from my superb outlook. The view from here must be extremely beautiful in any weather. Now my eye roved over the piny hills and dales as over fields of waving grain, and felt the light running in ripples and broad swelling undulations across the valleys from ridge to ridge, as the shining foliage was stirred by corresponding waves of air. Oftentimes these waves of reflected light would break up suddenly into a kind of beaten foam, and again, after chasing one another in regular order, they would seem to bend forward in concentric curves, and disappear on some hillside, like sea-waves on a shelving shore. The quantity of light reflected from the bent needles was so great as to make whole groves appear as if covered with snow, while the black shadows beneath the trees greatly enhanced the effect of the silvery splendor.

Excepting only the shadows there was nothing somber in all this wild sea of pines. On the contrary, notwithstanding this was the winter season, the colors were remarkably beautiful. The shafts of the pine and libocedrus were brown and purple, and most of the foliage was well tinged with yellow; the laurel groves, with the pale undersides of their leaves turned upward, made masses of gray; and then there was many a dash of chocolate color from clumps of manzanita, and jet of vivid crimson from the bark of the madroños, while the ground on the hillsides, appearing here and there through openings between the groves, displayed masses of pale purple and brown.

The sounds of the storm corresponded gloriously with this wild exuberance of light and motion. The profound bass of the naked branches and boles booming like waterfalls; the quick, tense vibrations of the pine-needles, now rising to a shrill, whistling hiss, now falling to a silky murmur; the rustling of laurel groves in the dells, and the keen metallic click of leaf on leaf—all this was heard in easy analysis when the attention was calmly bent.

The varied gestures of the multitude were seen to fine advantage, so that one could recognize the different species at a distance of several miles by this means alone, as well as by their forms and colors, and the way they reflected the light. All seemed strong and comfortable, as if really enjoying the storm, while responding to its most enthusiastic greetings. We hear much nowadays concerning the universal struggle for existence, but no struggle in the common meaning of the word was manifest here; no recognition of danger by any tree; no deprecation; but rather an invincible gladness as remote from exultation as from fear.

I kept my lofty perch for hours, frequently closing my eyes to enjoy the music by itself, or to feast quietly on the delicious fragrance that was streaming past. The fragrance of the woods was less marked than that produced during warm rain, when so many balsamic buds and leaves are steeped like tea; but, from the chafing of resiny branches against each other, and the incessant attrition of myriads of needles, the gale was spiced to a very tonic degree. And besides the fragrance from these local sources there were traces of scents brought from afar. For this wind came first from the sea, rubbing against its fresh, briny waves, then distilled through the redwoods, threading rich ferny gulches, and spreading itself in broad undulating currents over many a flower-enameled ridge of the coast mountains, then across the golden plains, up the purple foot-hills, and into these piny woods with the varied incense gathered by the way. . . .

Most people like to look at mountain rivers, and bear them in mind; but few care to look at the winds, though far more beautiful and sublime, and though they become at times about as visible as flowing water. When the north winds in winter are making upward sweeps over the curving summits of the High Sierra, the fact is sometimes published with flying snow-banners a mile long. Those portions of the winds thus embodied can scarce be wholly invisible, even to the darkest imagination. And when we look around over an agitated forest, we may see something of the wind that stirs it, by its effects upon the trees. Yonder it descends in a rush of water-like ripples, and sweeps over the bending pines from hill to hill. Nearer, we see detached plumes and leaves, now speeding by on level currents, now whirling in eddies, or, escaping over the edges of the whirls, soaring aloft on grand, upswelling domes of air, or tossing on flame-like crests. Smooth, deep currents, cascades, falls, and swirling eddies, sing around every tree and leaf, and over all the varied topography of the region with telling changes of form, like mountain rivers conforming to the features of their channels.

After tracing the Sierra streams from their fountains to the plains, marking where they bloom white in falls, glide in crystal plumes, surge gray and foam-filled in boulder-choked gorges, and slip through the woods in long, tranquil reaches—after thus learning their language and forms in detail, we may at length hear them chanting all together in one grand anthem, and comprehend them all in clear inner vision, covering the range like lace. But even this spectacle is far less sublime and not a whit more substantial than what we may behold of these storm-streams of air in the mountain woods.

We all travel the milky way together, trees and men; but it never occurred to me until this storm-day, while swinging in the wind, that trees are travelers, in the ordinary sense. They make many journeys, not extensive ones, it is true; but our own little journeys, away and back again, are only little more than tree-wavings—many of them not so much.

When the storm began to abate, I dismounted and sauntered down through the calming woods. The storm-tones died away, and, turning toward the east, I beheld the countless hosts of the forests hushed and tranquil, towering above one another on the slopes of the hills like a devout audience. The setting sun filled them with amber light, and seemed to say, while they listened, ''My peace I give unto you.''

As I gazed on the impressive scene, all the so-called ruin of the storm was forgotten, and never before did these noble woods appear so fresh, so joyous, so immortal.

CLARENCE KING

(1842–1901)

Clarence King differed from the other nineteenth-century naturalists who worked for the federal government. His personality was a flamboyant one driven by epicurean tastes and an ever-pressing need for money. While friends were pursuing academic careers or plotting the course of a nation, King was degenerating both mentally and physically. But when he chose to write about his youthful scientific experiences, his flashiness and imaginative flair led to some very fine prose.

King's career began conventionally enough, with a Yale degree from the Sheffield School of Science and a job working beside Josiah Whitney and William Brewer on the California Geological Survey. In 1867 he left the survey for Washington, D.C., where he convinced government officials of the need for a similar study of the route along the trans-

continental railroad. Twelve years later he was appointed
first director of the United States Geological Survey. When
his administrative capabilities were stretched and his $6,000
salary proved insufficient, however, he resigned. For twenty
years, then, he followed a tragic rainbow that led from un-
productive Mexican gold mines to the decadent streets of
Europe and from the tables of the wealthy to a lonely Bloom-
ingdale asylum.

If he accomplished nothing else, though, King wrote one
first-rate book about the West. *Mountaineering in the Sierra
Nevada* was created by an imagination completely in control.
Its pages display some of the very best qualities of Western
American literature—a heightened zest for adventure, a tendency to exaggerate, a tongue-in-cheek sense of humor, a
fluid idiomatic style. Based on King's own experiences while
working for the California Survey, including some other field
trips as well (the excerpt I'm including here describes a venture into Idaho), it treats the reader to scenic panoramas,
to feats of mountaineering prowess, and to lively anecdotes
about life on the trail.

It is so well written, in fact, that it's deceptive. Tall tales
and the truth obviously intermingle in chapters like "Kaweah's
Run," where man and horse prodigiously flee two highway-
men. But hyperbole also characterizes chapters as subtle as
"The Ascent of Mount Tyndall," where King and a friend
climb a spire "as upon a tree, cutting mere toe-holes and
embracing the whole column of ice." The view is terrific:
"a thousand sculptures of stone, hard, sharp, shattered by
cold into infiniteness of fractures and rift, springing up,
mutely severe, into the dark, austere blue of heaven; scarred
and marked, except where snow or ice, spiked down by ragged granite bolts, shields with its pale armor these rough
mountain shoulders; storm-tinted at summit, and dark where,

swooping down from ragged cliff, the rocks plunge over cañon-walls into blue, silent gulfs.''

Not all of *Mountaineering* is overstated, though. Many of its chapters, even in the midst of hilarity, contain thoughtful assessments about human beings and their environment. One such example sounds sadly ironic when measured against King's own life. In "The Newtys of Pike" the author talks about the "brave spirit of Westward Ho," the inward drive that forces men and women in pursuit of the American dream. Then he remarks about the negative pull that occurs when such spirit "degenerates into mere weak-minded restlessness" and creates a "race of perpetual emigrants who roam as dreary waifs over the West." King, himself, found such an unfortunate fate.

From "The Falls of the Shoshone" in *Mountaineering in the Sierra Nevada*

In October, 1868, with a small detachment of the United States Geological Survey of the 40th Parallel, the writer crossed Goose Creek Mountains, in northern Utah, and descended by the old Fort Boise road to the level of the Snake plain. A gray, opaque haze hung close to the ground, and shut out all distance. The monotony of sage-desert was overpowering. We would have given anything for a good outlook; but for three days the mists continued, and we were forced to amuse ourselves by chasing occasional antelopes.

The evening we camped on Rock Creek was signalized by a fierce wind from the northeast. It was a dry storm, which continued with tremendous fury through the night, dying away at daybreak, leaving the heavens brilliantly clear. We were breakfasting when the sun rose, and shortly afterward, mounting into the saddle, headed toward the cañon of the Shoshone. The air was cold and clear. The remotest mountain-peaks upon the horizon could be distinctly seen, and the forlorn details of their brown slopes stared at us as through a vacuum. A few miles in front the smooth surface of the plain was broken by a ragged, zigzag line of black, which marked the edge of the farther wall of the Snake cañon. A dull throbbing sound greeted us. Its pulsations were deep, and seemed to proceed from the ground beneath our feet. Leaving the cavalry to bring up the wagon, my two friends and I galloped on, and were quickly upon the edge of the cañon-wall. We looked down into a broad, circular excavation, three quarters of a mile in diameter, and nearly seven hundred feet deep. East and north, over the edges of the cañon, we looked across miles and miles of the Snake plain, far on to the blue boundary mountains. The wall of the gorge opposite us, like the cliff at our feet, sank in perpendicular bluffs nearly to the level of the river, the broad excavation being covered by rough piles of black lava and rounded domes of trachyte rock. An horizon as level as the sea; a circling wall, whose sharp edges were here and there battlemented in huge, fortress-like masses; a broad river, smooth and unruffled, flowing quietly into the middle of the scene, and then plunging into a labyrinth of rocks, tumbling over a precipice two hundred feet high, and moving westward in a still, deep current to disappear behind a black promontory. It is a strange, savage scene: a monotony of pale blue sky, olive and gray stretches of desert, frowning walls of jetty lava, deep beryl-green of river-stretches, reflecting, here and there, the intense solemnity of the cliffs, and in the centre a dazzling sheet of foam. In the early morning light, the shadows of the cliffs were cast over half the basin, defining themselves in sharp outline here and there on the river. Upon the foam of the cataract one point of the rock cast a cobalt-blue shadow. Where the river flowed around the western promontory, it was wholly in shadow, and of a deep sea-green. A scanty growth of coniferous trees fringed the brink of the lower cliffs, overhanging the river. Dead barrenness is the whole sentiment of the scene. The mere suggestion of trees clinging here and there along the walls serves rather to heighten than to relieve the forbidding gloom of the place. Nor does the flashing whiteness, where the river tears itself among the rocky islands, or rolls in spray down the cliff, brighten the aspect. In contrast with its brilliancy, the rocks seem darker and more wild. The descent of four hundred feet, from our stand-point to the level of the river above the falls, has to be made by a narrow, winding path, among rough ledges of lava. We were obliged to leave our wagon at the summit, and pack down the camp equipment and photographic apparatus upon carefully led mules. By midday we were comfortably camped on the margin of the left bank, just above the brink of the falls. My tent was pitched upon the edge of a cliff, directly overhanging the rapids. From my door I looked over the cataract, and, when-ever the veil of mist was blown aside, could see for a mile down the river. The lower half of the cañon is excavated in a gray, porphyritic trachyte. It is over this material that the Snake falls. Above the brink, the whole breadth of the river is broken by a dozen small, trachyte islands, which the water has carved into fantastic forms: rounding some into low domes, sharpening others into mere pillars, and now and then wearing out deep caves. At the very brink of the fall a few twisted evergreens cling with their roots to the rock, and lean over the abyss of foam with something of that air of fatal fascination which is apt to take possession of men.

In plan the fall recurves up stream in a deep horseshoe, resembling the outline of Niagara. The total breadth is about seven hundred feet, and the greatest height of the single fall about one hundred and ninety. Among the islands above the brink are several beautiful cascades, where portions of the river pour over in lace-like forms. The whole mass of cataract is one ever-varying sheet of spray. In the early spring, when swollen by the rapidly melted snows, the river pours over with something like the grand volume of Niagara, but, at the time of my visit, it was wholly white foam. Here and there, along the brink, the underlying rock shows through, and among the islands shallow green pools disclose the form of the underlying trachyte. Numberless rough shelves break the fall, but the volume is so great that they are only discovered by the glancing outward of the foam. The river below the falls is very deep. The right bank sinks into the water in a clear, sharp precipice, but on the left side a narrow, pebbly beach extends along the foot of the cliff. From the top of the wall, at a point a quarter of a mile below the falls, a stream has gradually worn a little stairway: thick growths of evergreens have huddled together in this ravine. By careful climbing, we descended to the level of the river. The trachytes are very curiously worn in vertical forms. Here and there an obelisk, either wholly or half detached from the cañon-wall, juts out like a buttress. Farther down, these projecting masses stand like a row of columns upon the left bank. Above them, a solid capping of black lava reaches out to the edge, and overhangs the river in abrupt black precipices. Wherever large fields of basalt have overflowed an earlier rock, and erosion has afterward laid it bare, there is found a strong tendency to fracture in vertical lines. The immense expansion of the upper surface from heat seems to cause deep fissures in the mass.

Under the influence of the cool shadow of cliffs and pine, and constant percolating of surface-waters, a rare fertility is developed in the ravines opening upon the cañon shore. A luxuriance of ferns and mosses, an almost tropical wealth of green leaves and velvety carpeting, line the banks. There are no rocks at the base of the fall. The sheet of foam plunges almost vertically into a dark, beryl-green, lake-like expanse of the river. Immense volumes of foam roll up from the cataract-base, and, whirling about in the eddying winds, rise often a thousand feet in the air. When the wind blows down the cañon, a gray mist obscures the river for half a mile; and when, as is usually the case in the afternoon, the breezes blow eastward, the foam-cloud curls over the brink of the fall, and hangs like a veil over the upper river. On what conditions depends the height to which the foam-cloud rises from the base of the fall, it is apparently impossible to determine. Without the slightest wind, the cloud of spray often rises several hundred feet above the cañon-wall, and again, with apparently the same conditions of river and atmosphere, it hardly reaches the brink. Incessant roar, reinforced by a thousand echoes, fills the cañon. Out of this monotone, from time to time, rise strange, wild sounds, and now and then may be heard a slow, measured beat, not unlike the recurring fall of breakers. From the white front of the cataract the eye constantly wanders up to the black, frowning parapet of lava. Angular bastions rise sharply from the general level of the wall, and here and there isolated blocks, profiling upon their sky-line, strikingly recall barbette batteries. To goad one's imagination up to the point of perpetually seeing resemblances of everything else in the forms of rocks, is the most vulgar vice of travellers. To refuse to see the architectural suggestions upon the Snake cañon, however, is to administer a flat snub to one's fancy. The whole edge of the cañon is deeply cleft in vertical *crevasses*. The actual brink is usually formed of irregular blocks and prisms of lava, poised upon their ends in an unstable equilibrium, ready to be tumbled over at the first leverage of the frost. Hardly an hour passes without the sudden boom of one of those rock-masses falling upon the ragged *débris* piles below.

Night is the true time to appreciate the full force of the scene. I lay and watched it many hours. The broken rim of the basin profiled itself upon a mass of drifting clouds where torn openings revealed gleams of pale moonlight and bits of remote sky trembling with misty stars. Intervals of light and blank darkness hurriedly followed each other. For a moment the black gorge would be crowded with forms. Tall cliffs, ramparts of lava, the rugged outlines of islands huddled together on the cataract's brink, faintly luminous foam breaking over black rapids, the swift, white leap of the river, and a ghostly, formless mist through which the cañon-walls and far reach of the lower river were veiled and unveiled again and again. A moment of this strange picture, and then a rush of black shadow, when nothing could be seen but the breaks in the clouds, the basin-rim, and a vague, white centre in the general darkness.

After sleeping on the nightmarish brink of the falls, it was no small satisfaction to climb out of this Dantean gulf and find myself once more upon a pleasantly prosaic foreground of sage. Nothing more effectually banishes a melotragic state of mind than the obtrusive ugliness and abominable smell of this plant. From my feet a hundred miles of it stretched eastward. A half-hour's walk took me out of sight of the cañon, and as the wind blew westward, only occasional indistinct pulsations of the fall could be heard. The sky was bright and cloudless, and arched in cheerful vacancy over the meaningless disk of the desert.

I walked for an hour, following an old Indian trail which occasionally approached within seeing distance of the river, and then, apparently quite satisfied, diverged again into the desert. When about four miles from the Shoshone, it bent abruptly to the north, and led to the cañon edge. Here again the narrow gorge widened into a broad theatre, surrounded, as before, by black vertical walls, and crowded over its whole surface by rude piles and ridges of volcanic rock. The river entered it from the east through a magnificent gateway of basalt, and, having reached the middle, flowed on either side of a low, rocky island, and plunges in two falls into a deep green basin. A very singular ridge of the basalt projects like an arm almost across the river, enclosing within its semi-circle a bowl three hundred feet in diameter and two hundred feet deep. Within this the water was of the same peculiar beryl-green, dappled here and there by masses of foam which swim around and around with a spiral tendency toward the centre. To the left of the island half the river plunges off an overhanging lip, and falls about one hundred and fifty feet, the whole volume reaching the surface of the basin many feet from the wall. The other half has worn away the edge, and descends in a tumbling cascade at an angle of about forty-five degrees. The river at this point has not yet worn through the fields of basaltic lava which form the upper four hundred feet of the plain. Between the two falls it cuts through the remaining beds of basalt, and has eroded its channel a hundred feet into underlying porphyritic trachyte. The trachyte erodes far more easily than the basalt, and its resultant forms are quite unlike those of the black lava. The trachyte islands and walls are excavated here and there in deep caves, leaving island masses in the forms of mounds and towers.

In general, spherical outlines predominate, while the erosion of the basalt results always in sharp, perpendicular cliffs, with a steeply inclined talus of ragged *débris*.

The cliffs around the upper cataract are inferior to those of the Shoshone. While the level of the upper plain remains nearly the same, the river constantly deepens the channel in its westward course. In returning from the upper fall, I attempted to climb along the very edge of the cliff, in order to study carefully the habits of the basalt; but I found myself in a labyrinth of side *crevasses* which were cut into the plain from a hundred to a thousand feet back from the main wall. These recesses were usually in the form of an amphitheatre, with black walls two hundred feet high, and a bottom filled with immense fragments of basalt rudely piled together.

By dint of hard climbing I reached the actual brink in a few places, and saw the same general features each time: the cañon successively widening and narrowing, its walls here and there approaching each other and standing like pillars of a gateway; the river alternately flowing along smooth, placid reaches of level, and rushing swiftly down rocky cascades. Here and there along the cliff are disclosed mouths of black caverns, where the lava seems to have been blown up in the form of a great blister, as if the original flow had poured over some pool of water, and, converted into steam by contact with the hot rock, had been blown up bubble-like by its immense expansion. I continued my excursions along the cañon west of the Shoshone. About a mile below the fall a very fine promontory juts sharply out and projects nearly to the middle of the cañon. Climbing with difficulty along its toppling crest, I reached a point which I found composed of immense angular fragments piled up in dangerous poise. Eastward, the battlemented rocks around the falls limited the view; but westward I could see down long reaches of river, where islands of trachyte rose above white cascades. A peculiar and fine effect is noticeable upon the river during all the midday. The shadow of the southern cliff is cast down here and there, completely darkening the river, but often defining itself upon the water. The contrast between the rich, gem-like green of the sunlit portions and the deep violet shadow of the cliff is of extreme beauty. The Snake River deriving its volume wholly from the melting of the mountain snows, is a direct gauge of the annual advance of the sun. In June and July it is a tremendous torrent, carrying a full half of the Columbia. From the middle of July it constantly shrinks, reaching its minimum in midwinter. At the lowest, it is a river equal to the Sacramento or Connecticut.

After ten days devoted to walking around the neighborhood and studying the falls and rocks, we climbed to our wagon, and rested for a farewell look at the gorge. It was with great relief that we breathed the free air of the plain, and turned from the rocky cañon where darkness, and roar, and perpetual cliffs had bounded our senses, and headed southward, across the noiseless plain.

JOHN C. VAN DYKE

(1856–1932)

For more than forty years John Charles Van Dyke was a professor of art history at Princeton University. That background, unique among *Words for the Wild* contributors, strongly influenced the way he perceived the natural environment and the manner in which he chose to describe it. More often than not, he wrote passages that are pictorial.

By pictorial I mean a scene rendered in such a way that it resembles a framable picture. Looking at his surroundings, an author like Van Dyke reconstitutes the scene artistically, paying close attention to shadows and light, to colors, to shapes and sizes, to the exact position where a rock or a bush or a tree stands. Indeed the primary characteristic of Van Dyke's prose is his use of color. Paragraph after paragraph appears rainbow-splashed, drawn from a palate of special shades.

You may have had doubts, too, about the intense lumi-
nosity of the blue sky; but look up at it along the walls
of rock to where it spreads in a thin strip above the jaws
of the canyon. Did you ever see such light coming out of
the blue before! See how it flashes from the long line of
tumbling water that pitches over the rocks! White as an
avalanche, the water slips through the air down to its
basin of stone; and white, again, as the snow are the
foam and froth of the pool.

The chiaroscuro effect—a sharp contrast between light and
dark—replicates exactly what one sees when gazing at a
desert canyon waterfall.

It is obvious, of course, that Van Dyke's prose is somewhat old-fashioned. A man educated in the nineteenth century, he naturally learned from reading an effusive Ruskin
extolling Turneresque beauties. But even though his adjec-
tives were quaint, Van Dyke's ideas about the landscape were
quite ahead of his time. After he fell in love with the arid
desert, he argued vociferously that it ought to be left alone.

"The deserts should never be reclaimed," he wrote in a
chapter describing the Salton Basin before the 1905 irriga-
tion project. "They are the breathing-spaces of the west and
should be preserved forever." Then Van Dyke focused his
artistic eye on emotional as well as environmental needs, suggesting that whatever is beautiful in nature must be saved
just because it is there. "The aesthetic sense—the power to
enjoy through the eye, the ear, and the imagination—is just
as important a factor in the scheme of human happiness as
the corporeal sense of eating and drinking."

Van Dyke concluded his argument with a paragraph
reminiscent of George Perkins Marsh. "When man is gone,
the sand and the heat will come back to the desert . . . the
opalescent mirage will waver skyward on wings of light,

serene in its solitude, though no human eye sees nor human tongue speaks its loveliness." Meanwhile, John C. Van Dyke's pictorial imagination etched a Southwest in colors his own generation was perhaps too blind to see.

From "Light, Air, and Color"
in *The Desert*

These deserts, cut through from north to south by a silent river and from east to west by two noisy railways, seem remarkable for only a few commonplace things, according to the consensus of public opinion. All that one hears or reads about them is that they are very hot, that the sunlight is very glaring, and that there is a sand-storm, a thirst, and death waiting for every traveller who ventures over the first divide.

There is truth enough, to be sure, in the heat and glare part of it, and an exceptional truth in the other part of it. It is intensely hot on the desert at times, but the sun is not responsible for it precisely in the manner alleged. The heat that one feels is not direct sunlight so much as radiation from the receptive sands; and the glare is due not to preternatural brightness in the sunbeam, but to there being no reliefs for the eye in shadows, in dark colors, in heavy foliage. The vegetation of the desert is so slight that practically the whole surface of the sand acts as a reflector; and it is this, rather than the sun's intensity, that causes the great body of light. . . .

It has been said that our atmosphere breaks, checks, and diffuses the falling sunlight like the globe of a lamp. It does something more. It acts as a prism and breaks the beam of sunlight into the colors of the spectrum. Some of these colors

it deals with more harshly than others because of their short-
ness and their weakness. The blue rays, for instance, are the
greatest in number; but they are the shortest in length, the
weakest in travelling power of any of them. Because of their
weakness, and because of their affinity (as regards size) with
the small dust particles of the higher air region, great quantities of these rays are caught, refracted, and practically held
in check in the upper strata of the atmosphere. We see them
massed together overhead and call them the "blue sky."
After many millions of these blue rays have been eliminated
from the sunlight the remaining rays come down to earth
as a white or yellow or at times reddish light, dependent upon
the density of the lower atmosphere.

Now it seems that an atmosphere laden with moisture particles obstructs the passage earthward of the blue rays, less
perhaps than an atmosphere laden with dust. In consequence,
when they are thus allowed to come down into the lower atmosphere in company with the other rays, their vast number
serves to dominate the others, and to produce a cool tone
of color over all. So it is that in moist countries like Scotland
you will find the sky cold-blue and the air tinged gray, pale-
blue, or at twilight in the mountain valleys, a chilly purple.
A dust-laden atmosphere seems to act just the reverse of this.
It obstructs all the rays in proportion to its density, but it
stops the blue rays first, holds them in the upper air, while
the stronger rays of red and yellow are only checked in the
lower and thicker air-strata near the earth. The result of this
is to produce a warm tone of color over all. So it is that in
dry countries like Spain and Morocco or on the deserts of
Africa and America, you will find the sky rose-hued or yellow, and the air lilac, pink, red, or yellow.

I mean now that the air itself is colored. Of course countless quantities of light-beams and dispersed rays break through

the aërial envelope and reach the earth, else we should not see color in the trees or grasses or flowers about us; but I am not now speaking of the color of objects on the earth, but of the color of the air. A thing too intangible for color you think? But what of the sky overhead? It is only tinted atmosphere. And what of the bright-hued horizon skies at sunrise and sunset, the rosy-yellow skies of Indian summer! They are only tinted atmospheres again. Banked up in great masses, and seen at long distances, the air-color becomes palpably apparent. Why then should it not be present in shorter distances, in mountain canyons, across mesas and lomas, and over the stretches of the desert plains?

The truth is all air is colored, and that of the desert is deeper dyed and warmer hued than any other for the reasons just given. It takes on many tints at different times, dependent upon the thickening of the envelope by heat and dust-diffusing winds. I do not know if it is possible for fine dust to radiate with heat alone; but certain it is that, without the aid of the wind, there is more dust in the air on hot days than at any other time. When the thermometer rises above 100°F., the atmosphere is heavy with it, and the lower strata are dancing and trembling with phantoms of the mirage at every point of the compass. It would seem as though the rising heat took up with it countless small dust-particles and that these were responsible for the rosy or golden quality of the air-coloring.

There is a more positive tinting of the air produced sometimes by high winds. The lighter particles of sand are always being drifted here and there through the aërial regions, and even on still days the whirlwinds are eddying and circling, lifting long columns of dust skyward and then allowing the dust to settle back to earth through the atmosphere. The stronger the wind, and the more of dust and sand, the brighter the coloring. The climax is reached in the dramatic sand-storm—a veritable sand-fog which often turns half the heavens into a luminous red, and makes the sun look like a round ball of fire.

The dust-particle in itself is sufficient to account for the warmth of coloring in the desert—sufficient in itself to produce the pink, yellow, and lilac hazes. And yet I am tempted to suggest some other causes. It is not easy to prove that a reflection may be thrown upward upon the air by the yellow face of the desert beneath it—a reflection similar to that produced by a fire upon a night sky—yet I believe there is something of the desert's air-coloring derived from that source. Nor is it easy to prove that a reflection is cast by blue, pink, and yellow skies, upon the lower air-strata, yet certain effects shown in the mirage (the water illusion, for instance, which seems only the reflection of the sky from heated air) seem to suggest it. And if we put together other casual observations they will make argument toward the same goal. For instance, the common blue haze that we may see any day in the mountains, is always deepest in the early morning when the blue sky over it is deepest. At noon when the sky turns gray-blue the haze turns gray-blue also. The yellow haze of the desert is seen at its best when there is a yellow sunset, and the pink haze when there is a red sunset, indicating that at least the sky has some part in coloring by reflection the lower layers of desert air.

Whatever the cause, there can be no doubt about the effect. The desert air is practically colored air. Several times from high mountains I have seen it lying below me like an enormous tinted cloud or veil. A similar veiling of pink, lilac, or pale yellow is to be seen in the gorges of the Grand Canyon; it stretches across the Providence Mountains at noon-day and is to be seen about the peaks and packed in the valleys at sunset; it is dense down in the Coahuila Basin; it is denser from range to range across the hollow of Death Valley; and it tinges the whole face of the Painted Desert in Arizona. In its milder manifestations it is always present, and during the summer months its appearance is often startling. By that I do not mean that one looks through it as through a highly colored glass. The impression should not be gained that this air is so rose-colored or saffron-hued that one has to rub his eyes and wonder if he is awake. The average unobservant traveller looks through it and thinks it not different from any other air. But it is different. In itself, and in its effect upon the landscape, it is perhaps responsible for the greater part of what everyone calls "the wonderful color" of the desert.

And this not to the obliteration of local hue in sands, rocks, and plants. Quite independent of atmospheres, the porphyry mountains are dull red, the grease-wood is dull green, the vast stretches of sand are dull yellow. And these large bodies of local color have their influence in the total sum-up. Slight as is the vegetation upon the desert, it is surprising how it seems to bunch together and count as a color-mass. Almost all the growths are "evergreen." The shrubs and the trees shed their leaves, to be sure, but they do it so slowly that the new ones are on before the old ones are off. The general appearance is always green, but not a bright hue, except after prolonged rains. Usually it is an olive, bordering on yellow. One can hardly estimate what a relieving note this thin thatch of color is, or how monotonous the desert might be without it. It is welcome, for it belongs to the scene, and fits in the color-scheme of the landscape as perfectly as the dark-green pines in the mountain scenery of Norway.

The sands, again, form vast fields of local color, and,

indeed, the beds of sand and gravel, the dunes, the ridges, and the mesas, make up the most widespread local hue on the desert. The sands are not "golden," except under peculiar circumstances, such as when they are whirled high in the air by the winds, and then struck broadside by the sunlight. Lying quietly upon the earth they are usually a dull yellow. In the morning light they are often gray, at noon frequently a bleached yellow, and at sunset occasionally pink or saffron-hued. Wavering heat and mirage give them temporary coloring at times that is beautifully unreal. They then appear to undulate slightly like the smooth surface of a summer sea at sunset; and the colors shift and travel with the undulations. The appearance is not common; perfect calm, a flat plain, and intense heat being apparently the conditions necessary to its existence.

The rocks of the upper peaks and those that make the upright walls of mountains, though small in body of color, are perhaps more varied in hue than either the sands or the vegetation, and that, too, without primary notes as in the Grand Canyon of the Yellowstone. The reds are always salmon-colored, terra-cotta, or Indian red; the greens are olive-hued, plum-colored, sage-green; the yellows are as pallid as the leaves of yellow roses. Fresh breaks in the wall of rock may show brighter colors that have not yet been weather-worn, or they may reveal the oxidation of various minerals. Often long strata and beds, and even whole mountain tops show blue and green with copper, or orange with iron, or purple with slates, or white with quartz. But the tones soon become subdued. A mountain wall may be dark red within, but it is weather-stained and lichen-covered without; long-reaching shafts of granite that loom upward from a peak may be yellow at heart but they are silver-gray on the surface. The colors have undergone years of "toning down" until they blend and run together like the faded tints of an Eastern rug.

But granted the quantity and the quality of local colors in the desert, and the fact still remains that the air is the medium that influences if it does not radically change them all. The local hue of a sierra may be gray, dark red, iron-hued, or lead-colored; but at a distance, seen through dust-laden air, it may appear topaz-yellow, sapphire-blue, bright lilac, rose-red—yes, fire-red. During the heated months of summer such colors are not exceptional. They appear almost every evening. I have seen at sunset, looking north from Sonora some twenty miles, the whole tower-like shaft of Baboquivari change from blue to topaz and from topaz to glowing red in the course of half an hour. I do not mean edgings or rims or spots of these colors upon the peak, but the whole upper half of the mountain completely changed by them. The red color gave the peak the appearance of hot iron, and when it finally died out the dark dull hue that came after was like that of a clouded garnet.

The high ranges along the western side of Arizona, and the buttes and tall spires in the Upper Basin region, all show these warm fire-colors under heat and sunset light, and often in the full of noon. The colored air in conjunction with light is always responsible for the hues. Even when you are close up to the mountains you can see the effect of the air in small ways. There are edgings of bright color to the hill-ridges and the peaks; and in the canyons, where perhaps a sunshaft streams across the shadow, you can see the gold or fire-color of the air most distinctly. Very beautiful are these golden sunshafts shot through the canyons. And the red shafts are often startling. It would seem as though the canyons were packed thick with yellow or red haze. And so in reality they are.

There is one marked departure from the uniform warm

colors of the desert that should be mentioned just here. It is the clear blue seen in the shadows of western-lying mountains at sunset. This colored shadow shows only when there is a yellow or orange hued sunset, and it is produced by the yellow of the sky casting its complementary hue (blue) in the shadow. At sea a ship crossing a yellow sunset will show a marvellous blue in her sails just as she crosses the line of the sun, and the desert mountains repeat the same complementary color with equal facility and greater variety. It is not of long duration. It changes as the sky changes, but maintains always the complementary hue.

The presence of the complementary color in the shadow is exceptional, however. The shadows cast by such objects as the sahuaro and the palo verde are apparently quite colorless; and so, too, are the shadows of passing clouds. The colored shadow is produced by reflection from the sky, mixed with something of local color in the background, and also complementary color. It is usually blue or lilac-blue, on snow for example, when there is a blue sky overhead; and lilac when shown upon sand or a blue stone road. Perhaps it does not appear often on the Mojave-Colorado because the surfaces are too rough and broken with coarse gravel to make good reflectors of the sky. The fault is not in the light or in the sky, for upon the fine sands of the dunes, and upon beds of fine gypsum and salt, you can see your own shadow colored an absolute indigo; and often upon bowlders of white quartz the shadows of cholla and greasewood are cast in almost cobalt hues.

All color—local, reflected, translucent, complementary— is, of course, made possible by light and has no existence apart from it. Through the long desert day the sunbeams are weaving skeins of color across the sands, along the sides of the canyons, and about the tops of the mountains. They stain the ledges of copper with turquoise, they burn the buttes to a terra-cotta red, they paint the sands with rose and violet, and they key the air to the hue of the opal. The reek of color that splashes the western sky at sunset is but the climax of the sun's endeavor. If there are clouds stretched across the west the ending is usually one of exceptional brilliancy. The reds are all scarlet, the yellows are like burnished brass, the oranges like shining gold.

But the sky and clouds of the desert are of such unique splendor that they call for a chapter of their own.

MARY AUSTIN

(1868–1934)

Mary Austin's life could not be characterized as easy. Fatherless at age ten, she moved with her mother and brothers from the family farm in Illinois to a California homestead. Married at age twenty-three, she moved countless times again as her husband sought work from Bakersfield to Bishop. Separated a few years later, she lived for a time in Carmel, tried New York City, finally settled in Santa Fe, New Mexico. Despite the troubling upheavals, though, she always found time to write.

Indeed, she was quite prolific. Short stories, novels, essays, and treatises poured from her pen. Uneven in quality, some of her books were excellent; others, best forgotten.

The essay collection called *The Land of Little Rain* ranks with the finest. Written while she lived in California's Owens Valley, it describes the arid landscape from salt flat to mountaintop and introduces the people who live there. More than most authors who created *Words for the Wild*, in fact, Mary

Austin was interested in the human dimension. A basket maker, a pocket hunter, the residents of Jimville, and other isolated types range through the pages of her prose, simultaneously making contact with the soil and fertilizing the author's imagination.

No reader can thumb through *The Land of Little Rain* without perceiving her sympathy for the land and its inhabitants. Austin's own personal relationships were somewhat erratic, but she was always sensitive to people in touch with their environment. "To understand the fashion of any life," she wrote, "one must know the land it is lived in and the procession of the year." Her depiction of the Owens Valley reveals precisely that kind of knowledge.

The Land of Little Rain is a land one doesn't love instinctively but one that takes hold of the soul. It took hold of Mary Austin's soul at the turn of the century, lifting her past her own problems and leading her into literary success. "Come away, you who are obsessed with your own importance in the scheme of things," she speaks directly at the final essay's close. "Come away by the brown valleys and full-bosomed hills to the even-breathing days, to the kindliness, earthiness, ease." Fortunately for us, she took her own advice.

From "The Land of Little Rain" in *The Land of Little Rain*

East away from the Sierras, south from Panamint and Amargosa, east and south many an uncounted mile, is the Country of Lost Borders.

Ute, Paiute, Mojave, and Shoshone inhabit its frontiers, and as far into the heart of it as a man dare go. Not the law, but the land sets the limit. Desert is the name it wears upon the maps, but the Indian's is the better word. Desert is a loose term to indicate land that supports no man; whether the land can be bitted and broken to that purpose is not proven. Void of life it never is, however dry the air and villainous the soil.

This is the nature of that country. There are hills, rounded, blunt, burned, squeezed up out of the chaos, chrome and vermilion painted, aspiring to the snow-line. Between the hills lie high level-looking plains full of intolerable sun glare, or narrow valleys drowned in a blue haze. The hill surface is streaked with ash drift and black, unweathered lava flows. After rains water accumulates in the hollows of small closed valleys, and, evaporating, leaves hard dry levels of pure desertness that get the local name of dry lakes. Where the mountains are steep and the rains heavy, the pool is never quite dry, but dark and bitter, rimmed about with the efflorescence of alkaline deposits. A thin crust of it lies along the marsh over the vegetating area, which has neither beauty nor freshness. In the broad wastes open to the wind the sand drifts in hummocks about the stubby shrubs, and between them the soil shows saline traces. The sculpture of the hills here is more wind than water work, though the quick storms do sometimes scar them past many a year's redeeming. In all the Western desert edges there are essays in miniature at the famed, terrible Grand Cañon, to which, if you keep on long enough in this country, you will come at last.

Since this is a hill country one expects to find springs, but not to depend on them; for when found they are often brackish and unwholesome, or maddening, slow dribbles in a thirsty soil. Here you find the hot sink of Death Valley, or high rolling districts where the air has always a tang of frost. Here are the long heavy winds and breathless calms on the tilted mesas where dust devils dance, whirling up into a wide, pale sky. Here you have no rain when all the earth cries for it, or quick downpours called cloud-bursts for violence. A land of lost rivers, with little in it to love; yet a land that once visited must be come back to inevitably. If it were not so there would be little told of it.

This is the country of three seasons. From June on to November it lies hot, still, and unbearable, sick with violent unrelieving storms; then on until April, chill, quiescent, drinking its scant rain and scanter snows; from April to the hot season again, blossoming, radiant, and seductive. These months are only approximate; later or earlier the rain-laden wind may drift up the water gate of the Colorado from the Gulf, and the land sets its seasons by the rain.

The desert floras shame us with their cheerful adaptations to the seasonal limitations. Their whole duty is to flower and fruit, and they do it hardly, or with tropical luxuriance, as the rain admits. It is recorded in the report of the Death Valley expedition that after a year of abundant rains, on the Colorado desert was found a specimen of Amaranthus ten feet high. A year later the same species in the same place matured in the drought at four inches. One hopes the land may breed like qualities in her human offspring, not tritely to "try," but to do. Seldom does the desert herb attain the full stature of the type. Extreme aridity and extreme altitude have the same dwarfing effect, so that we find in the high Sierras and in Death Valley related species in miniature that reach a comely growth in mean temperatures. Very fertile are the desert plants in expedients to prevent evaporation, turning their foliage edgewise toward the sun, growing silky hairs, exuding viscid gum. The wind, which has a long sweep, harries and helps them. It rolls up dunes about the stocky stems, encompassing and protective, and above the dunes, which may be, as with the mesquite, three times as high as a man, the blossoming twigs flourish and bear fruit.

There are many areas in the desert where drinkable water lies within a few feet of the surface, indicated by the mesquite and the bunch grass (*Sporobolus airoides*). It is this nearness of unimagined help that makes the tragedy of desert deaths. It is related that the final breakdown of that hapless party that gave Death Valley its forbidding name occurred in a locality where shallow wells would have saved them. But how were they to know that? Properly equipped it is possible to go safely across that ghastly sink, yet every year it takes its toll of death, and yet men find there sun-dried mummies, of whom no trace or recollection is preserved. To underestimate one's thirst, to pass a given landmark to the right or left, to find a dry spring where one looked for running water—there is no help for any of these things.

Along springs and sunken watercourses one is surprised to find such water-loving plants as grow widely in moist ground, but the true desert breeds its own kind, each in its particular habitat. The angle of the slope, the frontage of a hill, the structure of the soil determines the plant. South-looking hills are nearly bare, and the lower tree-line higher here by a thousand feet. Cañons running east and west will have one wall naked and one clothed. Around dry lakes and marshes the herbage preserves a set and orderly arrangement. Most species have well-defined areas of growth, the best index the voiceless land can give the traveler of his whereabouts.

If you have any doubt about it, know that the desert begins with the creosote. This immortal shrub spreads down into Death Valley and up to the lower timber-line, odorous and medicinal as you might guess from the name, wandlike, with shining fretted foliage. Its vivid green is grateful to the eye in a wilderness of gray and greenish white shrubs. In the spring it exudes a resinous gum which the Indians of those parts know how to use with pulverized rock for cementing arrow points to shafts. Trust Indians not to miss any virtues of the plant world!

Nothing the desert produces expresses it better than the unhappy growth of the tree yuccas. Tormented, thin forests of it stalk drearily in the high mesas, particularly in that triangular slip that fans out eastward from the meeting of the Sierras and coastwise hills where the first swings across the southern end of the San Joaquin Valley. The yucca bristles with bayonet-pointed leaves, dull green, growing shaggy with age, tipped with panicles of fetid, greenish bloom. After death, which is slow, the ghostly hollow network of its woody skeleton, with hardly power to rot, makes the moonlight fearful. Before the yucca has come to flower, while yet its bloom is a creamy cone-shaped bud of the size of a small cabbage, full of sugary sap, the Indians twist it deftly out of its fence of daggers and roast it for their own delectation. So it is that in those parts where man inhabits one sees young plants of *Yucca arborensis* infrequently. Other yuccas, cacti, low herbs, a thousand sorts, one finds journeying east from the coastwise hills. There is neither poverty of soil nor species to account for the sparseness of desert growth, but simply that each plant requires more room. So much earth must be preëmpted to extract so much moisture. The real struggle for existence, the real brain of the plant, is underground; above there is room for a rounded perfect growth. In Death Valley, reputed the very core of desolation, are nearly two hundred identified species.

Above the lower tree-line, which is also the snow-line, mapped out abruptly by the sun, one finds spreading growth of piñon, juniper, branched nearly to the ground, lilac and sage, and scattering white pines.

There is no special preponderance of self-fertilized or wind-fertilized plants, but everywhere the demand for and evidence of insect life. Now where there are seeds and insects there will be birds and small mammals and where these are, will come the slinking, sharp-toothed kind that prey on them. Go as far as you dare in the heart of a lonely land, you cannot go so far that life and death are not before you. Painted lizards slip in and out of rock crevices, and pant on the white hot sands. Birds, hummingbirds even, nest in the cactus scrub; woodpeckers befriend the demoniac yuccas; out of the stark, treeless waste rings the music of the night-singing mockingbird. If it be summer and the sun well down, there will be a burrowing owl to call. Strange, furry, tricksy things dart across the open places, or sit motionless in the conning towers of the creosote. The poet may have "named all the birds without a gun," but not the fairy-footed, ground-inhabiting, furtive, small folk of the rainless regions. They are too many and too swift; how many you would not believe without seeing the footprint tracings in the sand. They are nearly all night workers, finding the days too hot and white. In mid-desert where there are no cattle, there are no birds of carrion, but if you go far in that direction the chances are that you will find yourself shadowed by their tilted wings. Nothing so large as a man can move unspied upon in that country, and they know well how the land deals with strangers. There are hints to be had here of the way in which a land forces new habits on its dwellers. The quick increase of suns at the end of spring sometimes overtakes birds in their nesting and effects a reversal of the ordinary manner of incubation. It becomes necessary to keep eggs cool rather than warm. One hot, stifling spring in the Little Antelope I had occasion to pass and repass frequently the nest of a pair of meadowlarks, located unhappily in the shelter of a very slender weed. I never caught them sitting except near night, but at midday they stood, or drooped above it, half fainting with pitifully parted bills, between their treasure and the sun. Sometimes both of them together with wings spread and half lifted continued a spot of shade in a temperature that constrained me at last in a fellow feeling to spare them a bit of canvas for permanent shelter. There was a fence in that country shutting in a cattle range, and along its fifteen miles of posts one could be sure of finding a bird or two in every strip of shadow; sometimes the sparrow and the hawk, with wings trailed and beaks parted, drooping in the white truce of noon.

If one is inclined to wonder at first how so many dwellers came to be in the loneliest land that ever came out of God's hands, what they do there and why stay, one does not wonder so much after having lived there. None other than this long brown land lays such a hold on the affections. The rainbow hills, the tender bluish mists, the luminous radiance of the spring, have the lotus charm. They trick the sense of time, so that once inhabiting there you always mean to go away without quite realizing that you have not done it. Men who have lived there, miners and cattle-men, will tell you this, not so fluently, but emphatically, cursing the land and going back to it. For one thing there is the divinest, cleanest air to be breathed anywhere in God's world. Some day the world will understand that, and the little oases on the windy tops of hills will harbor for healing its ailing, house-weary broods. There is promise there of great wealth in ores and earths, which is no wealth by reason of being so far removed from water and workable conditions, but men are bewitched by it and tempted to try the impossible. . . .

The palpable sense of mystery in the desert air breeds fables, chiefly of lost treasure. Somewhere within its stark borders, if one believes report, is a hill strewn with nuggets; one seamed with virgin silver; an old clayey water-bed where Indians scooped up earth to make cooking pots and shaped them reeking with grain of pure gold. Old miners drifting about the desert edges, weathered into the semblance of the tawny hills, will tell you tales like these convincingly. After a little sojourn in that land you will believe them on their own account. It is a question whether it is not better to be bitten by the little horned snake of the desert that goes sidewise and strikes without coiling, than by the tradition of a lost mine.

And yet—and yet—is it not perhaps to satisfy expectation that one falls into the tragic key in writing of desertness? The more you wish of it the more you get, and in the mean time lose much of pleasantness. In that country which begins at the foot of the east slope of the Sierras and spreads out by less and less lofty hill ranges toward the Great Basin, it is possible to live with great zest, to have red blood and delicate joys, to pass and repass about one's daily performance an area that would make an Atlantic seaboard State, and that with no peril, and, according to our way of thought, no particular difficulty. At any rate, it was not people who went into the desert merely to write it up who invented the fabled Hassaympa, of whose waters, if any drink, they can no more see fact as naked fact, but all radiant with the color of romance. I, who must have drunk of it in my twice seven years' wanderings, am assured that it is worth while.

For all the toll the desert takes of a man it gives compensations, deep breaths, deep sleep, and the communion of the stars. It comes upon one with new force in the pauses of the night that the Chaldeans were a desert-bred people. It is hard to escape the sense of mastery as the stars move in the wide clear heavens to risings and settings unobscured.

They look large and near and palpitant; as if they moved on some stately service not needful to declare. Wheeling to their stations in the sky, they make the poor world-fret of no account. Of no account you who lie out there watching, nor the lean coyote that stands off in the scrub from you and howls and howls.

"The Streets of the Mountains" in *The Land of Little Rain*

All streets of the mountains lead to the citadel; steep or slow they go up to the core of the hills. Any trail that goes otherwhere must dip and cross, sidle and take chances. Rifts of the hills open into each other, and the high meadows are often wide enough to be called valleys by courtesy; but one keeps this distinction in mind,—valleys are the sunken places of the earth, cañons are scored out by the glacier ploughs of God. They have a better name in the Rockies for these hill-fenced open glades of pleasantness; they call them parks. Here and there in the hill country one comes upon blind gullies fronted by high stony barriers. These head also for the heart of the mountains; their distinction is that they never get anywhere.

All mountain streets have streams to thread them, or deep grooves where a stream might run. You would do well to avoid that range uncomforted by singing floods. You will find it forsaken of most things but beauty and madness and death and God. Many such lie east and north away from the mid Sierras, and quicken the imagination with the sense of purposes not revealed, but the ordinary traveler brings nothing away from them but an intolerable thirst.

The river cañons of the Sierras of the Snows are better

worth while than most Broadways, though the choice of them is like the choice of streets, not very well determined by their names. There is always an amount of local history to be read in the names of mountain highways where one touches the successive waves of occupation or discovery, as in the old villages where the neighborhoods are not built but grow. Here you have the Spanish California in *Cero Gordo* and piñon; Symmes and Shepherd, pioneers both; Tunawai, probably Shoshone; Oak Creek, Kearsarge,—easy to fix the date of that christening,—Tinpah, Paiute that; Mist Cañon and Paddy Jack's. The streets of the west Sierras sloping toward the San Joaquin are long and winding, but from the east, my country, a day's ride carries one to the lake regions. The next day reaches the passes of the high divide, but whether one gets passage depends a little on how many have gone that road before, and much on one's own powers. The passes are steep and windy ridges, though not the highest. By two and three thousand feet the snow-caps overtop them. It is even possible to wind through the Sierras without having passed above timber-line, but one misses a great exhilaration.

The shape of a new mountain is roughly pyramidal, running out into long shark-finned ridges that interfere and merge into other thunder-splintered sierras. You get the saw-tooth effect from a distance, but the near-by granite bulk glitters with the terrible keen polish of old glacial ages. I say terrible; so it seems. When those glossy domes swim into the alpenglow, wet after rain, you conceive how long and imperturbable are the purposes of God.

Never believe what you are told, that midsummer is the best time to go up the streets of the mountain—well—perhaps for the merely idle or sportsmanly or scientific; but for seeing and understanding, the best time is when you have the longest leave to stay. And here is a hint if you would attempt the stateliest approaches; travel light, and as much as possible live off the land. Mulligatawny soup and tinned lobster will not bring you the favor of the woodlanders.

Every cañon commends itself for some particular pleasantness; this for pines, another for trout, one for pure bleak beauty of granite buttresses, one for its far-flung irised falls; and as I say, though some are easier going, leads each to the cloud shouldering citadel. First, near the cañon mouth you get the low-heading full-branched, one-leaf pines. That is the sort of tree to know at sight, for the globose, resin-dripping cones have palatable, nourishing kernels, the main harvest of the Paiutes. That perhaps accounts for their growing accommodatingly below the limit of deep snow, grouped sombrely on the valleyward slopes. The real procession of the pines begins in the rifts with the long-leafed *Pinus jeffreyi*, sighing its soul away upon the wind. And it ought not to sigh in such good company. Here begins the manzanita, adjusting its tortuous stiff stems to the sharp waste of boulders, its pale olive leaves twisting edgewise to the sleek, ruddy, chestnut stems; begins also the meadowsweet, burnished laurel, and the million unregarded trumpets of the coral-red pentstemon. Wild life is likely to be busiest about the lower pine border. One looks in hollow trees and hiving rocks for wild honey. The drone of bees, the chatter of jays, the hurry and stir of squirrels, is incessant; the air is odorous and hot. The roar of the stream fills up the morning and evening intervals, and at night the deer feed in the buckthorn thickets. It is worth watching the year round in the purlieus of the long-leafed pines. One month or another you get sight or trail of most roving mountain dwellers as they follow the limit of forbidding snows, and more bloom than you can properly appreciate.

Whatever goes up or comes down the streets of the mountains, water has the right of way; it takes the lowest ground and the shortest passage. Where the rifts are narrow, and some of the Sierra cañons are not a stone's throw from wall to wall, the best trail for foot or horse winds considerably above the watercourses; but in a country of cone-bearers there is usually a good strip of swardy sod along the cañon floor. Pine woods, the short-leafed Balfour and Murryana of the high Sierras, are sombre, rooted in the litter of a thousand years, hushed, and corrective to the spirit. The trail passes insensibly into them from the black pines and a thin belt of firs. You look back as you rise, and strain for glimpses of the tawny valley, blue glints of the Bitter Lake, and tender cloud films on the farther ranges. For such pictures the pine branches make a noble frame. Presently they close in wholly; they draw mysteriously near, covering your tracks, giving up the trail indifferently, or with a secret grudge. You get a kind of impatience with their locked ranks, until you come out lastly on some high, windy dome and see what they are about. They troop thickly up the open ways, river banks, and brook borders; up open swales of dribbling springs; swarm over old moraines; circle the peaty swamps and part and meet about clean still lakes; scale the stony gullies; tormented, bowed, persisting to the door of the storm chambers, tall priests to pray for rain. The spring winds lift clouds of pollen dust, finer than frankincense, and trail it out over high altars, staining the snow. No doubt they understand this work better than we; in fact they know no other. "Come," say the churches of the valleys, after a season of dry years, "let us pray for rain." They would do better to plant more trees.

It is a pity we have let the gift of lyric improvisation die out. Sitting islanded on some gray peak above the encompassing wood, the soul is lifted up to sing the Iliad of the pines. They have no voice but the wind, and no sound of them rises up to the high places. But the waters, the evidences of their power, that go down the steep and stony ways, the outlets of ice-bordered pools, the young rivers swaying with the force of their running, they sing and shout and trumpet at the falls, and the noise of it far outreaches the forest spires. You see from these conning towers how they call and find each other in the slender gorges; how they fumble in the meadows, needing the sheer nearing walls to give them countenance and show the way; and how the pine woods are made glad by them.

Nothing else in the streets of the mountains gives such a sense of pageantry as the conifers; other trees, if they are any, are home dwellers, like the tender fluttered, sisterhood of quaking asp. They grow in clumps by spring borders, and all their stems have a permanent curve toward the down slope, as you may also see in hillside pines, where they have borne the weight of sagging drifts.

Well up from the valley, at the confluence of cañons, are delectable summer meadows. Fireweed flames about them against the gray boulders; streams are open, go smoothly about the glacier slips and make deep bluish pools for trout. Pines raise statelier shafts and give themselves room to grow,—gentians, shinleaf, and little grass of Parnassus in their golden checkered shadows; the meadow is white with violets and all outdoors keeps the clock. For example, when the ripples at the ford of the creek raise a clear half tone,— sign that the snow water has come down from the heated high ridges,—it is time to light the evening fire. When it drops off a note—but you will not know it except the Douglas squirrel tells you with his high, fluty chirrup from the pines' aerial gloom—sign that some star watcher has caught the first far glint of the nearing sun. Whitney cries it from his vantage tower; it flashes from Oppapago to the front of Williamson; LeConte speeds it to the westering peaks. The high rills wake and run, the birds begin. But down three thousand feet in the cañon, where you stir the fire under the cooking pot, it will not be day for an hour. It goes on, the play of light across the high places, rosy, purpling, tender, glint and glow, thunder and windy flood, like the grave, exulting talk of elders above a merry game.

Who shall say what another will find most to his liking in the streets of the mountains. As for me, once set above the country of the silver firs, I must go on until I find white columbine. Around the amphitheatres of the lake regions and above them to the limit of perennial drifts they gather flockwise in splintered rock wastes. The crowds of them, the airy spread of sepals, the pale purity of the petal spurs, the quivering swing of bloom, obsesses the sense. One must learn to spare a little of the pang of inexpressible beauty, not to spend all one's purse in one shop. There is always another year, and another.

Lingering on in the alpine regions until the first full snow, which is often before the cessation of bloom, one goes down in good company. First snows are soft and clogging and make laborious paths. Then it is the roving inhabitants range down to the edge of the wood, below the limit of early storms. Early winter and early spring one may have sight or track of deer and bear and bighorn, cougar and bobcat, about the thickets of buckthorn on open slopes between the black pines. But when the ice crust is firm above the twenty foot drifts, they range far and forage where they will. Often in midwinter will come, now and then, a long fall of soft snow piling three or four feet above the ice crust, and work a real hardship for the dwellers of these streets. When such a storm portends the weather-wise blacktail will go down across the valley and up to the pastures of Waban where no more snow falls than suffices to nourish the sparsely growing pines. But the bighorn, the wild sheep, able to bear the bitterest storms with no signs of stress, cannot cope with the loose shifty snow. Never such a storm goes over the mountains that the Indians do not catch them floundering belly deep among the lower rifts. I have a pair of horns, inconceivably heavy, that were borne as late as a year ago by a very monarch of the flock whom death overtook at the mouth of Oak Creek after a week of wet snow. He met it as a king should, with no vain effort or trembling, and it was wholly kind to take him so with four of his following rather than that the night prowlers should find him.

There is always more life abroad in the winter hills than one looks to find, and much more in evidence than in summer weather. Light feet of hare that make no print on the forest litter leave a wondrously plain track in the snow. We used to look and look at the beginning of winter for birds to come down from the pine lands; looked in the orchard and stubble; looked north and south on the mesa for their migratory passing, and wondered that they never came. Busy little grosbeaks picked about the kitchen doors, and woodpeckers tapped the eaves of the farm buildings, but we saw hardly any other of the frequenters of the summer cañons. After a while when we grew bold to tempt the snow borders we found them in the street of the mountains. In the thick pine woods where the overlapping boughs hung with snow-wreaths make wind-proof shelter tents, in a very community of dwelling, winter the bird-folk who get their living from the persisting cones and the larvae harboring bark. Ground inhabiting species seek the dim snow chambers of the chaparral. Consider how it must be in a hill-slope overgrown with stout-twigged, partly evergreen shrubs, more than man high, and as thick as a hedge. Not all the cañon's sifting of snow can fill the intricate spaces of the hill tangles. Here and there an overhanging rock, or a stiff arch of buckthorn, makes an opening to communicating rooms and runways deep under the snow.

The light filtering through the snow walls is blue and ghostly, but serves to show seeds of shrubs and grass, and berries, and the wind-built walls are warm against the wind. It seems that live plants, especially if they are evergreen and growing, give off heat; the snow wall melts earliest from within and hollows to thinness before there is a hint of spring in the air. But you think of these things afterward. Up in the street it has the effect of being done consciously; the buckthorns lean to each other and the drift to them, the little birds run in and out of their appointed ways with the greatest cheerfulness. They give almost no tokens of distress, and even if the winter tries them too much you are not to pity them. You of the house habit can hardly understand the sense of the hills. No doubt the labor of being comfortable gives you an exaggerated opinion of yourself, an exaggerated pain to be set aside. Whether the wild things understand it or not they adapt themselves to its processes with the greater ease. The business that goes on in the street of the mountain is tremendous, world-formative. Here go birds, squirrels, and red deer, children crying small wares and playing in the street, but they do not obstruct its affairs. Summer is their holiday; "Come now," says the lord of the street, "I have need of a great work and no more playing."

But they are left borders and breathing-space out of pure kindness. They are not pushed out except by the exigencies of the nobler plan which they adopt with a dignity the rest of us have not yet learned.

PART 3
More Recent Sojourners in the Natural World

If a single feature distinguishes contemporary nature writing from that of the nineteenth century, it is an increasing concern for the environment. As soon as Americans began understanding that their natural resources were finite and that progress was altering their landscape irrevocably, the tone of their essays changed. Mildly worried at first, as they watched forests leveled and dams built, they questioned man's right to tamper with the surroundings. Less sanguine after awhile, as they saw developers plan ever more complex projects, their essays became argumentative, aggressive, even strident. This is not to say that the term "political activist" can be applied to every twentieth-century American nature writer, but certainly the inclination to add political overtones to environmental appreciation is characteristic.

I also don't mean to imply that nineteenth-century essayists were unaware of what was happening around them, since many of them honestly were concerned about the land. Our old friend Henry David Thoreau, for example, objected to the unfortunate damming of nearby Concord River and surreptitiously advocated a little sabotage. Acknowledging that a man-made structure such as the Billerica Dam turned fish away from their natural spawning grounds, he mused:

> Still patiently, almost pathetically, with instinct not to be discouraged, not to be *reasoned* with, revisiting their old haunts, as if their stern fates would relent, and still met by the Corporation with its dam. Poor shad! where is thy redress? When Nature gave thee instinct, gave she thee the heart to bear thy fate? Still wandering the sea in thy scaly armor to inquire humbly at the mouths of rivers if man has perchance left them free for thee to enter.

Thoreau offered two solutions. "I for one am with thee," he announced, "and who knows what may avail a crowbar against that Billerica dam?" On the other hand, nature might ply the monkey wrench. "Perchance, after a few thousand years, if the fishes will be patient, and pass their summers elsewhere meanwhile, nature will have leveled the Billerica dam, and the Lowell factories, and the Grass-ground River run clear again."

Such insistent lines may suggest that Thoreau was eager to stand up for ecological imperatives. But such was not the case. While it is true that his famous essay, "Civil Disobedience," strongly influenced passive-resistance advocates like Mahatma Gandhi and Martin Luther King, Jr., there is no evidence that he took such measures into the environmental arena. As a matter of fact, at times he made surprisingly insensitive remarks. "We had soon launched and loaded our boat, and, leaving our fire blazing, were off again before breakfast. The lumberers rarely trouble themselves to put out their fires, such is the dampness of the primitive forest; and this is one cause, no doubt, of the frequent fires in Maine, of which we hear so much on smoky days in Massachusetts.'' No doubt!

So the man whose spiritual ideas stand behind so much contemporary nature writing did not lead the way toward conservation. However, most other Americans of his generation displayed even less understanding of environmental issues. A strike-it-rich mentality was driving them across the continent, sending them from one goldfield to another, from one homestead to the next, and encouraging them to level anything that got in the way. Very few stopped to consider what they were perpetrating.

One who did worry about man's assault on the landscape was George Perkins Marsh. His 1864 book, *Man and Nature*, asked some very hard questions. Afraid that an altered environment might never recover, Marsh called for impact studies and conservative measures. His peers paid little attention to what he wrote—*Man and Nature* went out of print almost immediately and remained largely unavailable for nearly fifty years—but twentieth-century readers laud him as a forerunner of environmentalist thinking. Certainly many of his predictions about the impact of so-called improvements like the Panama Canal have proved true.

I didn't intend to turn this introduction into an historical survey of wilderness encroachments and subsequent reclamation projects, but such an overview would coincide almost exactly with changing trends in American nature writing. The more that developers planned, the more those plans were discussed in print. John Muir's personal career as a writer followed a pattern typical of nature writing as a whole. His early essays extolled poetic praises about the wilderness, while his later ones grew argumentative and polemical. Then the

Hetch Hetchy controversy changed his writing completely, as political concerns overrode his naturalist enthusiasms. Rather than pen poetic effusions about the Range of Light, he exploded in a series of tirades against industrialists and politicians who would invade what remained of a shrinking wilderness.

It never occurred to Muir that he was an invader, too. In order to sell the concept of preservation and to convince the American public that public lands must be conserved, he had to bring more and more people to the California Sierras. Yosemite Valley had its hotel, the Sierra Club its base camps, Muir his host of famous guests, their servants, and their friends. As early as the turn of the century—and a prelude to what is happening now—the wilderness was being loved to death.

In retrospect it's easy to see the paradox, and Muir wasn't the only man whose point of view trapped him into contradictory behavior. Bob Marshall's passion for an untracked wilderness drew him to Alaska's unnamed rivers and unclimbed peaks where he promptly named the rivers and climbed the peaks. Olaus Murie, an astute advocate of wildlife preservation, got his start by killing an extraordinary number (by today's standards) of specimens and samples for his biological studies. Perhaps the major philosophical aboutface was the one made by Aldo Leopold after the champion of predator control decided he was wrong. Then his insistence on deer harvesting and predator protection completely baffled those who misunderstood his emerging conservationist theory. This is not to say that these men were confused or even horribly inconsistent. Rather, as the years passed, they realized that the old ways no longer were appropriate.

We used to bury tin cans. In the 1980s that sounds like heresy, but in the days before aluminum and foil packaging, in the days before hundreds of thousands of hikers beat down thousands of miles of trail, can burial was perfectly acceptable. We did it every time we went backpacking. We cut down green branches, too. Sticks for roasting marshmallows, poles to prop up sagging tarps, fir boughs to soften our beds—they all came from living trees. And before 1970 I never knew a soul who owned a camp stove. Because there was plenty of wood everywhere, it never occurred to us not to burn every available log. Now I rarely build a campfire, seldom even carry a tin can, and never cut a branch. What once was common practice is now bad form. Even so, I did all those terrible things when I was young.

The same is true, I suggest, of nature writing. Where essayists once had little need to sound like preservationists, they now are compelled to raise their voices. Even a man as little inclined to activism as Wallace Stegner has devoted more and more hours to writing and speaking about the endangered wilderness. Since his retirement from teaching, almost all his energy has been spent on environmental issues. Others, of course, have expounded more radical measures than Stegner, but few can claim responsibility for thwarting the Army Corps of Engineers. *This Is Dinosaur*, which he edited in 1950, helped create such unhappy awareness of the Echo Park controversy that this particular dam project was abandoned and an ill-conceived proliferation of dams was curtailed.

No recent writer, however, has as effectively stirred public lethargy and challenged bureaucratic policy as Rachel Carson. She held nothing back. "The bitter upland plains, the purple wastes of sage, the wild, swift antelope, and the grouse are then a natural system in perfect balance," she wrote in 1962. "Are?" She questioned her own conclusion. "The verb must be changed—at least in those already vast and growing areas where man is attempting to improve on nature's way.'' Carson detailed the fate of a Wyoming valley after the Forest Service sprayed the sage with chemicals. A year later, "the moose were gone and so were the beaver. Their principal dam had gone out for want of attention by its skilled architects, and the lake had drained away. None of the large trout were left. None could live in the tiny creek that remained, threading its way through a bare, hot land where no shade remained. The living world was shattered.''

The living world may have been shattered, but American nature writing was not, not after *The Sea Around Us* and *Silent Spring*. Now men and women were cognizant of the serious—perhaps fatal—possibilities that environmental tampering could produce. So even though the Love Canal existed only in the mid-twentieth-century imagination, authors already were foreseeing catastrophic patterns. The most perceptive ones were suggesting that a philosophy of anthropocentrism was no longer viable. As George Perkins Marsh had said a hundred years before, "Man is everywhere a disturbing agent,'' an essentially destructive power that pursues his victims recklessly. "Man has too long forgotten that the earth was given to him for usufruct alone, not for consumption, still less for profligate waste.''

Usufruct—the right of enjoying the use and advantages of another's property short of destruction or waste of its substance—is a somewhat archaic word that well expresses what a number of our contemporaries advocate in their prose. With the specter of urban sprawl chewing its way across the Southwest and engineers happily digging into the mountains nearby, the Edward Abbeys now plead with civilization to cease and desist. Abbey specifically fills his nonfiction collections with arguments for moderation and denigrates the so-called "mad machine'' that civilization has unleashed on the landscape. Like Thoreau, he believes firmly that we and the world will all be better off when we pare our existences down to the necessaries of life.

Not every twentieth-century nature writer, however, has embraced environmentalism as a major theme. While it is clear that almost every *Words for the Wild* author in this section worries about the subject, some have kept their voices lowered, content merely to share an appreciation and love for the land. John Graves, for example, sounds more placid than polemical as he nods farewell to a river scheduled for damming. Yet no reader could doubt the cogency of his words, "a certain enraged awe when you hear that a river that you've always known, and that all men of that place have known always back into the red dawn of men, will shortly not exist. A piece of river, anyhow, my piece. . . ."

An inward dimension of Graves' last trip between the Brazos' banks is as important as the outward. Modern tensions demand release. Time spent on a river, time spent escaping urban pressures, time spent rethinking one's priorities, time spent seeking an atmosphere conducive to creativity, time spent in the wilderness is time well spent. This, it seems to me, is a second variable that has directed American nature writing during the last fifty years. To find themselves, essayists look to the wilderness. No different from the millions of men and women who join Sierra Club outings or who seek Outward Bound adventures, who find pleasure in strolling through woods for an hour or in sitting by the sea for an afternoon, writers apprehend the natural world as a source for both physical and imaginative renewal.

Some see it in terms of personal challenge. Where John C. Fremont once crossed the Sierras in an escapade of winter bravery and the inexperienced Isabella Bird once assaulted Long's Peak, modern adventurers behave just as precipitously, producing dozens of books about deeds undertaken just because the author wanted to see if it—whatever it may be—could be done.

Not everyone has to climb Everest or El Capitan in order to produce credible nature writing however. As a matter of fact, spiritual adventure may involve very little physical testing at all. Joseph Wood Krutch, for example, found the Sonoran desert a haven from contemporary tension and stress, a place large enough to confirm his humanistic beliefs. Yet he "stuck close to my own little stretch of cactus and sand. I never wandered more than a few hours away." Like Krutch, Annie Dillard could find a whole tale in a bird sitting on a twig, a whole history in an abandoned cocoon, a whole miracle in miniature. And her narrow West Virginia landscape, populated by nothing more startling than burrowing creatures, bugs, and an occasional snake, had Darwinian boundaries that pulse and throb. She never walked farther than her creek, but under her scrutiny a simple butterfly or a lonesome frog took on new meaning. The same can be said of Aldo Leopold's Wisconsin farm, of Loren Eiseley's Nebraska plains. In almost any landscape, a nature writer can find a kind of wilderness, "exploring, in fear and trembling," as Dillard suggests, "some of the unmapped dim reaches and unholy fastnesses to which those tales and sights so dizzyingly lead."

In many ways contemporary nature writing hasn't developed much. Environmental concerns added a variety of political assertions and innuendos, but the basic pattern remains. A testing of the self, whether by exploration and high adventure or by observation and philosophic musings, dictates the content of *Words for the Wild*. And its essays strive toward an understanding of the self, through a series of individual experiences in the natural world.

ALDO LEOPOLD

(1887–1948)

Many call Aldo Leopold the father of the profession of wildlife management in America; perhaps he should be called the father of ecological ethics as well. From his youthful days in Arizona and New Mexico, where he worked for the Forest Service, to his later years when he taught Agricultural Economics at the University of Wisconsin, Leopold was evolving the land ethic that he would pass on to an entire generation. He spent his whole life teaching his students that man is responsible for the health of the land and convincing the public that man must cultivate an environmental conscience. While he was not always successful in altering public policy, his ideas have had a lasting impact on environmental philosophy.

A striking characteristic of the man was his ability to replace old ideas with new. Leopold changed his mind about the role of game management, for example, when too much deer protection led to serious deer overpopulation in several parts of the country. His own scientific knowledge, coupled with pressing conservation needs, showed him that too many predator controls were misguided and that large-scale herd reduction was imperative. Moreover, he recognized that any system of conservation based on economic self-interest would be hopelessly lopsided. So he argued persuasively for a broader ethic "dealing with man's relationship to the land and to the animals and plants which grow upon it."

Leopold believed that a man must learn to "think like a mountain," to conceive objectively and ecologically rather than narrowly and in a self-serving manner. If this meant that wolves must go unharmed, that deer occasionally must be slaughtered, and that forests must be protected from the inroads of man, so be it. Not all mid-twentieth-century Americans were ready for this somewhat radical view, but Leopold persisted. "A thing is right when it tends to preserve the integrity, stability and beauty of the biotic community. It is wrong when it tends otherwise." Trappers and loggers, recreationists, and all those responsible for managing the wilderness need to keep this truism uppermost in their minds.

During his lifetime, Aldo Leopold published a variety of books and essays designed to argue his evolving points of view. He penned game survey reports, texts like *Game Management* (1933), professional papers in scholarly journals and popular magazines. His best-known work, *A Sand County Almanac*, appeared after his death. This collection of nature essays and another group called *Sketches Here and There* show Leopold's philosophy of the heart as well as the head. "There are some who can live without the wild things," he announces in the *Almanac*'s foreword, "and some who cannot. These essays are the delights and dilemmas of one who cannot." They are also the words of one of America's fore-most theorists of environmental preservation.

From "March" in
A Sand County Almanac

THE GEESE RETURN

One swallow does not make a summer, but one skein of geese, cleaving the murk of a March thaw, is the spring.

A cardinal, whistling spring to a thaw but later finding himself mistaken, can retrieve his error by resuming his winter silence. A chipmunk, emerging for a sunbath but finding a blizzard, has only to go back to bed. But a migrating goose, staking two hundred miles of black night on the chance of finding a hole in the lake, has no easy chance for retreat. His arrival carries the conviction of a prophet who has burned his bridges.

A March morning is only as drab as he who walks in it without a glance skyward, ear cocked for geese. I once knew an educated lady, banded by Phi Beta Kappa, who told me that she had never heard or seen the geese that twice a year proclaim the revolving seasons to her well-insulated roof. Is education possibly a process of trading awareness for things of lesser worth? The goose who trades his is soon a pile of feathers.

The geese that proclaim the seasons to our farm are aware of many things, including the Wisconsin statutes. The south-bound November flocks pass over us high and haughty, with scarcely a honk of recognition for their favorite sandbars and sloughs. 'As a crow flies' is crooked compared with their undeviating aim at the nearest big lake twenty miles to the south, where they loaf by day on broad waters and filch corn by night from the freshly cut stubbles. November geese are aware that every marsh and pond bristles from dawn till dark with hopeful guns.

March geese are a different story. Although they have been shot at most of the winter, as attested by their buckshot-battered pinions, they know that the spring truce is now in effect. They wind the oxbows of the river, cutting low over the now gunless points and islands, and gabbling to each sandbar as to a long-lost friend. They weave low over the marshes and meadows, greeting each newly melted puddle and pool. Finally, after a few *pro-forma* circlings of our marsh, they set wing and glide silently to the pond, black landing-gear lowered and rumps white against the far hill. Once touching water, our newly arrived guests set up a honking and splashing that shakes the last thought of winter out of the brittle cattails. Our geese are home again!

It is at this moment of each year that I wish I were a muskrat, eye-deep in the marsh.

Once the first geese are in, they honk a clamorous invitation to each migrating flock, and in a few days the marsh is full of them. On our farm we measure the amplitude of our spring by two yardsticks: the number of pines planted, and the number of geese that stop. Our record is 642 geese counted in on 11 April 1946.

As in fall, our spring geese make daily trips to corn, but these are no surreptitious sneakings-out by night; the flocks move noisily to and from the corn stubbles through the day. Each departure is preceded by loud gustatory debate, and each return by an even louder one. The returning flocks, once thoroughly at home, omit their *pro-forma* circlings of the marsh. They tumble out of the sky like maple leaves, side-slipping right and left to lose altitude, feet spraddled toward the shouts of welcome below. I suppose the ensuing gabble deals with the merits of the day's dinner. They are now eating the waste corn that the snow blanket has protected over winter from corn-seeking crows, cottontails, meadow mice, and pheasants.

It is a conspicuous fact that the corn stubbles selected by geese for feeding are usually those occupying former prairies. No man knows whether this bias for prairie corn reflects some superior nutritional value, or some ancestral tradition transmitted from generation to generation since the prairie days. Perhaps it reflects the simpler fact that prairie cornfields tend to be large. If I could understand the thunderous debates that precede and follow these daily excursions to corn, I might soon learn the reason for the prairie-bias. But I cannot, and I am well content that it should remain a mystery. What a dull world if we knew all about geese!

In thus watching the daily routine of a spring goose convention, one notices the prevalence of singles—lone geese that do much flying about and much talking. One is apt to impute a disconsolate tone to their honkings, and to jump to the conclusion that they are broken-hearted widowers, or mothers hunting lost children. The seasoned ornithologist knows, however, that such subjective interpretation of bird behavior is risky. I long tried to keep an open mind on the question.

After my students and I had counted for half a dozen years the number of geese comprising a flock, some unexpected light was cast on the meaning of lone geese. It was found by mathematical analysis that flocks of six or multiples of six were far more frequent than chance alone would dictate. In other words, goose flocks are families, or aggregations of families, and lone geese in spring are probably just what our fond imaginings had first suggested. They are bereaved survivors of the winter's shooting, searching in vain for their kin. Now I am free to grieve with and for the lone honkers.

It is not often that cold-potato mathematics thus confirms the sentimental promptings of the bird-lover.

On April nights when it has become warm enough to sit outdoors, we love to listen to the proceedings of the convention in the marsh. There are long periods of silence when one hears only the winnowing of snipe, the hoot of a distant owl, or the nasal clucking of some amorous coot. Then, of a sudden, a strident honk resounds, and in an instant pandemonium echoes. There is a beating of pinions on water, a rushing of dark prows propelled by churning paddles, and a general shouting by the onlookers of a vehement controversy. Finally some deep honker has his last word, and the noise subsides to that half-audible small-talk that seldom ceases among geese. Once again, I would I were a muskrat!

By the time the pasques are in full bloom our goose-convention dwindles, and before May our marsh is once again a mere grassy wetness, enlivened only by redwings and rails.

"Thinking Like a Mountain" in *A Sand County Almanac*

A deep chesty bawl echoes from rimrock to rimrock, rolls down the mountain, and fades into the far blackness of the night. It is an outburst of wild defiant sorrow, and of contempt for all the adversities of the world.

Every living thing (and perhaps many a dead one as well)

pays heed to that call. To the deer it is a reminder of the way of all flesh, to the pine a forecast of midnight scuffles and of blood upon the snow, to the coyote a promise of gleanings to come, to the cowman a threat of red ink at the bank, to the hunter a challenge of fang against bullet. Yet behind these obvious and immediate hopes and fears there lies a deeper meaning, known only to the mountain itself. Only the mountain has lived long enough to listen objectively to the howl of a wolf.

Those unable to decipher the hidden meaning know nevertheless that it is there, for it is felt in all wolf country, and distinguishes that country from all other land. It tingles in the spine of all who hear wolves by night, or who scan their tracks by day. Even without sight or sound of wolf, it is implicit in a hundred small events: the midnight whinny of a pack horse, the rattle of rolling rocks, the bound of a fleeing deer, the way shadows lie under the spruces. Only the ineducable tyro can fail to sense the presence or absence of wolves, or the fact that mountains have a secret opinion about them.

My own conviction on this score dates from the day I saw a wolf die. We were eating lunch on a high rimrock, at the foot of which a turbulent river elbowed its way. We saw what we thought was a doe fording the torrent, her breast awash in white water. When she climbed the bank toward us and shook out her tail, we realized our error: it was a wolf. A half-dozen others, evidently grown pups, sprang from the willows and all joined in a welcoming mêlée of wagging tails and playful maulings. What was literally a pile of wolves writhed and tumbled in the center of an open flat at the foot of our rimrock.

In those days we had never heard of passing up a chance to kill a wolf. In a second we were pumping lead into the pack, but with more excitement than accuracy: how to aim a steep downhill shot is always confusing. When our rifles were empty, the old wolf was down, and a pup was dragging a leg into impassible slide-rocks.

We reached the old wolf in time to watch a fierce green fire dying in her eyes. I realized then, and have known ever since, that there was something new to me in those eyes— something known only to her and to the mountain. I was young then, and full of trigger-itch; I thought that because fewer wolves meant more deer, that no wolves would mean hunters' paradise. But after seeing the green fire die, I sensed that neither the wolf nor the mountain agreed with such a view.

Since then I have lived to see state after state extirpate its wolves. I have watched the face of many a newly wolfless mountain, and seen the south-facing slopes wrinkle with a maze of new deer trails. I have seen every edible bush and seedling browsed, first to anaemic desuetude, and then to death. I have seen every edible tree defoliated to the height of a saddlehorn. Such a mountain looks as if someone had given God a new pruning shears, and forbidden Him all other exercise. In the end the starved bones of the hoped-for deer herd, dead of its own too-much, bleach with the bones of the dead sage, or molder under the high-lined junipers.

I now suspect that just as a deer herd lives in mortal fear of its wolves, so does a mountain live in mortal fear of its deer. And perhaps with better cause, for while a buck pulled down by wolves can be replaced in two or three years, a range pulled down by too many deer may fail of replacement in as many decades.

So also with the cows. The cowman who cleans his range of wolves does not realize that he is taking over the wolf's job of trimming the herd to fit the range. He has not learned to think like a mountain. Hence we have dustbowls, and rivers washing the future into the sea.

We all strive for safety, prosperity, comfort, long life, and dullness. The deer strives with his supple legs, the cowman with trap and poison, the statesman with pen, the most of us with machines, votes, and dollars, but it all comes to the same thing: peace in our time. A measure of success in this is all well enough, and perhaps is a requisite to objective thinking, but too much safety seems to yield only danger in the long run. Perhaps this is behind Thoreau's dictum: In wildness is the salvation of the world. Perhaps this is the hidden meaning in the howl of the wolf, long known among mountains, but seldom perceived among men.

"Country" in *A Sand County Almanac*

There is much confusion between land and country. Land is the place where corn, gullies, and mortgages grow. Country is the personality of the land, the collective harmony of its soil, life, and weather. Country knows no mortgages, no alphabetical agencies, no tobacco road; it is calmly aloof to these petty exigencies of its alleged owners. That the previous occupant of my farm was a bootlegger mattered not one whit to its grouse; they sailed as proudly over the thickets as if they were guests of a king.

Poor land may be rich country, and vice versa. Only economists mistake physical opulence for riches. Country may be rich despite a conspicuous poverty of physical endowment, and its quality may not be apparent at first glance, nor at all times.

I know, for example, a certain lakeshore, a cool austerity of pines and wave-washed sands. All day you see it only as something for the surf to pound, a dark ribbon that stretches farther than you can paddle, a monotony to mark the miles by. But toward sunset some vagrant breeze may waft a gull across a headland, behind which a sudden roistering of loons reveals the presence of a hidden bay. You are seized with an impluse to land, to set foot on bearberry carpets, to pluck a balsam bed, to pilfer beach plums or blueberries, or perhaps to poach a partridge from out those bosky quietudes that lie behind the dunes. A bay? Why not also a trout stream? Incisively the paddles clip little soughing swirls athwart the gunwale, the bow swings sharp shoreward and cleaves the greening depths for camp.

Later, a supper-smoke hangs lazily upon the bay; a fire flickers under drooping boughs. It is a lean poor land, but rich country.

Some woods, perennially lush, are notably lacking in charm. Tall clean-boled oaks and tulip poplars may be good to look at, from the road, but once inside one may find a coarseness of minor vegetation, a turbidity of waters, and a paucity of wildlife. I cannot explain why a red rivulet is not a brook. Neither can I, by logical deduction, prove that a thicket without the potential roar of a quail covey is only a thorny place. Yet every outdoorsman knows that this is true. That wildlife is merely something to shoot at or to look at is the grossest of fallacies. It often represents the difference between rich country and mere land.

There are woods that are plain to look at, but not to look into. Nothing is plainer than a cornbelt wood-lot; yet, if it be August, a crushed pennyroyal, or an over-ripe mayapple, tells you here is a place. October sun on a hickory nut is irrefutable evidence of good country; one senses not only hickory but a whole chain of further sequences: perhaps of oak coals in the dusk, a young squirrel browning, and a distant barred owl hilarious over his own joke.

The taste for country displays the same diversity in aesthetic competence among individuals as the taste for opera, or oils. There are those who are willing to be herded in droves through 'scenic' places; who find mountains grand if they be proper mountains with waterfalls, cliffs, and lakes. To such the Kansas plains are tedious. They see the endless corn, but not the heave and the grunt of ox teams breaking the prairie. History, for them, grows on campuses. They look at the low horizon, but they cannot see it, as de Vaca did, under the bellies of the buffalo.

In country, as in people, a plain exterior often conceals hidden riches, to perceive which requires much living in and with. Nothing is more monotonous than the juniper foothills, until some veteran of a thousand summers, laden blue with berries, explodes in a blue burst of chattering jays. The drab sogginess of a March cornfield, saluted by one honker from the sky, is drab no more.

JOSEPH WOOD KRUTCH

(1893–1970)

Most of the time I've chosen *Words for the Wild* samples that demonstrate what an author likes and what an author does best. If he or she prefers mountains to desert, flora to fauna, adventure to aesthetics, community to contemplation, the excerpt does the same. The Joseph Wood Krutch selection, however, deviates somewhat from this pattern. "The Mystique of the Desert" is hardly typical. Instead of detailing his observations, as most of his desert essays do, or analyzing the ideas of others, as most of his critical studies do, it summarizes Krutch's own thoughts in a way quite philosophically direct.

Krutch began his career in academia. A professor at Columbia University for more than twenty years and a member of *The Nation*'s editorial staff, he wrote prolifically about literature, drama, and the plight of his fellow men. Perhaps his best-known book was *The Modern Temper* (1929), a pessimistic assessment of modern existence. With the advent of contemporary science and psychology, man's faith in the universe and in himself has been decimated. What, then, is left? Only the pursuit of knowledge, or so the scholar decided.

As the years went by, however, Krutch tempered his beliefs. Two things, I think, steered him away from skepticism and toward the humanism advocated later in his life. First, his literary interests led him to the Romantics and then to the Transcendentalists. In 1948 he even published a book on Thoreau. Second, he and his wife developed a passion for the desert Southwest. They first saw it in 1938, returned for three successive years, went back after the war ended, took a fifteen-month sabbatical there, and then moved permanently to Arizona when Krutch retired in 1952. A demonstration of just how much this author's attitudes had changed during the intervening years can be found in *The Measure of Man*, a 1954 reexamination of *The Modern Temper* from a humanistic point of view.

Krutch's desert writings are more significant, though, as words for the wild. Four of his books—*The Desert Year* (1952), *The Voice of the Desert* (1955), *Grand Canyon* (1958), and *The Forgotten Peninsula* (1961)—are special favorites of mine. Each one studies the desert environment with detailed, loving care. Krutch readily acknowledges that arid land isn't always easy to love, that to recognize its beauty isn't always an easy task, but he sees in its spaces "a new, undreamed of world . . . [a] combination of brilliant sun and high, thin, dry air with a seemingly limitless expanse of sky and earth," a place that captivated him both physically and philosophically.

To make that panorama meaningful, Krutch pulls the reader's eyes away from the expanses and shows a desert up close. Chapters in *The Desert Year* examine the rainfall, the cactus, bats, birds, a contemplative toad. Chapters in *The Voice of the Desert* are even more specific, as Krutch eyes a giant saguaro, a tarantula, a scorpion, gourds, the mouse that never drinks. Any one of these is a fascinating account.

But I have chosen instead a summary chapter, one that explains how Krutch finally interprets what he has seen and thought. It is also one that shows what has replaced Krutch's early skepticism—"a kind of pantheism," he says in another place. For me, then, "The Mystique of the Desert" is a kind of personal capstone to Krutch's career. Moreover, with only a few descriptive changes, it could be describing "the mystique of the wild" anywhere.

From "The Mystique of the Desert" in *The Voice of the Desert*

I happen to be one of those, and we are not a few, to whom the acute awareness of a natural phenomenon, especially of a phenomenon of the living world, is the thing most likely to open the door to that joy we cannot analyze. I have experienced it sometimes when a rabbit appeared suddenly from a bush to dash away to the safety which he values so much, or when, at night, a rustle in the leaves reminds me how many busy lives surround my own. It has also come almost as vividly when I suddenly saw a flower opening or a stem pushing out of the ground.

But what is the content of the experience? What is it that at such moments I seem to realize? Of what is my happiness compounded?

First of all, perhaps, there is the vivid assurance that these things, that the universe itself, really do exist, that life is not a dream; second, that the reality is pervasive and, it seems, unconquerable. The future of mankind is dubious. Perhaps the future of the whole earth is only somewhat less dubious. But one knows that all does not depend upon man, that possibly, even, it does not depend upon this earth. Should man disappear, rabbits may well still run and flowers may still open. If this globe itself should perish, then it seems not unreasonable to suppose that what inspires the stem and the flower may exist somewhere else. And I, it seems, am at least part of all this.

God looked upon the world and found that it was good. How great is the happiness of being able, even for a moment, to agree with Him! And how much easier that is if one is not committed to considering only some one section of the world or of the universe.

Long before I ever saw the desert I was aware of the mystical overtones which the observation of nature made audible to me. But I have never been more frequently or more vividly aware of them than in connection with the desert phenomena. And I have often wondered why.

Were I to believe what certain psychologists have been trying to tell me, the thing which I call a "mystique" and especially what I call "the mystique of the desert" is only the vague aura left behind by certain experiences of infancy and childhood. Should I search my memory of the latter I should certainly find there what nearly every other American or European would: a Christmas card showing Wise Men crossing the desert and also, in some school geography, another picture of rolling dunes, a camel and the caption, "Sahara Desert." Both seemed then to be things I should never see; both were remote from the scene of my sorrows—

whatever at the moment I found my sorrows to be. "Poof!" say those psychologists. The "mystique" is mysterious no longer. To adjust yourself to your environment would have been a simple matter. Had you been so adjusted you would never have gone to live in the American Southwest. And you would not give a damn whether Dipodomys drinks or not.

If those psychologists are right, then I am glad that I, at least, was not "adjusted" to everything and hence incapable of giving a damn about anything whatsoever. But I am not sure that they *are* right. Curiosity is not always the result of conditioning and there are words at which most imaginations kindle. Among them are all those words which suggest the untamed extravagances or the ultimate limits of nature in any one of her moods. We may prefer to live amid hills and meadows, fields and woodlots, or even, for that matter, surrounded by steel and concrete. But "wilderness," "jungle," and "desert" are still stirring words, as even moviemakers know. And it is just possible that they will continue to be such after the last Christmas card having anything to do with Christmas has disappeared from the shops and after school geographies have consented to confine themselves exclusively to "things relevant to the child's daily life." Perhaps the mind is not merely a blank slate upon which anything may be written. Perhaps it reaches out spontaneously toward what can nourish either intelligence or imagination. Perhaps it is part of nature and, without being taught, shares nature's intentions.

Most of the phrases we use glibly to exorcise or explain away the realities of our intimate experience are of quite recent origin—phrases like "emotional conditioning," "complex," "fixation," and even "reflex." But one of the most inclusive, and the most relevant here, is older. It was Ruskin, of all people, who invented the term "pathetic fallacy" to stigmatize as in some sense unjustified our tendency to perceive a smiling landscape as "happy," a somber one as "sad." But is it really a fallacy? Are we so separate from nature that our states are actually discontinuous with it? Is there nothing outside ourselves which is somehow glad or sad? Is it really a fallacy when we attribute to nature feelings analogous to our own?

Out of the very heart of the romantic feeling for nature the question arose. And it was Coleridge, again of all people, who gave the answer upon which the post-romantic "scientific" attitude rests: "Only in ourselves does nature live." But Wordsworth, who recorded Coleridge's dictum, was not himself always sure. When he was most himself it seemed to him that, on the contrary, the joy of nature was older than the joy of man and that what was transitory in the individual was permanent somewhere else. When the moment of happiness passed, it was not because the glory had faded but only because his own sight had grown dim.

> *There was a time when meadow, grove, and stream,*
> *The earth, and every common sight,*
>   *To me did seem*
> *Apparelled in celestial light,*
> *The glory and the freshness of a dream.*
>
> *Oh joy! that in our embers*
> *Is something that doth live,*
> *That nature yet remembers*
> *What was so fugitive!*

Something like this is what, in clumsy prose, I am trying to suggest. "Wilderness," "jungle," "desert," are not magic words because we have been "conditioned" to find them such but because they stand for things which only conditioning can make seem indifferent or alien. How could the part be greater than the whole? How can nature's meaning come wholly from man when he is only part of that meaning? "Only in ourselves does nature live" is less true than its opposite: "Only in nature do *we* have a being."

The most materialistic of historians do not deny the influence upon a people of the land on which they live. When they say, for instance, that the existence of a frontier was a dominant factor in shaping the character of the American people, they are not thinking only of a physical fact. They mean also that the idea of a frontier, the realization that space to be occupied lay beyond it, took its place in the American imagination and sparked the sense that there was "somewhere else to go" rather than that the solution of every problem, practical or spiritual, had to be found within the limits to which the man who faced them was confined.

In the history of many other peoples the character of their land, even the very look of the landscape itself, has powerfully influenced how they felt and what they thought about. They were woodsmen or plainsmen or mountaineers not only economically but spiritually also. And nothing, not even the sea, has seemed to affect men more profoundly than the desert, or seemed to incline them so powerfully toward great thoughts, perhaps because the desert itself seems to brood and to encourage brooding. To the Hebrews the desert spoke of God, and one of the most powerful of all religions was born. To the Arabs it spoke of the stars, and astronomy came into being.

Perhaps no fact about the American people is more important than the fact that the continent upon which they live is large enough and varied enough to speak with many different voices—of the mountains, of the plains, of the valleys and of the seashore—all clear voices that are distinct and strong. Because Americans listened to all these voices, the national character has had many aspects and developed in many different directions. But the voice of the desert is the one which has been least often heard. We came to it last, and when we did come, we came principally to exploit rather than to listen.

To those who do listen, the desert speaks of things with an emphasis quite different from that of the shore, the mountains, the valleys or the plains. Whereas they invite action and suggest limitless opportunity, exhaustless resources, the implications and the mood of the desert are something different. For one thing the desert is conservative, not radical. It is more likely to provoke awe than to invite conquest. It does not, like the plains, say, "Only turn the sod and uncountable riches will spring up." The heroism which it encourages is the heroism of endurance, not that of conquest.

Precisely what other things it says depends in part upon the person listening. To the biologist it speaks first of the remarkable flexibility of living things, of the processes of adaptation which are nowhere more remarkable than in the strange devices by which plants and animals have learned to conquer heat and dryness. To the practical-minded conservationist it speaks sternly of other things, because in the desert the problems created by erosion and overexploitation are plainer and more acute than anywhere else. But to the merely contemplative it speaks of courage and endurance of a special kind.

Here the thought of the contemplative crosses the thought of the conservationist, because the contemplative realizes that the desert is "the last frontier" in more senses than one. It is the last because it was the latest reached, but it is the last also because it is, in many ways, a frontier which *cannot* be crossed. It brings man up against his limitations, turns him in upon himself and suggests values which more indulgent regions minimize. Sometimes it inclines to contemplation men who have never contemplated before. And of all answers to the question "What is a desert good for?" "Contemplation" is perhaps the best.

The eighteenth century invented a useful distinction which we have almost lost, the distinction between the beautiful and the sublime. The first, even when it escapes being merely the pretty, is easy and reassuring. The sublime, on the other hand, is touched with something which inspires awe. It is large and powerful; it carries with it the suggestion that it might overwhelm us if it would. By these definitions there is no doubt which is the right word for the desert. In intimate details, as when its floor is covered after a spring rain with the delicate little ephemeral plants, it is pretty. But such embodiments of prettiness seem to be only tolerated with affectionate contempt by the region as a whole. As a whole the desert is, in the original sense of the word, "awful." Perhaps one feels a certain boldness in undertaking to live with it and a certain pride when one discovers that one can.

I am not suggesting that everyone should listen to the voice of the desert and listen to no other. For a nation which believes, perhaps rightly enough, that it has many more conquests yet to make, that voice preaches a doctrine too close to quietism. But I am suggesting that the voice of the desert might well be heard occasionally among the others. To go "up to the mountain" or "into the desert" has become part of the symbolical language. If it is good to make occasionally what the religious call a "retreat," there is no better place than the desert to make it. Here if anywhere the most faimiliar realities recede and others come into the foreground of the mind.

A world traveler once said that every man owed it to himself to see the tropics at least once in his life. Only there can he possibly realize how completely nature can fulfill certain potentialities and moods which the temperate regions only suggest. I have no doubt that he was right. Though I have never got beyond the outer fringe of the tropical lands, I hope that some day I shall get into their heart. But I am sure that they are no more necessary than the desert to an adequate imaginative grasp of the world we live in. Those who have never known it are to be pitied, like a man who has never read *Hamlet* or heard the *Jupiter Symphony*. He has missed something which is unique. And there is nothing else which can give him more than a hint of what he has missed. To have experienced it is to be prepared to see other landscapes with new eyes and to participate with a fresh understanding in the life of other natural communities.

EDWIN WAY TEALE

(1899–   )

A tantalizing list of credits shows how closely Edwin Way Teale has been allied to *Words for the Wild* subjects. President of the Thoreau Society in 1958, he later was awarded the John Burroughs Medal for distinguished nature writing. Editor of *The Wilderness World of John Muir*, he received the Pulitzer Prize for one of his own books about the American landscape. Meanwhile, he has written hundreds of articles and dozens of volumes, most of which deal with a naturalist's activities in the twentieth century.

Teale sees his role as paradoxical. The modern naturalist is "something of a contradiction," he observed in 1965. He is "assisted in innumerable ways by the products of modern technology. But at the same time he wants wildness. He wants escape from a too-civilized world." Teale's books explore that dilemma.

My favorites are the ones that seek a naturalist's milieu

by automobile. Teale and his wife, Nellie, drove back and forth across the United States four different times. Their leisurely travels resulted in a quartet of books that survey "the natural history of the American seasons." *North with the Spring* (1951) describes a 17,000-mile trip from the Gulf of Mexico to New Hampshire's Mount Washington. *Autumn Across America* (1956) heads west across the northern tier of states, then concludes with a meander down the Pacific Coast. *Journey into Summer* (1960) angles somewhat southwest from the author's Connecticut home, taking time for a lengthy investigation of the Great Lakes region and ending with a stretch in Colorado. The final volume (and winner of the Pulitzer Prize), *Wandering Through Winter* (1965), tracks the cold season from San Diego to Texas, then up through the midwest and north toward home.

Obviously the two travellers spent much of the time outside their car. They found absolutely charming characters— the Texas owners of seventy-nine cats, for example, the Ohio comet collector, the dedicated bird watcher of traffic-encircled Van Cortlandt Park. Down byways and country lanes, they avoided plastic America and looked for the unique—the rock rabbits, the monarch butterflies, the kit fox, and the desert sardine, the showy lady's slipper, the Colorado tundra, the floating islands that drift freely on Orange Lake. To accompany them is a very special reading treat.

When the last mile had been driven and the last page written, Teale concluded: "No two other persons in history had ever known the experience we had shared. We had observed first-hand the infinite diversity of the American seasons. We had crisscrossed, from sea to sea, this land unsurpassed for the variety and magnificence of its scenery, for the interest of its wild inhabitants. And, it seemed to us, we had seen it in the nick of time."

This touch of nostalgia is what makes Teale's prose so vital. Even as his naturalist's eye perceives a landscape threatened by interstate highways and unlimited development, his naturalist's pen shares that vision without sounding the knell of doom. To the contrary, in these books Teale recreates a happily perceptive incantation of America's denizens a generation ago.

From "Craters of the Moon" in *Autumn Across America*

I started out that morning with a dull mind fit only for entering figures in our expense account. But we had not gone far before a change in the country around us kindled to life vivid memories of an experience 2,000 miles away, on the border of North Carolina and Tennessee, in the spring of the year. Then we had come from lush Appalachian forests into the blighted, manmade desert of the Copper Basin. Now, once again, we rode through a stricken land. As far as we could see around us extended only hills and plains of cinders and barren lava. We seemed to have slipped swiftly backward through immense reaches of time. We were in the third day of creation. We wandered in a land new made.

For 200,000 square miles across south central Idaho, in the region of the Craters of the Moon, the earth presents a face hard, almost untouched by time. It is America's newest landscape. Only a few thousand years ago, in some cases only 500 years ago—a mere second as geological ages run—the molten, smoking lava had welled from fissures in the earth. The blue glaze of its exterior was still unmarked by storms. The centuries of gradual transformation and breaking down, of erosion and decay, were only just beginning. In the Copper Basin of the east the topsoil had been carried away. Here the soil had never been. Here was a hard, lifeless land. Or so we thought. Here was a countryside untouched by the seasons. Or so it seemed. The great adventure of this day was the discovery of life where life appeared impossible, the revelation that, in hundreds of ways, even in this dead land the turning wheel of the seasons had left its track.

By midmorning we reached the roads and trails of the Craters of the Moon National Monument, an eighty-square-mile area near Arco set aside by the federal government in 1924. It was autumn. The tourist season was over. We wandered almost alone through its black, eerie world of broken lava, tree molds, cinder cones and natural bridges. We had gone but a short distance before we were reminded afresh of how almost pathetically small are the basic requirements of life. Put a teaspoonful of dust in any crack and some seed will find it. All across this land of seeming emptiness and desolation seeds had discovered little accumulations of airborne dust. Even clumps of that bushy western relative of the goldenrod, rabbitbrush, here and there amazingly rose from the lava, rooted in invisible soil.

Our first surprise came when we entered a stretch of open cinders, our feet crunching along as though we were walking on dry toast. These cinder fields are formed of the froth or molten spray thrown off by fire fountains during volcanic activity. Sometimes they have a brownish cast, occasionally a reddish hue as though they were still uncooled, but most of the time they are ebony black. From a distance they look like rich loam plowed and harrowed and ready for planting. As we emerged on this sloping plain of cinders we saw scattered across its surface hundreds of what appeared to be small, white, lace doilies. Each was from three inches to a foot across. Each, on closer examination, proved to be composed of low-lying, silver-hued, woolly-textured leaves. Variously known as the umbrella plant, the silver plant and woolly knees, these cinder dwellers were one of the wild buckwheats. Long since the yellow flowers had withered. The upright stems were now dry and shriveled. Only a few more weeks and this year's installment of the life of the plant would be rounded out. But the perennial roots below, as well as the seeds, already formed and hardened, insured that its blooms would appear again the following summer in this arid and improbable garden.

Looking down at these silver clusters of the wild buckwheat we were, once more, making contact with the eccentric pioneer naturalist whose trail we first encountered at Cape May. For it was Thomas Nuttall who, a century ago, bestowed on this western plant its scientific name, *Eriogonum ovalifolium*.

There were other plants—small, sere, sparse, widely spaced—growing on the cinder fields. Only the *Eriogonum* now showed signs of life. But in June and July the white of bitterroot blooms and the red of monkey flowers are scattered over the black background of the cinders. Growth, blooming and seedtime come swiftly here as they do on a mountain meadow. Down some of the slopes of the cinder cones that favorite food of bears, the wild parsnip, grows almost abundantly. And in shaded cracks and recesses in the lava the dainty *Woodsia* fern sometimes obtains a foothold. Lichens, liverworts, mosses and algae—primitive plants all—are widely scattered in the Craters of the Moon. All through the so-called Devil's Orchard we found the ragged, jumbled masses—the slag of primal furnaces—splotched with brilliant patches of algae, orange and scarlet and sulphur yellow.

It was while we were wandering through this colorful,

eerie landscape that we came upon the juncos. They were no ordinary juncos. They were juncos our eyes had never encountered before. A little flock of a dozen or more flitted about, calling, alighting on the ground, feeding. Each bird was brownish of back, grayish of head, with a flush of rusty pink running back along its sides and across its breast. Amid these bizarre surroundings we were meeting our first pink-sided juncos.

As the afternoon advanced the wind rose. It pummeled us on the rises and raced overhead in long screeching blasts when we descended into the hollows. It drove cinder dust into our mouths and ears and noses. Once we struggled for an eighth of a mile—like flies on the rim of a bowl—around the edge of a deep cinder crater. In this exposed position the fifty-mile-an-hour gale caught us full force. We struggled down into a depression beyond, pounded and panting as though we had battled our way through heavy surf. There, protected from the great gusts and warmed by the sun a dancing, yellow-winged grasshopper crackled in the air. And above the sound of the wind we caught low cricket music somewhere amid the sparse vegetation.

It was in this depression that I picked a fernlike leaf from a low shrub. Absently, I crushed it between my fingers. Fragrance filled the air around us. For hours afterward my hand was scented with the perfume of this redolent leaf. The low shrub was that medicinal plant of the pioneers, mountain misery, bear clover, bearmat, tarweed, kittikit or kit-kit-dizze. Its aromatic leaves are evergreen. Where the white-petaled blossoms of summer had been, autumn had brought the dry, one-seeded hips of this curious relative of the wild rose.

When the early pioneers first came to the Craters of the Moon region they were mystified by low mounds found here and there among the lava fields. Each mound consisted of alternating layers of cinders and sagebrush. The riddle was solved when an aged Indian at the Fort Hall Reservation recalled that it was thus his ancestors had marked their paths, the sagebrush being laid lengthwise to indicate the direction of the trail. For three miles, past Great Owl Cavern and on to the tree molds west of Big Cinder Butte, we followed one of these ancient Indian trails. The path led along the line where lava fields and cinder slopes met. Here and there, dwarfed and wind-wracked limber pines huddled together, their branches contorted and grotesque. One of these trees, in 1926, was struck by lightning near Big Crater. When park service men felled it they found it measured thirty-four and a half inches in diameter. Its annual growth rings numbered 461. It was rooted there, already a good-sized tree, before the *Santa Maria* sailed from Spain on its epic voyage of discovery.

The sun was well down in the west by the time we passed Great Owl Cavern. Not far beyond we came upon deer tracks in the cinders and near by, where a dry, fallen tree lay shaggy in a brilliant sheathing of green lichen, a chipmunk had dug its burrow. Twice we glimpsed these striped rodents scurrying away across the rolling waves of lava. On occasions they explore the lava plains as much as half a mile from their cinderfield homes. We, like the chipmunks, emerged on the open lava as we neared the tree molds. There a remarkable sight met our eyes, as beautiful as it was unexpected.

All across the black, wind-buffeted expanse to the west— shot through with the iridescent, metallic glintings of the lava beneath—was a streaming sea of silken threads. A vast multitude of ballooning spiderlings had come to earth in this forbidding place. Across thousands upon thousands of acres the silver of the autumn gossamer was streaming in the wind, catching the low rays of the sun, shimmering and flickering in constant motion—the ephemeral silk of a few days' duration bringing its delicate beauty to the hard, enduring, centuries-old face of the lava.

It is amid this gossamer that we came at last to those almost miraculous features of the lava beds, the tree molds. At this spot, once upon a time, a group of trees had stood in the path of the molten flood. The round holes, where the trunks had been, extended deep into the hardened lava. When that lava had issued incandescent from fissures in the The Great Rift, its temperature had been about 2,000 degrees F. How then did the trees avoid being consumed like celluloid? What enabled them to survive long enough to leave their forms in the hardening rock? Scientists believe the lava was slowing down and cooling rapidly when it reached the spot. Moisture and sap in the trunks formed a layer of steam that accelerated the cooling process and formed a protective shell of rock around the wood. Later the tree trunks rotted away leaving the molds behind. In a few rare instances, the top of a burning tree would fall on the surface of the cooling lava and leave there, by the same sequence of events, a perfect mold of its upper branches.

Retracing our steps in the sunset, we stopped on the flank of a cinder cone to watch a slim bird flitting flycatcherwise along the slope from pine to sagebrush and back to pine again. Each time it landed its support reared and bucked in the wind while the bird gripped its twig and rode out the great gusts. White feathers ran down either side of its tail. Brown patches stood out on its dark gray wings. And a white line encircled each eye. Here, in this solitary place, we were seeing for the first time a Townsend's solitaire. And once more we were touching the life of Old Curious.

For it was during the 1834 Wyeth Expedition across the

South Pass of Wyoming to the Columbia River that Nuttall's young companion, John Kirk Townsend, had collected the first specimen of this bird known to science, a bird named for its discoverer by John James Audubon. It is the only North American representative of a group of thrushes, mostly tropical, famed for their glorious voices. Here, in the Craters of the Moon, the two pioneer naturalists who had journeyed west so long before were, after a fashion, united again, one remembered for the silver plant he had named, the other for a dark, slender bird christened in his honor.

At one point I tried a short cut across an arm of the open lava. I learned in a dozen steps how slow and laborious and hazardous is the walking. In places the lava is jagged and broken. No horse can be ridden across it. Snakes are entirely absent from the region. The local belief is that they cannot stand the abrasion of the hard furrows. Pioneers who penetrated the area on foot often returned with their shoes nearly eaten away by the rasp of the lava.

Out of the fastness of this dangerous land they brought tales of ice-cold pools surrounded by sun-heated rocks too hot to touch. And, unlike those legends of hidden treasure with which the region abounds, these reports were true. Here and there are small water holes where the temperature rarely exceeds thirty-four degrees. They are not springs. They are not connected with subterranean streams. Their origin, for a long time a baffling mystery, is now known to be associated with caches of winter ice and snow. Packing into deep pits and fissures during the seven months of cold weather, the frozen water in time forms a solid base of impermeable ice. Lava is a poor conductor of heat. Only the upper layers of the snow and ice melt in summer and the resulting water never gets much more than two degrees above the freezing point. Yet in this frigid water green algae sometimes grow.

At first the riddle of these water holes was believed to be connected with another mystery, a mystery of lost rivers. For all this area of the Craters of the Moon is a land of disappearing streams. Beneath the lava run the subterranean conduits of rivers flowing underground. Not a single stream flows across the surface of the whole Snake River Plateau. Fifty miles to the north of us, as we followed the trail back, rose Borah Peak, the highest mountain in Idaho, its summit 12,655 feet above sea level. And all along the horizon in that direction we saw the lofty rampart of the snowclad Sawtooth Mountains. Down their slopes the Big Lost River, the Little Lost River, and numerous other streams descend until they reach the lava plain. Then they sink out of sight. Draining into innumerable cracks and crevices they flow beneath the lava layer across a gently tilting plain to the gorge of the Snake River. There, in some cases after running unseen for upward of 200 miles, they emerge near Hagerman in the spectacular display of a host of fountains gushing from the sheer face of the river wall. These are the famous Thousand Springs marveled at by the early pioneers as their covered wagons crept along the opposite bank of the river on the road to Oregon.

Looking across the greenish water of the Snake from this same vantage point the next day, Nellie and I spent an hour watching the emerging rivers plunging down the rocks in sheets of spray. Some descended in long plumes and veils, others dropped to the river in walls of white water. The year around the temperature of the emerging flood is between sixty and sixty-two degrees. All the way from the Salmon River to the town of Bliss, a distance of eighteen miles, fountains flow from the northern wall of the canyon. But it is in a stretch of hardly more than half a mile near Hagerman that the dramatic display of the Thousand Springs is concentrated. Here the precipice towers as much as 185 feet above the river and some of the springs pour out their long-pent-up flood close to the top.

At the turn of the century it was estimated that water flowed down the face of the canyon wall at this point at the rate of 20,000 cubic feet a second. At the lowest point of the Snake, during the latter days of summer, the fountains of the Thousand Springs were said to add a volume of water that equaled the entire previous flow of the river. What we witnessed, half a century later, while still beautiful was only a maimed and diminished show. Where some of the falls had been there were now the slanting metal flumes of a power company. We remembered Thoreau's observation when owners began cutting down the beautiful Walden Woods: "It concerns us all whether these proprietors choose to cut down all the woods this winter or not." The wild beauty of America is a national possession. The preservation of this heritage is everybody's affair. No land on earth has been more superlatively blessed with varied and priceless forms of natural beauty. Whatever mars or destroys it robs the future as well as the present. What "These Proprietors" choose to do—even in a far-off corner of the land—is of more than personal, more than local concern. It is the concern of all.

From "Barrier Island"
in *North with the Spring*

About sunset we packed our knapsack with extra sweaters, sandwiches, oranges, and a thermos of hot tea and, after a day of uncertain weather, set out for the ocean beach. Beside the road a Carolina wren sang, sounding loud and shrill so close at hand—as though someone were sharpening shears on a lop-sided grindstone. Once we walked through an island of perfume beside a mound of jessamine, and just before we reached the shore we came to stunted trees behind a low ridge of dunes, trees with their tops sheared flat by the wind and all their twisted branches flaring away from the sea. Beyond was the barrier beach. It stretched away, deserted from end to end, as lonely as some primitive shore facing a pre-Columbian sea.

We sat down on the warm sand and leaned back against a beam from a wrecked ship, half buried in the beach. The play of sunset colors changed moment by moment over the expanse of water before us. Two hundred yards from shore a long raft of scaup rode the breakers, rising and falling, appearing and disappearing, as the waves rolled under them. The tide was out. Veils of falling rain, rain that had circled and missed us, increased in number over the sea. The east was serene and blue while in the west the sun was setting in a wild and broken sky.

We wandered along the shore, examining shells and gathering firewood for the night. Twice in succession, shells I reached for began sliding away on the wet sand, propelled by the feet of hermit crabs. High on the beach, where a dead palm tree had been thrown by storm waves, I broke off a decaying frond and discovered the massed white bodies of termites riddling the interior. Steadily the pile of wood increased beside the weathered timber. Gathering driftwood for a fire is a comforting occupation. It is direct and obvious in a world of confusing complexities. The benefits are seen at once. There are no lost or hidden links in the chain of action. Cause and effect, effort and result, are apparent at a glance.

A sprinkle of fine rain ran across the sand and then passed

out to sea. A moment later the last rays of the sun streamed suddenly through a long gap in the clouds just above the black trees on the western horizon. Horizontally they shot over the sea, tinting the wave tips pink. They struck the fine shower that had passed us and the colors of a rainbow swiftly brightened. One end of the arch rested on the sea, the other on the northern end of the island. A faint band of red strengthened below the green—the beginning of a rainbow within a rainbow.

Rarely have I seen a more brilliant arch in the sky. The distinctness of its colors probably resulted from the fact that the sheet of falling rain contained an unusual number of small droplets of water. The finer and more numerous the water droplets in the air the more distinct is the rainbow, just as in a half-tone illustration the finer the screen—the more and smaller the dots—the more distinct the picture.

A small cloud of shore birds scudded past us; they seemed to fly in and out of the arc of the rainbow. They were followed by three least terns, flying single-file. These dainty, butterfly-like creatures were so persecuted on Bull's Island, half a century ago, that feather hunters from the North, in a single season, wiped out the entire breeding colony. The scaup, more than one hundred of them among the outer breakers, rode the rise and fall of the darkening water— under the sunset, under the rainbow, as they would ride it under the stars. Finally their bobbing forms grew indistinct, part of the vast darkness that was enveloping us.

The tide had changed. The turn of the tide and the turn of the day had come at almost the same time. The waves were advancing on the shore; the night was advancing on land and sea alike. By our flickering campfire we sat on the edge of two mysterious realms, the realm of the sea and the realm of the night.

At seven-fifteen the first star became visible to our eyes. It was Sirius, the Dog Star. From then on, the glint and glitter of the stars and planets increased. Clouds rimmed the horizon where sheet lightning brightened and faded; but the great dome overhead was clear. Infinitely far above us, lost among the stars, we heard a lonely plane thrumming across the sky. Once in the dark, as we gathered fresh firewood, we debated without decision whether a light on the ocean's rim was a rising star or a ship standing offshore. Even our field glasses failed to dispel our uncertainty. Later two ships, like luminous hyphens an inch apart, crept northward along the horizon line.

This was Saturday night. All over the country, in cities and villages, in stores and theaters and dance halls, along Main Street and Broadway, Saturday night was something special. On our barrier beach, with the sea and the dark for our companions, it was something special too. The city man, in his neon-and-mazda glare, knows nothing of nature's midnight. His electric lamps surround him with synthetic sunshine. They push back the dark. They defend him from the realitites of the age-old night. A hundred years after he asked it, the answer is still "yes" to Henry Thoreau's question: "Is not the midnight like Central Africa to most of us?"

When the postmidnight hours came, faint clouds formed in streaks or furrows or shoals of vapor. They seemed thicker to the south, and above Charleston, 20 miles away, the reflected light from thousands of street lamps formed a luminous patch on the sky, a kind of celestial lighthouse marking the site of the city.

Each time we piled driftwood on our fire the flames leaped high, brilliantly colored by salts of the sea impregnating the flotsam. They lighted the dunes and the ribbed sand of the beach and the white waves of the flood tide. With our fire as the hub of our activity, we wandered north and south along the beach. Swinging the beams of flashlights over the sand, we stalked ghost crabs, watching them scuttle back into their burrows at our approach. From grass clumps fringing the dunetops came the metallic bandsaw buzzing of seaside grasshoppers. And beyond, just over the low ridge of dunes, a chuck-will's-widow called hour after hour.

It had fallen silent by the time we packed up and threw sand over the embers of our fire. The night was far gone and "the world and all the Sons of Care lay hushed in sleep." We started back through a gap in the dunes. We had gone no more than a hundred yards before a grayish, dusky bird leaped into the air from the sandy ground. It was the chuck-will's-widow. I caught it in the beam of my flashlight and held it for thirty feet or so as it fluttered upward. This voice of the night was silent as it rose on rapidly beating wings, shining and ghostly in the spotlight.

A still stranger sight was to greet us farther on. Cottonmouth moccasins—the "mackasin snake" of William Bartram—hunt in the night. We moved with caution along the narrow road bordered on either side by water and marshy tracts. We played the beams of our two flashlights along the path ahead of us. Lizards rattled over the palmetto fronds with a dry hissing sound. Frogs leaped from the grass over our feet. Once our flashlights picked out a huge shape bearing down upon us with shining eyes. It was Solo on one of his nocturnal rambles.

It was under such conditions that we came on a scene of eerie beauty. Twenty yards ahead of us we caught sight of a half-moon of green, glowing light shining in the darkness of the roadside. It appeared to be about the size of a silver dollar half thrust into the earth. At first I wondered if it was some animal eye reflecting back the rays of our flashlights.

We swung the beams down. The spot glowed as eerily green as before.

Approaching closer, we discovered a large, whitish grub bearing luminous spots along its sides. Almost two inches long, it was nearly out of its burrow, curving in a semicircle. With both flashlight beams concentrated on it, it began backing into the ground. I pried it out with a bamboo stick. It curled up like a cutworm, lying on its side, the row of glowing dots shining as brightly as though formed of neon tubes. We watched it for a long time, then placed it back on the soft earth where its tunnel had brought it to the surface.

This glowing apparition was the wingless, larvaform female of a beetle, a relative of the familiar firefly. To scientists it is *Phengodes*. To people in parts of the South it is the "neon worm." To us, appearing as it did when the new day was almost beginning, it was the final memory of our night on the barrier beach.

HARVEY BROOME

(1902–1968)

Harvey Broome is probably better known because of who he was and what he did than because of what he wrote. One of the eight organizers of the Wilderness Society, he served as a member of its governing council from the beginning, became its vice president in 1948, its president in 1957. He held that office until his death.

The list of his accomplishments seems endless. Not only was he a trustee of the Robert Marshall Wilderness Fund, but he played an active role in the preservation and protection of wild areas all across the country. Along with the late Howard Zahniser, Broome led both populace and politicians toward the establishment of the National Wilderness Preservation System. His first love was the wilderness landscape outside his Tennessee home, the Great Smoky Mountains, but he respected any untouched land. His career was marked by hikes, canoe trips, and backcountry horseback rides from coast to coast.

Descriptions of some of those trips can be found in *Faces of the Wilderness*, a collection of essays recounting Broome's wilderness travels. Many of the excerpts describe those Wilderness Society council meetings held in remote areas, while others tell of trips made privately with his wife and friends. The entries, extending chronologically over a twenty-five-year period of time, are more personal than political, although they reflect, as Broome says, "a deepening concern over abuses of the land and a parallel concern for the future of man."

They are most powerful, I think, when they contemplate a landscape that is diminishing before Broome's very eyes or when they ask the hard questions. In Oregon, sand dunes move forests. Why not? Or, rather, why should the federal government attempt to stop them? In Idaho, "the primitive area seemed to have become a gigantic elk factory, which was proliferating beyond expectation." Broome wonders what Aldo Leopold would say. In New Mexico he knows "the battle is joined—not for particular parks or monuments in forests or wilderness but for a philosophy of land use." Yet he remembers that state best for a stand of aspen, "as though all the riches of the earth had been gathered into that spot and flung broadcast through the air."

We all should remember Broome best for the time and expertise he gave to the embryonic environmental movement. Without such personal energy and sacrifice, I believe wilderness as we know it today would not exist. The *Washington Post*, just after Broome's death, concurs: "Conservationists and naturalists all over the country owe him a debt of gratitude for his work." Then the editorial adds, "He found relaxation and renewal of the inner spirit in the beauty of a forest, the gleam of a glacier, the song of a bird and the quiet whisper of the teeming wilderness. These are the values he helped to preserve for America." These also are the values expressed in Harvey Broome's writing.

From "Big Horn Crags" in *Faces of the Wilderness*

IDAHO
1961

Few periods in my life have matched the prolonged, relentless, and intense anxiety of the three days just past. It arose over the disappearance in the Big Horn Crags within the Idaho Primitive Area of a woman botanist named Anna.

The day started disarmingly enough. Brandy proposed a hike from the site of our camp, which was about a half mile below Welcome Lake. A great bulging formation of granite came down to the very cook tent. It was an offshoot of the ridge which protruded from a higher divide and separated our camp from Welcome Lake.

We started up this pebble-faced granite and ascended it to the dividing ridge. As its slopes became more precipitous we angled off into the timber on the west face. Here there were scattered grass, loose talus, small bluffs, and sparse stands of timber. It was not easy going but it was not hazardous and we made progress both laterally and vertically with infrequent rests. Eventually we intercepted the trail from Welcome Lake a few hundred feet from the top of the divide.

The divide at that spot was broad, level, and gritty, and broken by a scattered stand of pine. The elevation was around nine thousand feet. We eased off its south face into the timber and began to catch glimpses of a remarkable collection of lakes in the basin below. This was the Puddin Lake basin— a very wild area, untrailed, and hemmed in by savagely ragged mountains. There were a few meadows. By a quiet approach we hoped to see elk and other game. We proceeded as quietly as nine people could proceed and examined the area with some frequency with field glasses. Below us was forest, small meadows and emerald lakes. We finally counted a total of nine lakes, the most entrancing of which was one of considerable size, and the highest in the basin. It was far to the west of us and seemed to offer the most in beauty of surroundings and in remoteness. Edging slowly off the ridge, we moved in the general direction of this unnamed lake.

Four of the party grew impatient and dropped steeply into the basin. The other five of us held up for fear of dashing rocks on those who had gone on. Eventually we followed, but less precipitately, working through a bench of lodgepole pines to one of the meadows.

We were all very thirsty and found a string of slowly running pools from which we drank. Moving on another hundred yards, we found in a deep groin a freely running rivulet of very cold water coursing down flower-lined banks. We stopped and drank again. We were now at the lower edge of a shallow timbered ridge which we had glimpsed from above. Brandy thought if we got on its back we could follow it through the timber to the northwest and reach a point just above our unnamed lake.

As we started to rise, Anna demurred, saying she needed to rest. So we settled down again in moss along the banks of a freely running rivulet and enjoyed this very wild spot. Some, including Anna, ate a little, but I jokingly said the day was not over and I was saving my sandwich for an emergency. After perhaps twenty minutes we moved on through the covering woods. We reached the rounded back of the ridge and after a half hour found ourselves in sight of the green-black waters of our nameless lake. It lay so high, it was perhaps no more than fifty feet below the forested ridge crest we had been following. On our side there was a small beach, and a huge tree which had fallen parallel with the shore and slightly into the water.

There was a fringe of trees around the entire lake from which protruded rocky bluffs and above which were the stark chalky-gray angles of high above-timber line ridges. It was untrailed, remote. The lake lay open to the sky in a vast maze of intersecting ridges. It was a wild and beautiful lake.

Above the forest on the north and west were gray-fractured, angular faces of cliffs. Again I had reached a spot completely given over to wild game and seldom visited. The ruff of trees and beach, the rays of grass and flowering draws stretching up from the shore did not dilute my feeling. All around were gaunt pyramids of broken rock pushing above the forest into the domain of the thunderbolts. And back of us was the wide basin laced only with game ways. This was indeed wilderness—perhaps the wildest place I had ever been—and a part of the great Idaho wilderness.

In this grimly beautiful setting, we were soon to be chilled by fear for the safety of one who was then close by. . . .

When I reached the top of the bluff, no more than ten minutes had elapsed since I had passed Anna. I could see two figures at her post and assumed that one of the fellows had stopped to talk to her. I then walked back along the shore to the main draw below the pass.

Thinking I would be the first at the pass, I climbed slowly taking photos and observing the birds and flowers. As I was nearing the top, I was surprised to see two figures and realized Doc and Paul had preceded me. Clouds and rain were gather-

ing to the south among the crags across the lake and there
was a sharp flash or two of lightning. Paul and Doc descended toward me to get out of lightning range, but we soon
climbed again to the pass where we had agreed to rendezvous. It was a grim and bleak prospect to the north. Everywhere I looked were harsh, angular contours of nothing but
rock.

I took the glasses and studied the frightening slopes of
a pass into the Welcome Lake area. I wondered if we could
drag our party up to it. There were too many bare, vertical
bluffs to please me. The only hope lay in a fuzz of timber
between which rock slides had torn ghastly perpendicular
paths. Even if we could climb this slope, could we descend
on the far side? Again a few straggling trees seemed to offer
some hope. But it was not a certainty and I wished the others
would come so we could get at it in daylight.

I whiled the time until Brandy should arrive, and when
he did come Anna was missing. It did not alarm me but it
was annoying. We were already late. Several went back to
call her. Their shouts and rolling echoes were unanswered.
The situation took on a serious aspect. If she could not hear,
where was she? Had she fallen in that apron of giant boulders
above the flowering draw where she had been sitting? There
is nothing more potent, nor agonizingly eloquent, than silence
in an area as cruel as this. She could be anywhere—unnoticed
in those terrifying piles of rocks.

She did not come. Things were becoming serious. We
abandoned our plan to circle back to Welcome Lake, and
resolved to sweep that tilted boulder field above the flowers.
There was hazard in this. The slopes were barely in repose
and we stumbled across fragments of cliff which rocked
under our weight. We had to spread far to protect those on
the slopes below. It was hard tense work, and as the elastic

spring of our search drew into a knot in the draw, there was no sign of Anna. There was no inert form twisted among the car-size boulders—no answering cry to our anxious shouts— nothing.

That she had disappeared was incredible. She had been in sight of everyone. I had spoken to her, and yet she had vanished in the short ten minutes from the time I had re-passed her until Ross Bennett and Tom Leggat had sat in the sun at the very spot where I had spoken to her. Had she ranged up the boulders and fallen? Had she followed a screen of trees to reach the pass ahead of the Greaveses and gone on down the bleak gorge beyond? Had she crossed under the bluff above her resting spot and fallen down the cliffs to the east? Had she reascended the shallow forested rim by which we had reached the lake and was even then making her way through the meadows and forest toward camp?

By a kind of consensus we decided she had gone back by the way we had arrived. But there remained that gnawing uncertainty. We swept the cliffs back of us with the glasses and spread out through the woods before we reached the meadows, peering and looking, straining our eyes at the gloomy shadows in the woods for the secret they might hide. As we gained the open woods above the meadows, Brandy thought he found the track of a woman heading in our direc-tion. He felt sure it was Anna's track and we were relieved. We had only to verify this when we reached camp. Our anx-iety was dulled for the time.

As we slanted up the ridge, we intercepted a steep trail, which by short switchbacks went almost straight up. It was an elk trail and we followed it, clawing and slipping in the churned earth and gravel. On top we found ourselves only a few hun-dred feet west of the cairn marking the Welcome Lake trail.

We hustled down this trail and walked into camp about 6:30 and received the numbing news that Anna had not returned.

It is hard to describe the effect. There was an amalgam of misgivings, forebodings, bewilderment, and incredulity. How could she have vanished with people all around her? What had happened to her; what was her condition?

The camp was galvanized. Amidst half-swallowed suppers, maps were drawn, plans laid, flashlights and extra batteries assembled, horses saddled, revolvers buckled on, rescue routes discussed and searching assignments made.

Three packers and Doc and Brandy were to ride as far as they could, hitch the horses, and descend again into the Puddin Lake basin and search it by flashlight. Two of the fellows were to go down Wilson Creek to a point commanding the ascent ridge and divide and build a signal fire in case she should return that way. Jim Moles, one of the packers, and I were to go up by the ascent of the morning, build another fire by which we hoped to guide her in.

We started out in deep dusk. I was tired from heavy exertions during the day. I knew in that thin air I would be no match for Jim. But we pushed on in half moonlight, never using our torches. We called continually and reached a point far higher on the ridge than we had made that morning.

We came to a pocket in a great balding face of the cliff. There were dead trees all around and a few fifteen-foot seedling firs. The site of our fire was a rocky niche overlooking Welcome Lake. I gathered squaw wood, Jim made shavings, and soon our signal fire roared up in the darkness. Jim was restless and decided to climb higher. He went on in the moonlit darkness. I kept in touch with him by shouts. The ridge, he reported, was like the comb of a roof and he stopped where he could command the divide and built another signal fire.

For a time I was alone with the lower fire and with my worries and thoughts. Under different circumstances the scene about me would have been a fantasy of beauty. I was on an eyrie of rock in the center of a vast basin of crags and pyramids. Below was the sheen of a lake and the shadow of a forest. The moon was obscured from me, but it shone through great windows of clear sky onto the cliffs behind me, touching them with unearthly light. It was a world one almost never sees, halfway between the brightness of day and the obscurity of full dark. The half-light showed a world which had never existed for man. He is not gifted for seeing in the darkness. Who would climb those rugged cliffs at night to see something which couldn't be imagined? Who would brave the chill of such an exposed place? And yet because of Anna's disappearance, I was high on a crag at night amidst scenes of haunting and spectral beauty. The cliffs which dropped precipitously all around me, my own weariness and half-thoughts, contributed eerily to the experience.

Suddenly there was a flare-up in my fire and a crackling explosion of light. I hastened around the screen of firs. The fire had crept close to a seedling fir four feet high. It became too hot and flared into flame—a blazing torch from a living tree. I was sorry.

The clouds thickened. Lightning flickered around us—the crags and pyramids flashed into sight and then went black again. There was a patter of drops on the rocks; I drew my jacket closer about me. Then I heard a shout. Jim was making his way back to me. We talked in low voices. There were no signal fires on the divide. Below we could see a light at the camp and the other signal fire down Wilson Creek. In the void below us we could hear the bells on the tethered horses.

Then Jim remembered that in our anxiety the horses had

not been fed or watered. I thought this over, and decided that no one would now be descending those cliffs alone. We had accomplished our purpose in giving her a guide fire in the early evening. We decided to return.

So greatly does one become accustomed to the darkness, we hardly needed our lights. Each feature has a different gradient and shading. A shadow would mark a fallen tree. Our boots gripped perfectly. My only fear was loose gravel. We got into camp about 11 p.m. And as we went to feed the horses, out of the vastness behind us, there came the undulating wail and barking of coyotes. The wilderness had taken over.

I went to my sleeping bag about 12:20 a.m. and dozed fitfully, to be awakened at 3:30 a.m. by the sound of horses. I counted them as they stomped by. There were six horses, but the silence of the riders was ominous. I slipped on my boots and trousers and jacket and found Brandy down in the meadow with the horses. On their trip they had tied the horses on the divide and had descended by foot into the basin. With their torches they had again found our lake, had searched the draws and copses up to the pass. No Anna answered their shouts, or came into the beams of their flashlights.

At dawn we discussed further search plans. Richie would go to the roadhead and give the alarm to the road crew. Brandy would go down Wilson Creek. I would lead Tom Leggat and Jack Sheridan back to the lake. Jim Moles and Ross would ascend the ridge again and search the divide east and west. John Bradford and his father would take a stand on the divide at the Welcome Lake trail and pass on any signals from our party. Three shots if we needed help; two if we found her and all was well.

Tom, Jack, and I made up an emergency pack with a

blanket, a pillow slip for splints, a gun for signaling, a canteen, and jackets. We had matches and flashlights. Tom carried the pack all day.

The night-searching party had been unable to ride the horses up the switchbacks of the Welcome Lake trail. On those violent slopes, horses were almost useless and we walked the whole distance and did not have the care of the horses. On top we checked on our signals with John Bradford and hunted the descending elk trail, the head of which John would mark with cairns.

When we descended to a lake, it had a rough, ugly shore with a ten-foot drawdown. We had never seen it before. It began to rain and the rocks were slick. We didn't know where we were. Instead of going back to a known point, we decided to circle to the right. This was an act of faith. Dimly visible in a low, overcast of clouds, the lake seemed to drain through a low rim into an unknown creek. Through holes in the clouds, we saw unfamiliar ridges. It was a bad moment. We went over several ridges, expecting every time to see *our* lake over its crest. But no. We were thoroughly confused.

Eventually we climbed a little meadow, caught a glimpse of dark water through a thinness in the trees. I said, "This is it."

It was our lake; its features had been so burned in my memory, I could never have been mistaken about it. But we were very high on bluffs opposite the spot where we had eaten the previous day. And we had to find a way down off those bluffs to the shore. This we were able to do, and walked out on the prominence from which I had taken photographs less than twenty-four hours before.

We first combed the lake shore between the big draw and grassy draw, examining every copse of trees where she might have crept for warmth had she been injured. We then climbed the rocks beneath the big butte and looked east. Tom thought she might have fallen there, and we saved it for a going-over on our return. We then worked back and forth between the two draws toward the pass and ridge crest. We were in sight and call of each other. There was no possible place of concealment which we did not examine.

Eventually we worked into the pass—a spot as empty and bleak as our search had been. I descended the far side to the bench which had blocked our view to the north on the previous day. The ravine was empty. Back to the pass for lunch. We heard a whistle and saw a figure to the east, high on the loose pyramid of rocks. On a hunch, I called,

"Is that you, Jim?" and Jim Moles worked down the rocks and through scattered trees to us at the pass. His shoes were almost in shreds. He had come alone across the lonely reaches above timber line.

While the others ate, I again descended from the pass to the north. I found a rudimentary trail made by game. There was nothing else. No signs. I wondered if any man had ever been there before. I went on down (dreading the climb on my return) until I could see a tiny empty meadow at the bottom and the violent, vertical cliffs guarding the pass. They were perpendicular—no ledges, no benches. After I had toiled back to the pass I cautioned Jim not to risk those crumbling cliffs, and he agreed, saying he would go to the foot of the ravine first. When we last saw him he was plunging down the rocks—his legs slightly bowed, the only living creature in sweeping Vs of talus which converged upon him from all sides. He had no pack or supplies. Audacious, fearless, conscientious, and tireless, he was one of the roughest, toughest, and most admirable persons I have ever known.

We again ran our three-toothed comb over the boulder field beneath the big butte. Jack wanted to examine the rim above the lake. Tom and I crossed the divide and searched the benches and troughs to its base. We called Anna's name at intervals. We heard nothing but worthless echoes. We met at the base. I felt somewhat encouraged that we had not found her injured, or any sign of her. She had surely, I thought, become separated from the party while she was still well. There was no sign of camera, pack, notebook, or discarded garments. I was sure she had not crossed the pass where we had just left Jim Moles. Tom felt she must have descended into the lower part of the main Puddin Lakes basin.

This made sense, as we were to learn later. Jim Moles eliminated the violent country to the north of the pass. Tom and I debated going down to the Puddin Lakes basin that afternoon, but we had promised to be back at camp by dark and to delay would add to the anxieties of those who remained.

As we were crossing the meadows, a helicopter came over the pass to the west, banked steeply and came to rest near us. The pilot had been instructed to pick up one of our party and search for an hour before dark. He was in a hurry—an overcast was coming in. Tom Leggat went with him in that open bubble which had stretchers for running boards. It swept back and forth a time or two, dashed toward the ground and then mounted upward and disappeared over the pass to the west.

At camp there was nothing to report. After supper Brandy announced plans to evacuate the party the next day by way of the Crags campground. We climbed a bluff above camp with a Forest Service walkie-talkie and sent messages to Brandy's father, to the Chamber of Commerce at Salmon for transport, and requested helicopters and searchers and ordered supplies for those who were staying.

We spent the last night around the campfire, taking the statements of those who had been on the hike with Anna or who had taken part in the search. I was to go out to help coordinate matters with the Forest Service. . . .

We were faced also with hellish uncertainties. Suppose she should not be found, either alive or dead, for how long should we press the search? That was a bottomless pit— a kind of circumstantial quicksand.

The following day, when Floyd Iverson, the Regional Forester in Ogden, gave instructions for the Forest Service to do all that it could with its own forces, the men sprang into activity. There was a great bustle as packs and supplies were assembled for the search crews, along with brawny out-doorsmen who were bursting with vitality.

Brandy senior had to get some new boots for young Brandy, who had walked the feet out of his old boots. Brandy senior and I came back to Denny's office about 11 a.m. We were sitting on the floor indulging in desultory conversation with Denny and his assistant, when the radio squawked and there came over it the electrifying words:

"Lost woman found; lost woman found. In good condition; in good condition."

All the tenseness of the past seventy hours drained away.

There was of course much to be done—recalling the search parties; relaying the word to Anna's sister; getting word to young Brandy; talking to Gene Powers—thus disassembling the web of communication and activity which had built up so rapidly around the disappearance. But the sense of relief and relaxation was massive and deep-felt. It was not until late afternoon when we had a scheduled radio contact with Brandy that he heard of the rescue. This spread of several hours between our receiving the news and passing it on to him, even with all the modern gadgets available to us, reflects the ruggedness of the area involved.

Although the details are not clear, Anna on the day she became separated from the party had climbed from her place by the lake to the rendezvous pass. Apparently she arrived there at the precise moment that Doc Greaves and his son had vacated it because of the storm. She decided she had missed the party and determined to return by our route in. How she missed intercepting the five of our party who were then ascending to the pass is the prime mystery. She returned by the Puddin Lakes basin, missed the turn off over the ridge to camp and proceeded on down the drainage to Wilson Creek along the banks of which she was spotted from the air three days later.

A few more comments are pertinent. As I consider those days, I think how precious in such an environment and under such circumstances is one human life. All the terrific complex of experience, knowledge, intelligence, and aspiration which inheres in a human life we were determined to save (that is, if it were not already lost). In that massive, untrailed and jagged terrain, a single human was the focus of all thought, activity, and anxiety. Wilderness had become a place where a human being could be seen and valued as an individual.

It is one of our problems today that our huge cities have become frightening colossi. The individual exists, for himself and a few who know him. Otherwise he is one of a mass to be thought of in the mass and shunted about in streams of traffic, in streams of thought, and in easy academic classifications. It took this wilderness experience to etch again the importance of a single person.

MARGARET E. MURIE

(1902–   )

For several reasons I've chosen *Two in the Far North* as a kind of model narration of a woman's life in the wilderness. First of all, Mardy Murie's attitude is exemplary; her voice, a happy one. Despite laughable setbacks (her bridegroom was late for his own wedding) and more consequential difficulties (caring for an eight-month-old while camped on a motorless scow in the mosquito-infested Old Crow Basin), she joyously communicates her love for her husband and her zest for the path they have followed. The teamwork between the two adds a welcome dimension to the frontier spirit they embrace. "Gone were those treacherous stubs and stumps and tussocks, that strain of watching every step, of yanking and tugging at handle bars which flounced around as though alive. We had come through on our feet, and my husband was saying lovely words about its being the toughest trail he had ever seen and there weren't many women. . . ."

Unlike many who confronted hardships and discomforts by imposing civilized amenities onto the wilderness life, this couple adapted themselves to their surroundings. Whether pursuing caribou to the Koyukuk or banding geese along the Yukon or watching grizzlies near Lobo Lake, Mardy and Olaus camped simply and quietly, pausing frequently to revere the land. Sometimes the view was spectacular—"one perfect cone of a white mountain standing there alone against that indescribable midnight-blue sky of a winter twilight, and riding triumphant on the white mountain's shoulder, Mars, flaming red, magnificent." Sometimes they found beauty in miniature—"tundra, the velvety sphagnum hummocks, the myriad tiny arctic plants gleaming in the moss, in the golden light." Always, they took time to see.

They took time to worry about the fragile Alaskan environment, too, about the changes that float planes and civilization and a growing population would bring. In fact, the Muries' ecological concerns dominate the activities and the publications of both. Their first years together were spent in Alaska, where Olaus worked as a field biologist. Later he became Director of the Wilderness Society, a task he performed half-time while the couple continued living on a ranch near Moose, Wyoming. There he wrote *Elk of North America*, a classic treatise abut the Jackson Hole herd. Meanwhile he and Mardy successfully worked together to establish the Arctic Wildlife Refuge under the jurisdiction of the Fish and Wildlife Service. "At Lobo Lake" outlines a happy month in 1956 spent with three other environmental scientists while researching the potential of that Alaskan wildlife range.

Other descriptions of the Muries' life can be found in *Wapiti Wilderness* (1966) and *Island Between* (1977). Because of its special intrepid spirit, though, my favorite remains *Two in the Far North*. From its pages we learn what it really meant to be the kind of twentieth-century pioneer who never lost her love for the wilderness experience.

From "At Lobo Lake" in
Two in the Far North

It was easy here to forget the world of man, to relax into this world of nature. It was a world that compelled all our interest and concentration and put everything else out of mind. As we walked over the tundra our attention was completely held by the achievements of that composition of moss, lichens, small plants, and bright flowers, yet we were ever on the alert to identify every bird, to note every evidence of bears—moss and roots dug up, tracks in the mud at the edge of pools. And since our way always led by either the river or one of the many lakes, we were identifying shore-birds, ducks, grebes, loons, gulls. How could we be anything but absorbed?

The three young people and I worked hard the first two days getting the camp in order. Bob, the master camp crafts-man, built a "cupboard" from scraps of poles and limbs, wire, and a few nails. He placed it against a clump of small spruces, just below the fireplace, so that all manner of things could be handily hung on the spruce branches; and being able to stand up to prepare food made my life entirely different! Brina, George, and I ransacked the whole outfit. We got the main food supply into the steel drum, whose clamp-on cover kept the food safe from bears, and placed it in the shade at the back of the cook tent. All the other supplies were set in a row on each side of the "cook tent," which we rarely cooked in. Near the kitchen we fixed a box of staple supplies, along with another box, christened the "snack box," where all the food for lunches was kept. After this labor we soon settled into a routine of work and exploration.

Each morning after breakfast everyone delved into the snack box and packed his own lunch—Jersey Cream biscuits, cheese, raisins, apricots, figs, chocolate—and with rucksack on back, camera and binoculars slung on, set off. Thus four or five different localities were explored on each trip. And the big news in our lives, related each evening as we sat at dinner, went something like this:

George: "Three ptarmigan nests, one with seven eggs, two with six. Two tree sparrow nests. One yellowlegs nest. I marked them all. I saw three bands of caribou and got close enough to photograph a cow and calf, and by that little lake just north of this one I stood behind a clump of spruce and a beautiful bull with a good set of antlers came right by and I got two pictures before he heard the camera."

Brina: "I found a least-sandpiper nest and the female stayed right around me, making little sounds, and getting back on the eggs right there within five feet of me while I kept on taking pictures."

And Bob: "I got movies of a cross fox; maybe the same one we heard the other night. He still had a beautiful brush, and trotted and galloped clear across that flat by the river right in front of me. I don't think these animals up here know about man—they don't seem to have fear."

Our lake, by far the largest in the region, was the richest in animal activity. On the days when we stayed in camp to write in our journals, put up specimens, or perform camp chores, the animal world still claimed us. The girdle of water next to the shore widened each day, but for ten days after we landed the ice was still a highway for animals. One after-

noon Bob sat just below camp watching the performance of
three muskrats. Suddenly they all dived. He glanced around.
A fine big gray wolf stood above him on the slope. There
is no knowing who was more surprised, but Lobo did not
run; he merely turned and trotted back, and down to the
ice. Bob called to us with utmost urgency in his deep tones.
We all rushed out, and stood entranced, watching our first
wolf going away unhurriedly to the far shore. And that is
how our lake came to be named Lobo. . . .

When we landed on the ice of Lobo on June 1, the snow
was gone from the land and the prevailing color was brown;
there was no green vegetation except for the little spruce trees.
But there was one flower blooming, flat on the ground, a
single deep red-purple saxifrage, a lone but definite announce-
ment of winter's end—*Saxifraga oppositifolia*. Multitudes
of others were crowding close behind it, and in only one week
Lobo was a different place. The first week of June in the
Arctic must be the most exciting time of the year. Dwarf
birch, Labrador tea, heather, cranberry, all sorts of annuals
and grasses and alpine blossoms came into bud, into leaf,
into flower, so fast we were bewildered. The botanists could
hardly keep up with the show. On June 5 George made a
trip to the north shoulder of Table Mountain (the one named
mountain), east of Lobo. We called this north shoulder "the
Ridge." He came striding home across the ice at six o'clock,
three and a half hours from the top, after a long day and
many miles of hiking and climbing with nothing to eat but
a pocketful of raisins. "What a country! Those clear mountain streams, and those slopes, full of flowers, and such valleys! And from on top, the mountains just go like this, up
and down, up and down—you want to keep going, up one
ridge and down another!"

Then he proceeded to empty onto the moss a gorgeous

assortment of alpine flowers. These had to be sorted out, laid carefully flat on the plant-press papers, each sheet labeled with locality, date, elevation, and other pertinent information, and pressed between the blotter sheets of the press. All this had to be done before George could eat, and we were all clustered around him, trying to help, and admiring the tiny gentians, forget-me-nots, and others we did not even know.

Two days later Olaus announced at breakfast that he wanted to go "over to the mountain" to the foot of the Ridge. . . .

Our route led around the base of the ridge on which we were camped. It extended back from camp and back from the lake, north along the river, then out across a big belt of tundra pools and scattered spruce forest to a rather large lake half free of ice. In it were twenty white-winged scoters, several greater scaups, and some pintails. Olaus sat down with the glasses. I said: "Come look here. There's something that looks like a grebe, and I don't know . . ."

Then followed the usual routine. He looked for a while, saying nothing, and then handed me the glasses. I, hesitating, said: "Well—horned grebe?"

"Yes, that's right; and I'm sure George and Brina haven't that one listed yet."

So that was a highlight of the day, news to carry back to Brina.

We had left camp at nine; at ten we were enjoying the lake and the ducks. At eleven we had sloshed and hopped and slogged across a great wet muskeg flat and were in the spruce again at the foot of the Ridge. At twelve we were halfway up, still in spruce and some willow, but at the edge of the great slate slide that marked that side of the mountain. There were alpine-type moss-covered rocks and mossy hummocks, with the roar of a stream in a draw near by. We went over to it and sat on soft hummocks in a fairyland of tiny moss plants, and ate our lunch, drinking icy-clear water from the stream.

We then began traversing, gaining altitude up over the treeless top third of the slope, among yellow, purple, and blue alpine flowers, with pipits "pipit-ing" and once the sudden "snore" of a rock ptarmigan which flew off in front of us. We were really climbing, but I think we both noticed the helpful difference from our home altitude in the Tetons of Wyoming, for here our base was only 2,500 feet rather than 6,500. We were only slightly out of breath, and felt no heart pumping. The weariness in our long-unused climbing muscles was the main reason for the stops. And it was this muscle-weariness that crept upon us toward the end of the long trek back at the end of the day. But the day was worth the price.

On top, across a carpet of mountain avens, heather, dwarf willows, and dozens of other lovely small plants, a balmy breeze blew. The sun was high and blazing. I lay flat on the moss and heather, hat over my face, and felt absolutely content. This cannot be put into words. Here I was, privileged to lie on top of a mountain in the Arctic, an observer of the richness of this short summer pageant. Through half-closed eyes I looked across the valley to the west and north. The mountains made an unearthly beautiful frieze against the blue: numberless, snowy, streaked with dark rocks, various in shape—shoulders, domes, spires, and castles—and cliffs and screes on the slopes reaching to the darkness of the belt of forest. And then the broad valley, the winding Sheenjek, the countless lakes. I know nothing of painting, but I felt for a moment the urge a landscape painter must experience—to brush great strokes of brown and fawn and purple-gray and silver upon canvas. Gazing at such a scene, through half-closed eyes, from a mountaintop strikes through to your inmost heart. The place, the scene, the breeze, the bird song, the fragrance of myriad brave burgeoning mosses and flowers—all blend into one clear entity, one jewel. It is the Arctic in its unbelievably accelerated summer life. It is also the personal well-being purchased by striving—by lifting and setting down your legs, over and over, through the muskeg, up the slopes, gaining the summit—man using himself. This wondrous mingling of weariness and triumph and sudden harmony with the exquisite airs, the burgeoning life of the bird and plant world of the tops, is part of the "glad tidings," surely, which John Muir meant when he said: "Climb the mountains and get their glad tidings."

When Olaus came back from his "little look at the other side," we stood and took a long view before starting down. Facing west, we looked across the "wide, lake-dotted valley floor" with the river winding in great broad loops through it and on to the southeast. Far to our right, to the north, was the head of the valley, up against the crest, or backbone, of the main range itself, which runs east and west. From that crest, all the way to Table Mountain, short steep mountain masses, also running east and west, rise on both sides of the river. The mountain world here seems to multiply itself—mountain and valley, mountain and valley, all the canyons emptying into the Sheenjek. Each valley made me wonder what was at the head of it, what was on the other side. But the heart of the whole region is, of course, the river.

Coming down the little channels of turf over the limestone formation was fun, and when we hit the forest we followed it all the way back, avoiding the big muskeg flat to the north. The last miles through the springy soft moss stretched themselves out; we had to stop and rest several times though it was getting late and I thought Bob might be worrying about us.

We passed a lot of bear diggings. I said: "If we meet him now I'm just going to lie down and let him have me!"

"Oh no, you won't. All you have to remember is to *stand*, not run."

I wondered about this—and still do! However, no bear appeared, and half a mile from camp, sure enough, we met Bob, who was out looking for us. Bless them, he and Brina had dinner all ready—vegetable soup, corned beef, mashed potatoes. And we found the weariness fading away in the stimulation of food and comfort and good company.

Lying in the little tent that night, bandana tied over my eyes to keep out the light of this twenty-four-hour day, I listened to the sounds of Lobo. The ptarmigan, robust and comical: "Come here, come here, come here—go back go back, go back"; the tree sparrow, a cascade of sweet notes; the whitecrown, plaintive, questioning, but strong. Always these three voices, and from the lake the ducks, the loons, the gulls. This was their world. We were the fortunate visitors.

From the diary:

"June 8: This morning we were up early, but were still fussing along with various chores when suddenly someone hissed: 'Caribou coming on the ice!'

"Bob grabbed his movie camera and went up the hill to shoot down on them, and Olaus went along with his still camera. The rest of us went on with packing our lunches until in the middle of a word I saw a whole bunch coming on up, right near camp. Brina and George dove for their cameras, I for my glasses, and we flung ourselves down on the moss. Seventeen caribou, bulls, cows, and yearlings, clicking along, right past camp, silhouetted against the ice, heels clicking on it—blue sky and low brown hills to the south behind them. This clicking sound is thought by some scientists to be a snapping of tendons in the ankle. They seemed not aware of us at all. Brina exclaimed in a hushed voice: 'How many people in the world ever get to see anything like this? How lucky can one be? The pattern of those long legs— the sound of their feet! What a memory to have!'

"And George: 'Yes, but it's *over* so fast—you have that *feeling* of the thing, and then it's already just a memory!'

"Bob and Olaus came back happy; Bob's only complaint was that he had run out of film. Olaus and I then left on another trip upriver, covering some of the same tundra muskeg, bars, and ridges that we had traveled over the other day, but going further, counting several bands of caribou, watching the ducks on their favorite pond again. We also came upon many quite recent bear diggings in the mixed tundra and spruce on higher ground, so that I found myself looking to both sides and behind as we went along. But it was good walking, and sweetly, tangily fragrant in the spruce taiga. One has to lift a foot a bit higher springing through the moss, but we've discovered that if we keep a very relaxed, almost lazy, attitude about it and just slosh and slog along with no muscles tense, it is not tiring, and certainly much easier than hippety-hopping through the tussock-type muskeg places. After so much of that in years past in the Koyukuk and the Old Crow, we bless the Sheenjek for its variety; we can nearly always avoid the tussock patches.

"We came down to the river again where a little muddy creek wound in from the east. It was too wide to jump, and too deep to wade, so at its mouth we sat on a sandy bank and ate lunch and drank good muddy water. A beautiful blue day, and so quiet—still no mosquitoes! A pair of American widgeons drifted past, the male calling his whistling note now and then: "Whee, *whee* whew." Then from upstream came a long, lonesome "Wah, ah-a," and into view came a single bird. I handed Olaus the glasses. The same routine, he looking, handing me the glasses without a word, and I, quaveringly: 'A loon? Some kind of loon—it has a red throat!'

"'Yes, that's right. Red-throated loon, true bird of the Arctic!'

"So we sat watching as he floated by us and on down around the bend of the river, and as he went he kept turning his head, that beautiful soft gray head, to the left and right, as though searching the banks of the river for something, and three times as he went by us he uttered that long, dreamlike, lonely cry. 'Is he looking for another loon?' I asked.

"'Oh, I don't know. Maybe. That's just the call they have,' the scientist said.

"'Yes, but he sounds so lonesome; he sounds just the way I'd *feel* like sounding if I had lost *you* and couldn't find you!'

"We came home by way of the long wet sand bar, which bore wolf tracks, hundreds of caribou tracks, and one big moose track. We looked in every spot of gravel for fossil bones for Otto, but found none. Reaching camp, we found Bob and George just arriving jubilantly from their day southeast of Lobo at the grayling stream flowing out of a little lake, which Bob had discovered the day before. Five big grayling for our dinner!

"The day was warmer than ever today, and I could feel my face and hands 'cooking' despite nylon fisherman's hat, baby lotion, and mentholatum. But the land is deceptive; you are quite comfortable in the sun in cotton flannel shirt and heavy trousers and rubber pacs, because there is always a little cool breeze. There is no shade anyway; the sun is high and the spruces so scattered. And when the day is over, or rather when you call it a day and crawl in, and catch a glimpse of yourself in the camp mirror, you realize you are becoming the color of old leather, pouches swollen round your eyes, queer bumps on your cheeks. But it is part of the adventure, and none of us would think of criticizing this weather!

"June 10: Olaus and I had another long day afield. We were walking through ptarmigan all day, but it is impossible to find their nests except by sitting down somewhere and just watching the female until she goes to the nest—such protective mechanisms I never saw before. Even when Brina led me to the one on the hill behind camp and pointed right at the bird, it took me a few moments to distinguish the streaky brown feathers down at the base of a dwarf birch bush.

"At lunchtime we were far over near the base of the hills, and Olaus wanted to go across the big flat to the river and home that way. I was not bubbling over with enthusiasm, but we started across, through real old-time Alaska muskeg tussocks. You have to try to find a space for your rubber pac in the wet squishy moss between the tussocks, for if you step on top of one you will be tipped off balance every time. I was just beginning to worry about where we would find the energy for the return across these acres of 'footstools' when we came to an unsuspected stream, clear and sparkling, spread out in the grass. Olaus had to admit we couldn't cross this one without getting wet, so we sloshed and slogged back to the ridge and started the homeward trek. After about five hours I seem to reach a back-achy, heavy-in-the-legs state, in which I get pretty mad because Olaus went so far, and it's too far back to camp, and why do we *always* have to go so far, etc., etc. And always at this point some sweet inhabitant of this land furnishes relief. This time each of us found a tree-sparrow nest. Brina is making a study of their nesting and is delighted with every find. Mine had five eggs. Nice, the reciprocal living in the wilderness—the tree sparrow lines her nest with ptarmigan feathers! . . ."

The mosquitoes arrived on June 13, but were nothing compared with the swarm at Old Crow. Our breezy camp site was a blessing, and the repellent seemed to deal with them satisfactorily. Well smeared, knowing they wouldn't bite, one could ignore them, almost forget them, and this is what we did until late July, when they died away. But none of us ever said we enjoyed their song!

Next morning at six-thirty there was a cry of "Grizzly!" from George. I don't know how Brina got into her clothes so fast, but she joined the race. The three of them returned, puffing, just as Olaus got the fire going. It had been a small light grizzly, on the flat at the east end of Lobo. He had run off promptly, a fact I was not too sorry about. We proceeded to our breakfast of fruit, oatmeal, scrambled powdered eggs, and new bread, but midway in the meal George spied a big cow moose galloping along on the flat at the west end of the lake. I couldn't remember ever having seen a moose gallop. Olaus said perhaps it was because our Jackson Hole moose have no enemies and have become phlegmatic—like humans!

On June 14 George departed, pack on back, for a three-day exploration trip east and north along the mountainsides; Brina and Olaus and I went eastward too, then separated. She was working through the hillside habitat and we were headed for the first, or southernmost, of the Table Mountain group, where George had reported some great cliffs on top, with peregrine falcons—the duck hawks of Old Crow memories. Bob had gone off southwestward with movie camera and fishing gear.

This was the hottest day yet; we went over two lines of ridges, with long muskeg between, past the grayling lake and stream, over another ridge, down into the deep bed of a big mountain stream of clear water rushing over gravel. It was split into channels in such a way that it was easy to wade, and it seemed like a Wyoming mountain scene for those moments. And there we discovered the one and only cottonwood tree, a beautiful balm of Gilead at least thirty feet tall and still in the fragrant sticky bud stage.

After a long time of tramping upward through moss-floored spruce forest and then copses of dwarf birch, we at last came to the timber line, the bare heath dotted with purple anemones and yellow dwarf daisies and mountain avens, and this should have been pure pleasure. But there is a test involved in all this climbing. After miles of muskeg your leg muscles are heavy and complaining. The test, of course, is to keep your mind on other subjects. The best I could do was think of mountaineers and all the famous climbs I had read about. That helped some, but at last, as we neared the top, I said: "If I just sat down here, would you find me on your way down?"

"No," Olaus said emphatically. "I don't want to come back this way; I want to go down over there to the left, on that other slope. You're doing fine—just fine—you can make it!"

So I did. On the top there were no mosquitoes, and I went sound asleep on the turf with my hat over my face while Olaus went around the shoulder to the cliffs and back to join me, having seen no duck hawks.

How grateful we were that night to those two young people who had dinner ready when we got home and waited on us! We also learned that the helicopter we had spotted from on top had landed right on the knoll back of camp just after Bob had arrived home—Messrs. Foley and Myer, of the U.S. Geological Survey camp at Old John Lake. They "just dropped in" to see how we were getting along, which was very good of them. Olaus and I were sorry we hadn't been able to meet them. They were mapping the Sheenjek and surrounding country.

Talking about mapping led to a disussion of the future of this wilderness. When Keith came over unexpectedly on his Arctic Village run a few days before, he had said as we walked over to camp: "I know you want to be quiet up here and I don't want to disturb the atmosphere for you, but I thought I'd better find out about what time you thought you'd want to move on upriver."

Keith was sincere in this thought; he was not being facetious. One Cessna on floats skimming quietly onto a lake, and departing again, leaving no tracks, does not seem to alter the "spirit of the place." But suppose some real lovers of the wilderness were camped here and six float planes full of people came skimming in—what then? So it resolves itself into the same old problem—people and their attitudes and sensitivities. We cannot blame the plane, the motors, the machines, the inventions. In every phase of life, from the cold war to building new towns, machines will be the destroyers or benefactors according to the way in which they are used by man. I could not help recalling a little piece I read in the *Wildlife Review* of the British Columbia Game Commission, about a couple who hiked many miles into the Canadian wilderness for a much-needed quiet vacation. It was wonderful. Two days later a plane came clattering in and landed on their lake—acquaintances of theirs who thought they "would just fly over and see how you were getting along."

We discussed this problem many times at our campfire (a campfire, by the way, which burned only dry dead trees and branches, never a standing tree), and we all agreed that many people could see and live in and enjoy this wilderness in the course of a season, if they would just come a very few at a time, never a party larger than six, and then leave the camp site absolutely neat. It is possible, and this attitude of consideration, and reverence, is an integral part of an attitude toward life, toward the unspoiled, still evocative places on our planet. If man does not destroy himself through his idolatry of the machine, he may learn one day to step gently on his earth.

LOREN EISELEY

(1907–1977)

"I can at best report only from my own wilderness," wrote Loren Eiseley forty years ago. "The important thing is that each man possess such a wilderness and that he consider what marvels are to be observed there."

Loren Eiseley's wilderness differs somewhat from others' in *Words for the Wild*, but it is no less the terrain of what is wild and what is free. An anthropology professor, a paleontologist, a scientist, and a contributor to journals both technical and popular, Eiseley cared most about the history of man in his environment rather than about the environment in isolation. The interrelatedness between life forms and the landscape, the continuity of past and future, the mysteries of evolution, the ironies of existence—these were the topics that interested him and that spurred the writing of books from a generalist's point of view.

His best-known one, *The Immense Journey*, traces man's

course through time. He disclaims its words as science in the usual sense. Rather, he sees it as a record of thoughts that crossed his mind while he pursued the more technical demands of his profession. Its subject matter ranges from the Piltdown Man to the freshwater Crossopterygian (nicknamed the Snout), from the lonely screech of a crow to the busy chatter of a prairie-dog town, from the Badlands and the open plains to the depths of the ocean and on to the crush of New York.

Despite the widespread locales of the chapters, however, Eiseley's wilderness exists in his own mind. The landscape he evokes is one of intellectual rather than physical challenge. His background and training, for example, lead Eiseley to a definition of man's place in the universe that is expressed anthropologically rather than environmentally, pitting man against the evolutionary process rather than against the elements. The conclusion is the same one many other naturalists make—mankind is not the center—but the way Eiseley gets there is different.

First he voices a party line that I've heard less articulately said by a number of Nevada politicians. "We see ourselves as the culmination and the end," he suggests, "and if we do indeed consider our passing, we think that sunlight will go with us and the earth be dark. We are the end. For us continents rose and fell, for us the waters and the air were mastered, for us the great living web has pulsated and grown more intricate." The attitude of the early Puritans and pioneers, this is the mind set that spirited the westward movement.

Eiseley doesn't tell his readers that, however. Instead, he quietly shows the fallaciousness of such reasoning. If one believes in evolution, one must believe in constant change— "the hope of life," he insists. And if one affirms the principle of change, one cannot think that a single organism ever acquires an unsurpassable form. His conclusion is foregone. "We are one of many appearances of the thing called Life; we are not its perfect image." Man is neither the center nor the acme of the natural world.

Loren Eiseley challenges his readers to reconsider any assumptions about the nature of life. Combining detail with abstractions, science with mystery, intellect with imagination, he invites us into a different sort of environment. It is a place of vast dimensions, a wilderness circumscribed only by the boundaries of the mind.

From "The Flow of the River" in *The Immense Journey*

If there is magic on this planet, it is contained in water. Its least stir even, as now in a rain pond on a flat roof opposite my office, is enough to bring me searching to the window. A wind ripple may be translating itself into life. I have a constant feeling that some time I may witness that momentous miracle on a city roof, see life veritably and suddenly boiling out of a heap of rusted pipes and old television aerials. I marvel at how suddenly a water beetle has come and is submarining there in a spatter of green algae. Thin vapors, rust, wet tar and sun are an alembic remarkably like the mind; they throw off odorous shadows that threaten to take real shape when no one is looking.

Once in a lifetime, perhaps, one escapes the actual confines of the flesh. Once in a lifetime, if one is lucky, one so merges with sunlight and air and running water that whole eons, the eons that mountains and deserts know, might pass in a single afternoon without discomfort. The mind has sunk away into its beginnings among old roots and the obscure tricklings and movings that stir inanimate things. Like the charmed fairy circle into which a man once stepped, and upon emergence learned that a whole century had passed in a single night, one can never quite define this secret; but it has something to do, I am sure, with common water. Its substance reaches everywhere; it touches the past and prepares the future; it moves under the poles and wanders thinly in the heights of air. It can assume forms of exquisite perfection in a snowflake, or strip the living to a single shining bone cast up by the sea.

Many years ago, in the course of some scientific investigations in a remote western county, I experienced by chance, precisely the sort of curious absorption by water—the extension of shape by osmosis—at which I have been hinting. You have probably never experienced in yourself the meandering roots of a whole watershed or felt your outstretched fingers touching, by some kind of clairvoyant extension, the brooks of snow-line glaciers at the same time that you were flowing toward the Gulf over the eroded debris of worn-down mountains. A poet, MacKnight Black, has spoken of being "limbed . . . with waters gripping pole and pole." He had the idea, all right, and it is obvious that these sensations are not unique, but they are hard to come by; and the sort of extension of the senses that people will accept when they put their ear against a sea shell, they will smile at in the confessions of a bookish professor. What makes it worse is the fact that because of a traumatic experience in childhood, I am not a swimmer, and am inclined to be timid before any large body of water. Perhaps it was just this, in a way, that contributed to my experience.

As it leaves the Rockies and moves downward over the high plains towards the Missouri, the Platte River is a curious stream. In the spring floods, on occasion, it can be a mile-wide roaring torrent of destruction, gulping farms and bridges. Normally, however, it is a rambling, dispersed series of streamlets flowing erratically over great sand and gravel fans that are, in part, the remnants of a mightier Ice Age stream bed. Quicksands and shifting islands haunt its waters. Over it the prairie suns beat mercilessly throughout the summer. The Platte, "a mile wide and an inch deep," is a refuge for any heat-weary pilgrim along its shores. This is particularly true on the high plains before its long march by the cities begins.

The reason that I came upon it when I did, breaking through a willow thicket and stumbling out through ankle-deep water to a dune in the shade, is of no concern to this narrative. On various purposes of science I have ranged over a good bit of that country on foot, and I know the kinds of bones that come gurgling up through the gravel pumps, and the arrowheads of shining chalcedony that occasionally spill out of water-loosened sand. On that day, however, the sight of sky and willows and the weaving net of water murmuring a little in the shallows on its way to the Gulf stirred me, parched as I was with miles of walking, with a new idea: I was going to float. I was going to undergo a tremendous adventure.

The notion came to me, I suppose, by degrees. I had shed my clothes and was floundering pleasantly in a hole among some reeds when a great desire to stretch out and go with this gently insistent water began to pluck at me. Now to this bronzed, bold, modern generation, the struggle I waged with timidity while standing there in knee-deep water can only seem farcical; yet actually for me it was not so. A near-drowning accident in childhood had scarred my reactions; in addition to the fact that I was a nonswimmer, this "inch-deep river" was treacherous with holes and quicksands.

Death was not precisely infrequent along its wandering and illusory channels. Like all broad wastes of this kind, where neither water nor land quite prevails, its thickets were lonely and untraversed. A man in trouble would cry out in vain.

I thought of all this, standing quietly in the water, feeling the sand shifting away under my toes. Then I lay back in the floating position that left my face to the sky, and shoved off. The sky wheeled over me. For an instant, as I bobbed into the main channel, I had the sensation of sliding down the vast tilted face of the continent. It was then that I felt the cold needles of the alpine springs at my fingertips, and the warmth of the Gulf pulling me southward. Moving with me, leaving its taste upon my mouth and spouting under me in dancing springs of sand, was the immense body of the continent itself, flowing like the river was flowing, grain by grain, mountain by mountain, down to the sea. I was streaming over ancient sea beds thrust aloft where giant reptiles had once sported; I was wearing down the face of time and trundling cloud-wreathed ranges into oblivion. I touched my margins with the delicacy of a crayfish's antennae, and felt great fishes glide about their work.

I drifted by stranded timber cut by beaver in mountain fastnesses; I slid over shallows that had buried the broken axles of prairie schooners and the mired bones of mammoth. I was streaming alive through the hot and working ferment of the sun, or oozing secretively through shady thickets. I *was* water and the unspeakable alchemies that gestate and take shape in water, the slimy jellies that under the enormous magnification of the sun writhe and whip upward as great barbeled fish mouths, or sink indistinctly back into the murk out of which they arose. Turtle and fish and the pinpoint chirpings of individual frogs are all watery projections, concentrations—as man himself is a concentration—of that inde-

scribable and liquid brew which is compounded in varying
proportions of salt and sun and time. It has appearances,
but at its heart lies water, and as I was finally edged gently
against a sand bar and dropped like any log, I tottered as
I rose. I knew once more the body's revolt against emergence
into the harsh and unsupporting air, its reluctance to break
contact with that mother element which still, at this late point
in time, shelters and brings into being nine tenths of everything alive.

As for men, those myriad little detached ponds with their
own swarming corpuscular life, what were they but a way
that water has of going about beyond the reach of rivers?
I, too, was a microcosm of pouring rivulets and floating
driftwood gnawed by the mysterious animalcules of my own
creation. I was three fourths water, rising and subsiding according to the hollow knocking in my veins: a minute pulse
like the eternal pulse that lifts Himalayas and which, in the
following systole, will carry them away.

From "The Bird and the Machine" in *The Immense Journey*

The cabin had not been occupied for years. We intended to
clean it out and live in it, but there were holes in the roof
and the birds had come in and were roosting in the rafters.
You could depend on it in a place like this where everything
blew away, and even a bird needed some place out of the
weather and away from coyotes. A cabin going back to nature in a wild place draws them till they come in, listening
at the eaves, I imagine, pecking softly among the shingles
till they find a hole and then suddenly the place is theirs and
man is forgotten.

Sometimes of late years I find myself thinking the most beautiful sight in the world might be the birds taking over New York after the last man has run away to the hills. I will never live to see it, of course, but I know just how it will sound because I've lived up high and I know the sort of watch birds keep on us. I've listened to sparrows tapping tentatively on the outside of air conditioners when they thought no one was listening, and I know how other birds test the vibrations that come up to them through the television aerials.

"Is he gone?" they ask, and the vibrations come up from below, "Not yet, not yet."

Well, to come back, I got the door open softly and I had the spotlight all ready to turn on and blind whatever birds there were so they couldn't see to get out through the roof. I had a short piece of ladder to put against the far wall where there was a shelf on which I expected to make the biggest haul. I had all the information I needed just like any skilled assassin. I pushed the door open, the hinges squeaking only a little. A bird or two stirred—I could hear them—but nothing flew and there was a faint starlight through the holes in the roof.

I padded across the floor, got the ladder up and the light ready, and slithered up the ladder till my head and arms were over the shelf. Everything was dark as pitch except for the starlight at the little place back of the shelf near the eaves. With the light to blind them, they'd never make it. I had them. I reached my arm carefully over in order to be ready to seize whatever was there and I put the flash on the edge of the shelf where it would stand by itself when I turned it on. That way I'd be able to use both hands.

Everything worked perfectly except for one detail—I didn't know what kind of birds were there. I never thought about it at all, and it wouldn't have mattered if I had. My orders were to get something interesting. I snapped on the flash and sure enough there was a great beating and feathers flying, but instead of my having them, they, or rather he, had me. He had my hand, that is, and for a small hawk not much bigger than my fist he was doing all right. I heard him give one short metallic cry when the light went on and my hand descended on the bird beside him; after that he was busy with claws and his beak was sunk in my thumb. In the struggle I knocked the lamp over on the shelf, and his mate got her sight back and whisked neatly through the hole in the roof and off among the stars outside. It all happened in fifteen seconds and you might think I would have fallen down the ladder, but no, I had a professional assassin's reputation to keep up, and the bird, of course, made the mistake of thinking the hand was the enemy and not the eyes behind it. He chewed my thumb up pretty effectively and lacerated my hand with his claws, but in the end I got him, having two hands to work with.

He was a sparrow hawk and a fine young male in the prime of life. I was sorry not to catch the pair of them, but as I dripped blood and folded his wings carefully, holding him by the back so that he wouldn't strike again, I had to admit the two of them might have been more than I could have handled under the circumstances. The little fellow had saved his mate by diverting me, and that was that. He was born to it, and made no outcry now, resting in my hand hopelessly, but peering toward me in the shadows behind the lamp with a fierce, almost indifferent glance. He neither gave nor expected mercy and something out of the high air passed from him to me, stirring a faint embarrassment.

I quit looking into that eye and managed to get my huge carcass with its fist full of prey back down the ladder. I put the bird in a box too small to allow him to injure himself by struggle and walked out to welcome the arriving trucks. It had been a long day, and camp still to make in the darkness. In the morning that bird would be just another episode. He would go back with the bones in the truck to a small cage where he would spend the rest of his life. And a good thing, too. I sucked my aching thumb and spat out some blood. An assassin has to get used to these things. I had a personal reputation to keep up.

In the morning, with the change that comes on suddenly in that high country, the mist that had hovered below us in the valley was gone. The sky was a deep blue, and one could see for miles over the high outcroppings of stone. I was up early and brought the box in which the little hawk was imprisoned out onto the grass where I was building a cage. A wind as cool as a mountain spring ran over the grass and stirred my hair. It was a fine day to be alive. I looked up and all around me and at the hole in the cabin roof out of which the other little hawk had fled. There was no sign of her anywhere that I could see.

"Probably in the next county by now," I thought cynically, but before beginning work I decided I'd have a look at my last night's capture.

Secretively, I looked again all around the camp and up and down and opened the box. I got him right out in my hand with his wings folded properly and I was careful not to startle him. He lay limp in my grasp and I could feel his heart pound under the feathers but he only looked beyond me and up.

I saw him look that last look away beyond me into a sky so full of light that I could not follow his gaze. The little breeze flowed over me again, and nearby a mountain aspen shook all its tiny leaves. I suppose I must have had an idea then of what I was going to do, but I never let it come up into consciousness. I just reached over and laid the hawk on the grass.

He lay there a long minute without hope, unmoving, his eyes still fixed on that blue vault above him. It must have been that he was already so far away in heart that he never felt the release from my hand. He never even stood. He just lay with his breast against the grass.

In the next second after that long minute he was gone. Like a flicker of light, he had vanished with my eyes full on him, but without actually seeing even a premonitory wing beat. He was gone straight into that towering emptiness of light and crystal that my eyes could scarcely bear to penetrate. For another long moment there was silence. I could not see him. The light was too intense. Then from far up somewhere a cry came ringing down.

I was young then and had seen little of the world, but when I heard that cry my heart turned over. It was not the cry of the hawk I had captured; for, by shifting my position against the sun, I was now seeing further up. Straight out of the sun's eye, where she must have been soaring restlessly above us for untold hours, hurtled his mate. And from far up, ringing from peak to peak of the summits over us, came a cry of such unutterable and ecstatic joy that it sounds down across the years and tingles among the cups on my quiet breakfast table.

I saw them both now. He was rising fast to meet her. They met in a great soaring gyre that turned to a whirling circle and a dance of wings. Once more, just once, their two voices, joined in a harsh wild medley of question and response, struck and echoed against the pinnacles of the valley. Then they were gone forever somewhere into those upper regions beyond the eyes of men.

WALLACE STEGNER
(1909–   )

"In gaining the lovely and the usable, we have given up the incomparable."

So Wallace Stegner describes Glen Canyon's replacement, Lake Powell, in a way that also characterizes the way he personally envisions the process of historical change across the American continent. Seen through his eyes, the New World landscape always fluctuates, but it doesn't always metamorphose into something admirable. Too often, it just becomes something new.

All of his books, fiction and nonfiction alike, judge historical change. His best ones show forces in conflict—established beliefs versus radical imagination, civilized values versus nomadic compulsion, middle-aged conservatism versus youthful zealotry, east versus west, parent versus child. Lately his arguments have focused more directly on a conservationist theme—developers versus the environment, humans versus the land.

Instead of drumming up passion with his prose, though, he relies on intellectual conversion to his cause. No pulpit thumper or monkey-wrench tactician, but a master of rhetorical understatement and the subtle word, Stegner induces a quiet kind of blessed rage. The pages of his Glen Canyon essay are typical. While he never directly denigrates Lake Powell, no reader can fail to see his dismay at its existence or be touched by his concomitant sense of loss. Today he speaks and writes more forthrightly than he did two decades ago, but he still invokes sensitivity instead of sensation.

His latest collection of essays, *One Way to Spell Man* (1982), manages to combine easy reminiscence with uneasy prophecy in deceptively gentle tones. His other nonfiction books softly spell out the ways of our past, present, and future, too—"the human response to a set of environmental and temporal circumstances," Stegner admitted in an interview—another way of saying that all his writing examines one man's notion of the pulsations of historical flux.

Aside from that thematic constant, the novels sound somewhat divergent notes. His best one, Pulitzer Prize–winning *Angle of Repose* (1971), fictionalizes the life of Mary Hallock Foote's marriage, a nineteenth-century relationship that replicated the grievous contrast between eastern culture and the movement west. His other fiction ranges from an imaginative recreation of his *Big Rock Candy Mountain* (1943) boyhood to a retrospective analysis of its repercussions, and from a distressing look at *All the Little Live Things* (1967)—hippie life on the Big Sur—to a book-length flashback of its protagonist's life a generation earlier.

History doesn't exactly repeat itself in Wallace Stegner's worlds, but it certainly provokes change and contemplation. So does the landscape through which his characters tiptoe, a fragile environment ever receptive to their footprints, their voices, and their dreams. His people are among my favorites in western American literature; so are his words for the wild.

"Overture: The Sound of Mountain Water" in *The Sound of Mountain Water*

I discovered mountain rivers late, for I was a prairie child, and knew only flatland and dryland until we toured the Yellowstone country in 1920, loaded with all the camp beds, auto tents, grub-boxes, and auxiliary water and gas cans that 1920 thought necessary. Our road between Great Falls, Montana, and Salt Lake City was the rutted track that is now Highway 89. Beside a marvelous torrent, one of the first I ever saw, we camped several days. That was Henry's Fork of the Snake.

I didn't know that it rose on the west side of Targhee Pass and flowed barely a hundred miles, through two Idaho counties, before joining the Snake near Rexburg; or that in 1810 Andrew Henry built on its bank near modern St. Anthony the first American post west of the continental divide. The divide itself meant nothing to me. My imagination was not stretched by the wonder of the parted waters, the Yellowstone rising only a few miles eastward to flow out toward the Missouri, the Mississippi, the Gulf, while this bright pounding stream was starting through its thousand miles of canyons to the Columbia and the Pacific.

All I knew was that it was pure delight to be where the land lifted in peaks and plunged in canyons, and to sniff air thin, spray-cooled, full of pine and spruce smells, and to be so close-seeming to the improbable indigo sky. I gave my heart to the mountains the minute I stood beside this river with its spray in my face and watched it thunder into foam, smooth to green glass over sunken rocks, shatter to foam again. I was fascinated by how it sped by and yet was always there; its roar shook both the earth and me.

When the sun dropped over the rim the shadows chilled sharply; evening lingered until foam on water was ghostly and luminous in the near-dark. Alders caught in the current sawed like things alive, and the noise was louder. It was rare and comforting to waken late and hear the undiminished shouting of the water in the night. And at sunup it was still there, powerful and incessant, with the slant sun tangled in its rainbow spray, the grass blue with wetness, and the air heady as ether and scented with campfire smoke.

By such a river it is impossible to believe that one will ever be tired or old. Every sense applauds it. Taste it, feel its chill on the teeth: it is purity absolute. Watch its racing current, its steady renewal of force: it is transient and eternal. And listen again to its sounds: get far enough away so that the noise of falling tons of water does not stun the ears, and hear how much is going on underneath—a whole symphony of smaller sounds, hiss and splash and gurgle, the small talk of side channels, the whisper of blown and scattered spray gathering itself and beginning to flow again, secret and irresistible, among the wet rocks.

"Glen Canyon Submersus" in *The Sound of Mountain Water*

Glen Canyon, once the most serenely beautiful of all the canyons of the Colorado River, is now Lake Powell, impounded by the Glen Canyon Dam. It is called a great recreational resource. The Bureau of Reclamation promotes its beauty in an attempt to counter continuing criticisms of the dam itself, and the National Park Service, which manages the Recreation Area, is installing or planning facilities for all the boating, water skiing, fishing, camping, swimming, and plain sightseeing that should now ensue.

But I come back to Lake Powell reluctantly and skeptically, for I remember Glen Canyon as it used to be.

Once the river ran through Glen's two hundred miles in a twisting, many-branched stone trough eight hundred to twelve hundred feet deep, just deep enough to be impressive without being overwhelming. Awe was never Glen Canyon's province. That is for the Grand Canyon. Glen Canyon was for delight. The river that used to run here cooperated with the scenery by flowing swift and smooth, without a major rapid. Any ordinary boatmen could take anyone through it. Boy Scouts made annual pilgrimages on rubber rafts. In 1947 we went through with a party that contained an old lady of seventy and a girl of ten. There was superlative camping anywhere, on sandbars furred with tamarisk and willow, under cliffs that whispered with the sound of flowing water.

Through many of those two hundred idyllic miles the view was shut in by red walls, but down straight reaches or up side canyons there would be glimpses of noble towers and buttes lifting high beyond the canyon rims, and somewhat more than halfway down there was a major confrontation where the Kaiparowits Plateau, seventy-five hundred feet high, thrust its knife-blade cliff above the north rim to face the dome of Navajo Mountain, more than ten thousand feet high, on the south side. Those two uplifts, as strikingly different as if designed to dominate some gigantic world's fair, added magnificence to the intimate colored trough of the river.

Seen from the air, the Glen Canyon country reveals itself

as a bare-stone, salmon-pink tableland whose surface is a chaos of domes, knobs, beehives, baldheads, hollows, and potholes, dissected by the deep corkscrew channels of streams. Out of the platform north of the main river rise the gray-green peaks of the Henry Mountains, the last-discovered mountains in the contiguous United States. West of them is the bloody welt of the Waterpocket Fold, whose westward creeks flow into the Escalante, the last-discovered river. Northward rise the cliffs of Utah's high plateaus. South of Glen Canyon, like a great period at the foot of the fifty-mile exclamation point of the Kaiparowits, is Navajo Mountain, whose slopes apron off on every side into the stone and sand of the reservation.

When cut by streams, the Navajo sandstone which is the country rock forms monolithic cliffs with rounded rims. In straight stretches the cliffs tend to be sheer, on the curves undercut, especially in the narrow side canyons. I have measured a six-hundred-foot wall that was undercut a good five hundred feet—not a cliff at all but a musical shell for the multipication of echoes. Into these deep scoured amphitheaters on the outside of bends, the promontories on the inside fit like thighbones into a hip socket. Often, straightening bends, creeks have cut through promontories to form bridges, as at Rainbow Bridge National Monument, Gregory Bridge in Fiftymile Canyon, and dozens of other places. And systematically, when a river cleft has exposed the rock to the lateral thrust of its own weight, fracturing begins to peel great slabs from the cliff faces. The slabs are thinner at top than at bottom, and curve together so that great alcoves form in the walls. If they are near the rim, they may break through to let a window-wink of sky down on a canyon traveler, and always they make panels of fresh pink in weathered and stained and darkened red walls.

Floating down the river one passed, every mile or two on right or left, the mouth of some canyon, narrow, shadowed, releasing a secret stream into the taffy-colored, whirlpooled Colorado. Between the mouth of the Dirty Devil and the dam, which is a few miles above the actual foot of the Glen Canyon, there are at least three dozen such gulches on the north side, including the major canyon of the Escalante; and on the south nearly that many more, including the major canyon of San Juan. Every such gulch used to be a little wonder, each with its multiplying branches, each as deep at the mouth as its parent canyon. Hundreds of feet deep, sometimes only a few yards wide, they wove into the rock so sinuously that all sky was shut off. The floors were smooth sand or rounded stone pavement or stone pools linked by stone gutters, and nearly every gulch ran, except in flood season, a thin clear stream. Silt pockets out of reach of flood were gardens of fern and redbud; every talus and rockslide gave footing to cottonwood and willow and single-leafed ash; ponded places were solid with watercress; maidenhair hung from seepage cracks in the cliffs.

Often these canyons, pursued upward, ended in falls, and sometimes the falls came down through a slot or a skylight in the roof of a domed chamber, to trickle down the wall into a plunge pool that made a lyrical dunk bath on a hot day. In such chambers the light was dim, reflected, richly colored. The red rock was stained with the dark manganese exudations called desert varnish, striped black to green to yellow to white along horizontal lines of seepage, patched with the chemical, sunless green of moss. One such grotto was named Music Temple by Major John Wesley Powell on his first exploration, in 1869; another is the so-called Cathedral in the Desert, at the head of Clear Water Canyon off the Escalante.

That was what Glen Canyon was like before the closing of the dam in 1963. What was flooded here was potentially a superb national park. It had its history, too, sparse but significant. Exploring the gulches, one came upon ancient chiseled footholds leading up the slickrock to mortared dwellings or storage cysts of the Basket Makers and Pueblos who once inhabited these canyons. At the mouth of Padre Creek a line of chiseled steps marked where Fathers Escalante and Dominguez, groping back toward Santa Fe in 1776, got their animals down to the fjord that was afterward known as the Crossing of the Fathers. In Music Temple men from Powell's two river expeditions had scratched their names. Here and there on the walls near the river were names and initials of men from Robert Brewster Stanton's party that surveyed a water-level railroad down the canyon in 1889–90, and miners from the abortive goldrush of the 1890's. There were Mormon echoes at Lee's Ferry, below the dam, and at the slot canyon called Hole-in-the-Rock, where a Mormon colonizing party got their wagons down the cliffs on their way to the San Juan in 1880.

Some of this is now under Lake Powell. I am interested to know how much is gone, how much left. Because I don't much like the thought of power boats and water skiers in these canyons, I come in March, before the season has properly begun, and at a time when the lake (stabilized they say because of water shortages far downriver at Lake Mead) is as high as it has ever been, but is still more than two hundred feet below its capacity level of thiry-seven hundred feet. Not everything that may eventually be drowned will be drowned yet, and there will be none of the stained walls and exposed mudflats that make a drawdown reservoir ugly at low water.

Our boat is the Park Service partol boat, a thirty-four-foot diesel workhorse. It has a voice like a bulldozer's. As we back away from the dock and head out deserted Wah-weap Bay, conversing at the tops of our lungs with our noses a foot apart, we acknowledge that we needn't have worried about motor noises among the cliffs. We couldn't have heard a Chriscraft if it had passed us with its throttle wide open.

One thing is comfortingly clear from the moment we back away from the dock at Wahweap and start out between the low walls of what used to be Wahweap Creek toward the main channel. Though they have diminished it, they haven't utterly ruined it. Though these walls are lower and tamer than they used to be, and though the whole sensation is a little like looking at a picture of Miss America that doesn't show her legs, Lake Powell *is* beautiful. It isn't Glen Canyon, but it is something in itself. The contact of deep blue water and uncompromising stone is bizarre and somehow exciting. Enough of the canyon feeling is left so that traveling up-lake one watches with a sense of discovery as every bend rotates into view new colors, new forms, new vistas: a great glowing wall with the sun on it, a slot side canyon buried to the eyes in water and inviting exploration, a half-drowned cave on whose roof dance the little flames of reflected ripples.

Moreover, since we float three hundred feet or more above the old river, the views out are much wider, and where the lake broadens, as at Padre Creek, they are superb. From the river, Navajo Mountain used to be seen only in brief, distant glimpses. From the lake it is often visible for minutes, an hour, at a time—gray-green, snow-streaked, a high mysterious bubble rising above the red world, incontrovertibly the holy mountain. And the broken country around the Crossing of the Fathers was always wild and strange as a moon landscape, but you had to climb out to see it. Now, from the bay that covers the crossing and spreads into the mouths of tributary creeks, we see Gunsight Butte, Tower Butte, and the other fantastic pinnacles of the Entrada formation surging up a sheer thousand feet above the rounding platform of the Navajo. The horizon reels with surrealist forms, dark red at the base, gray from there to rimrock, the profiles rigid and angular and carved, as different as possible from the Navajo's filigreed, ripple-marked sandstone.

We find the larger side canyons, as well as the deeper reaches of the main canyon, almost as impressive as they used to be, especially after we get far enough up-lake so that the water is shallower and the cliffs less reduced in height. Navajo Canyon is splendid despite the flooding of its green bottom that used to provide pasture for the stolen horses of raiders. Forbidden Canyon that leads to Rainbow Bridge is lessened, but still marvelous: it is like going by boat to Petra. Rainbow Bridge itself is still the place of magic that it used to be when we walked the six miles up from the river, and turned a corner to see the great arch framing the dome of Navajo Mountain. The canyon of the Escalante, with all its tortuous side canyons, is one of the stunning scenic experiences of a lifetime, and far easier to reach by lake than it used to be by foot or horseback. And all up and down these canyons, big or little, is the constantly changing, nobly repetitive spectacle of the cliffs with their contrasts of rounding and sheer, their great blackboard faces and their amphitheaters. Streaked with desert varnish, weathered and lichened and shadowed, patched with clean pink fresh-broken stone, they are as magically colored as shot silk.

And there is God's plenty of it. This lake is already a hundred and fifty miles long, with scores of tributaries. If it ever fills—which its critics guess it will not—it will have eighteen hundred miles of shoreline. Its fishing is good and apparently getting better, not only catfish and perch but rainbow trout and largemouth black bass that are periodically sown broadcast from planes. At present its supply and access points are few and far apart—at Wahweap, Hall's Crossing, and Hite—but when floating facilities are anchored in the narrows below Rainbow Bridge and when boat ramps and supply stations are developed at Warm Creek, Hole-in-the-Rock, and Bullfrog Basin, this will draw people. The prediction of a million visitors in 1965 is probably enthusiastic, but there is no question that as developed facilities extend the range of boats and multiply places of access, this will become one of the great water playgrounds.

And yet, vast and beautiful as it is, open now to anyone with a boat or the money to rent one, available soon (one supposes) to the quickie tour by float-plane and hydrofoil, democratically accessible and with its most secret beauties captured on color transparencies at infallible exposures, it strikes me, even in my exhilaration, with the consciousness of loss. In gaining the lovely and the usable, we have given up the incomparable.

The river's altitude at the dam was about 3150 feet. At 3490 we ride on 340 feet of water, and that means that much of the archaeology and most of the history, both of which were concentrated at the river's edge or near it, are as drowned as Lyonesse. We chug two hundred feet over the top of the square masonry tower that used to guard the mouth of Forbidden Canyon. The one small ruin that we see up Navajo Canyon must have been nearly inaccessible, high in the cliff. Somehow (though we do not see them) we think it ought to have a line of footholds leading down into and under the water toward the bottom where the squash and corn gardens used to grow.

The wildlife that used to live comfortably in Glen Canyon is not there on the main lake. Except at the extreme reach of the water up side canyons, and at infrequent places where the platform of the Navajo sandstone dips down so that the lake spreads in among its hollows and baldheads, this reservoir laps vertical cliffs, and leaves no home for beaver or waterbird. The beaver have been driven up the side canyons, and have toppled whole groves of cottonwoods ahead of the rising water. While the water remains stable, they have a home; if it rises, they move upward; if it falls, the Lord knows what they do, for falling water will leave long mud flats between their water and their food. In the side canyons we see a few mergansers and redheads, and up the Escalante Arm the blue herons are now nesting on the cliffs, but as a future habitat Lake Powell is as unpromising for any of them as for the beaver.

And what has made things difficult for the wildlife makes them difficult for tourists as well. The tamarisk and willow bars are gone, and finding a campsite, or even a safe place to land a boat, is not easy. When the stiff afternoon winds sweep up the lake, small boats stay in shelter, for a swamping could leave a man clawing at a vertical cliff, a mile from any crawling-out place.

Worst of all are the places I remember that are now irretrievably gone. Surging up-lake on the second day I look over my shoulder and recognize the swamped and truncated entrance to Hidden Passage Canyon, on whose bar we camped eighteen years ago when we first came down this canyon on one of Norman Nevills' river trips. The old masked entrance is swallowed up, the river rises almost over the shoulder of the inner cliffs. Once that canyon was a pure delight to walk in; now it is only another slot with water in it, a thing to poke a motorboat into for five minutes and then roar out again. And if that is Hidden Passage, and we are this far out in the channel, then Music Temple is straight down.

The magnificent confrontation of the Kaiparowits and Navajo Mountain is still there, possibly even more magnificent because the lake has lifted us into a wider view. The splendid sweep of stained wall just below the mouth of the San Juan is there, only a little diminished. And Hole-in-the-Rock still notches the north rim, though the cove at the bottom where the Mormons camped before rafting the river and starting across the bare rock-chaos of Wilson Mesa is now a bay, with sunfish swimming among the tops of drowned trees. The last time I was here, three years ago, the river ran in a gorge three hundred feet below where our boat ties up for the night, and the descent from rim to water was a longer, harder way. The lake makes the feat of those Mormons look easier than it was, but even now, no one climbing the thousand feet of cliff to the slot will ever understand how they got their wagons down there.

A mixture of losses, diminishments, occasional gains, precariously maintained by the temporary stabilization of the lake. There are plenty of people willing to bet that there will never be enough water in the Colorado to fill both Lake Mead, now drawn far down, and Lake Powell, still 210 feet below its planned top level, much less the two additional dams proposed for Marble and Bridge canyons, between these two. If there ever is—even if there is enough to raise Lake Powell fifty or a hundred feet—there will be immediate drastic losses of beauty. Walls now low, but high enough to maintain the canyon feeling, will go under, walls now high will be reduced. The wider the lake spreads, the less character it will have. Another fifty feet of water would submerge the Gregory Natural Bridge and flood the floor of the Cathedral in the Desert; a hundred feet would put both where Music Temple is; two hundred feet would bring water and silt to the very foot of Rainbow Bridge. The promontories that are now the most feasible camping places would go, as the taluses and sandbars have already gone. Then indeed the lake would be a vertical-walled fjord widening in places to a vertical-walled lake, neither as beautiful nor as usable as it still is. And the moment there is even twenty or thirty feet of draw-down, every side canyon is a slimy stinking mudflat and every cliff is defaced at the foot by a band of mud and minerals.

By all odds the best thing that could happen, so far as the recreational charm of Lake Powell is concerned, would be a permanently stablized lake, but nobody really expects that. People who want to see it in its diminished but still remarkable beauty should go soon. And people who, as we do, remember this country before the canyons were flooded, are driven to dream of ways by which some parts of it may still be saved, or half-saved.

The dream comes on us one evening when we are camped up the Escalante. For three days we have been deafened by the noise of our diesel engines, and even when that has been cut off there has been the steady puttering of the generator that supplies our boat with heat, light, and running water. Though we weakly submit to the comforts, we dislike the smell and noise: we hate to import into this rock-and-water wilderness the very things we have been most eager to escape from. A wilderness that must be approached by power boat is no wilderness any more, it has lost its magic. Now, with the engines cut and the generator broken down, we sit around a campfire's more primitive light and heat and reflect that the best moments of this trip have been those in which the lake and its powerboat necessities were least dominant—eating a quiet lunch on a rock in Navajo Canyon, walking the 1.7 miles of sandy trail to the Rainbow Bridge or the half mile of creek botton to the Cathedral in the Desert, climbing up the cliff to Hole-in-the-Rock. Sitting on our promontory in the Escalante Canyon without sign or sound of the mechanical gadgetry of our civilization, we feel descending on us, as gentle as evening on a blazing day, the remembered canyon silence. It is a stillness like no other I have experienced, for at the very instant of bouncing and echoing every slight noise off cliffs and around bends, the canyons swallow them. It is as if they accentuated them, briefly and with a smile, as if they said, "Wait!" and suddenly all sound has vanished, there is only a hollow ringing in the ears.

We find that whatever others may want, we would hate to come here in the full summmer season and be affronted with the constant roar and wake of power boats. We are not, it seems, water-based in our pleasures; we can't get a thrill out of doing in these marvelous canyons what one can do on any resort lake. What we most liked on this trip has been those times when ears and muscles were involved, when the foot felt sand or stone, when we could talk in low voices, or sit so still that a brilliant collared lizard would come out of a crack to look us over. For us, it is clear, Lake Powell is not a recreational resource, but only a means of access; it is the canyons themselves, or what is left of them, that we respond to.

Six or seven hundred feet above us, spreading grandly from the rim, is the Escalante Desert, a basin of unmitigated stone furrowed by branching canyons as a carving platter is furrowed by gravy channels. It is, as a subsidiary drainage basin, very like the greater basin in whose trough once lay Glen Canyon, now the lake. On the north this desert drains from the Circle Cliffs and the Aquarius Plateau, on the east from the Waterpocket Fold, on the west from the Kaiparowits. In all that waste of stone fifty miles long and twenty to thirty wide there is not a resident human being, not a building except a couple of cowboy shelter shacks, not a road except the washed-out trail that the Mormons of 1880 established from the town of Escalante to Hole-in-the-Rock. The cattle and sheep that used to run on this desert range have ruined it and gone. That ringing stillness around us is a total absence of industrial or civilized decibels.

Why not, we say, sitting in chilly fire-flushed darkness under mica stars, why not throw a boom across the mouth of the Escalante Canyon and hold this one precious arm of Lake Powell for the experiencing of silence? Why not, giving the rest of that enormous water to the motorboats and the waterskiers, keep one limited tributary as a canoe or rowboat wilderness? There is nothing in the way of law or regulation to prevent the National Park Service from managing the Recreation Area in any way it thinks best, nothing that forbids a wilderness or primitive or limited-access area within the larger recreational unit. The Escalante Desert is already federal land, virtually unused. It and its canyons are accessible by packtrain from the town of Escalante, and will be accessible by boat from the facility to be developed at Hole-in-the-Rock. All down the foot of the Kaiparowits, locally called Fiftymile Mountain or Wild Horse Mesa, the old Mormon road offers stupendous views to those who from choice or necessity want only to drive to the edge of the silence and look in.

I have been in most of the side gulches off the Escalante—Coyote Gulch, Hurricane Wash, Davis Canyon, and the rest. All of them have bridges, windows, amphitheaters, grottoes, sudden pockets of green. And some of them, including the superlative Coyote Gulch down which even now it is possible to take a packtrain to the river, will never be drowned even if Lake Powell rises to its planned thirty-seven-hundred-foot level. What might have been done for Glen Canyon as a whole may still be done for the higher tributaries of the Escalante. Why not? In the name of scenery, silence, sanity, why not?

For awe pervades that desert of slashed and channeled stone overlooked by the cliffs of the Kaiparowits and the Aquarius and the distant peaks of the Henrys; and history, effaced through many of the canyons, still shows us its dim marks here: a crude *mano* discarded by an ancient camp-site, a mortared wall in a cave, petroglyphs picked into a cliff face, a broken flint point glittering on its tee of sand on some blown mesa, the great rock where the Mormons danced on their way to people Desolation. This is country that does not challenge our identity as creatures, but it lets us shed most of our industrialized gadgetry, and it shows us our true size.

Exploring the Escalante basin on a trip in 1961, we probed for the river through a half dozen quicksand gulches and never reached it, and never much cared because the side gulches and the rims gave us all we could hold. We saw not a soul outside our own party, encountered not a vehicle, saw no animals except a handful of cows and one mule that we scared up out of Davis Gulch when we rolled a rock over the rim. From every evening camp, when the sun was gone behind the Kaiparowits rim and the wind hung in suspension like a held breath and the Henrys northeastward and Navajo Mountain southward floated light as bubbles on the distance, we watched the eastern sky flush a pure, cloudless rose, darker at the horizon, paler above; and minute by minute the horizon's darkness defined itself as the blue-domed sha-dow of the earth cast on the sky, thinning at its upward arc to violet, lavender, pale lilac, but clearly defined, steadily darkening upward until it swallowed all the sky's light and the stars pierced through it. Every night we watched the earth-shadow climb the hollow sky, and every dawn we watched the same blue shadow sink down toward the Kaiparowits, to disappear at the instant when the sun splintered sparks off the rim.

In that country you cannot raise your eyes—unless you're in a canyon—without looking a hundred miles. You can hear coyotes who have somehow escaped the air-dropped poison baits designed to exterminate them. You can see in every sandy pocket the pug tracks of wildcats, and every water-pocket in the rock will give you a look backward into geologic time, for every such hole swarms with triangular crablike creatures locally called tadpoles but actually first cousins to the trilobites who left their fossil skeletons in the Paleozoic.

In the canyons you do not have the sweep of sky, the long views, the freedom of movement on foot, but you do have the protection of cliffs, the secret places, cool water, arches and bridges and caves, and the sunken canyon stillness into which, musical as water falling into a plunge pool, the canyon wrens pour their showers of notes in the mornings.

Set the Escalante Arm aside for the silence, and the boatmen and the water skiers can have the rest of that lake, which on the serene, warm, sun-smitten trip back seems more beautiful than it seemed coming up. Save this tributary and the desert back from it as wilderness, and there will be something at Lake Powell for everybody. Then it may still be possible to make expeditions as rewarding as the old, motorless river trips through Glen Canyon, and a man can make his choice between forking a horse and riding down Coyote Gulch or renting a houseboat and chugging it up somewhere near the mouth of the Escalante to be anchored and used as a base for excursions into beauty, wonder, and the sort of silence in which you can hear the swish of falling stars.

JOHN GRAVES

(1920–   )

No collection of American writing of any sort would be complete without a representative from Texas. Contrary to popular mythology, however, that sample need not be noisy, garish, or verbose. As a matter of fact, the soft-spoken pen of a John Graves belies the stereotype, for his wilderness words are among the most pensive in this anthology.

Most of Graves' writing reaches back to his roots, roots sunk deeply into a soil that threatens to blow away with time. His first Texas book, *Goodbye to a River*, relives a solitary canoe trip with only a fussy dachsund—The Passenger—for company, and recalls younger days spent on that now-endangered section of the Brazos (a couple of hundred miles dammed shortly after the farewell journey). "It was a good-bye trip," he says, "with a main part of its pleasure in the rehearsal of old things. . . ."

Graves' second extended essay, *Hardscrabble*, nods hello

to a past instead of goodbye. It describes the farm he bought in lieu of an urban lot—"something less than four hundred acres of rough limestone hill country, partly covered with cedar and hardwood brush and partly open pasture, with some fair trees of various kinds and a few little creekbottom fields more or less amenable to cultivation." There he struggles, hard, to eke twentieth-century amenities from a staunchly recalcitrant land.

His third book, *From a Limestone Ledge*, gathers a series of reflections about the place he loves. (He calls the volume a footnote to *Hardscrabble*.) The last essay in the collection tells an anecdote about "A Loser." The man's farm was up for sale, his equipment up for auction. Looking around the disheveled yard and listening to the disheartened bidding, Graves realizes how close to home the gavel strikes. "The Loser had made us view the fragility of all we had been working toward," he admits, "had opened our ears to the hollow low-pitched mirth of the land against mere human effort." A metaphor for unwarranted change, the Loser is a blemish not only on the land but on the imagination.

Between the author and the Loser, though, stand three volumes and countless articles, millions of words of Texas prose. Through Graves' writing, Texas isn't lost at all. To the contrary, it is rescued from the banal superficialities and the glib phrase; the limestone country, restored to its rightful beauty.

From *Goodbye to a River*

That morning I was up before dawn to blow away the ashes from the orange-velvet embers underneath, and to build more fire on them with twigs and leaves and brittle sticks of dead cottonwood. I huddled over it in the cold, still, graying darkness and watched coffee water seethe at the edges of a little charred pot licked by flame, and heard the horned owl stop that deceptively gentle five-noted comment he casts on the night. The geese at the island's head began to talk among themselves, then to call as they rose to go to pastures and peanut fields, and night-flushed bobwhites started whistling *where-you? where-you?* to one another somewhere above the steep dirt river bank. Drinking coffee with honey in it and canned milk, smoking a pipe that had the sweetness pipes only have in cold quiet air, I felt good if a little scratchy-eyed, having gone to sleep the night before struck with the romance of stars and firelight, with the flaps open and only the blanket over me, to wake at two thirty chilled through.

On top of the food box alligator-skin corrugations of frost had formed, and with the first touch of the sun the willows began to whisper as frozen leaves loosed their hold and fell side-slipping down through the others that were still green. Titmice called, and flickers and a redbird, and for a moment, on a twig four feet from my face, a chittering kinglet jumped around alternately hiding and flashing the scarlet of its crown. . . . I sat and listened and watched while the world woke up, and drank three cups of the syrupy coffee, better I thought than any I'd ever tasted, and smoked two pipes.

You run a risk of thinking yourself an ascetic when you enjoy, with that intensity, the austere facts of fire and coffee and tobacco and the sound and feel of country places. You aren't, though. In a way you're more of a sensualist than a fat man washing down sauerbraten and dumplings with heavy beer while a German band plays and a plump blonde kneads his thigh. . . . You've shucked off the gross delights, and those you have left are few, sharp, and strong. But they're sensory. Even Thoreau, if I remember right a passage or so on his cornbread, was guilty, though mainly he was a real ascetic.

Real ones shouldn't care. They ought to be able to live on pâté and sweet peaches and roast suckling pig or alternatively on cheese and garlic in a windmill or the scraps that housewives have thrown in begging bowls. Groceries and shelter should matter only as fuel and frame for life, and life as energy for thought or beyond-communion or (Old Man Goodnight has to fit somewhere, and a fraught executive or two I've known, and maybe Davis Birdsong hurling his bulldozer against the tough cedar brush in a torn shirt and denim pants, coughing yellow flu sputum while the December rain pelts him, not caring) for action.

But I hadn't set up as an ascetic, anyhow. I sat for a long time savoring the privilege of being there, and didn't overlay the taste of the coffee with any other food. A big red-brown butterfly sat spread on the cottonwood log my ax was stuck in, warming itself in the sun. I watched until it flew stiffly away, then got up and followed, for no good reason except that the time seemed to have come to stir and I wanted a closer look at the island than I'd gotten the evening before.

It was shaped like an attenuated teardrop or the cross section of an airplane's wing, maybe three quarters of a mile long and 100 yards or so wide at its upper, thicker end. Its foundation everywhere appeared to be a heavy deposit of the multicolored gravel, and its flat top except for a few high dunes of the padding sand was eight or ten feet above the present level of the river. All around, it dropped off steeply, in spots directly to the water, in others to beaches, and toward the pointed tail the willows and weeds stood rank. I rooted about there and found nothing but coon tracks and a few birds still sleepy and cold on their roosts, but, emerging among cockleburs above a beach by the other channel, scared four ducks off a quiet eddy. I'd left the gun in the tent; shots from here and there under the wide sky's bowl reminded me that busier hunters than I were finding game.

Let them. I considered that maybe in the evening I'd crouch under a bush at the island's upper end and put out sheets of notepaper on the off chance that more geese would come, and the off-off chance that if they did they'd feel brotherly toward notepaper. You can interest them sometimes in newspapers.

And maybe I wouldn't.

The shores on either side of the river from the island were dirt and steep, twenty feet high, surmounted by pecans and oaks with the bare sky of fields or pastures beyond. They seemed separate from the island; it was big enough, with a strong enough channel on either side, to seem to have a kind of being of its own distinct from that of the banks—a sand and willow and cottonwood and driftwood biome— though in dry times doubtless there would be only one channel and no island, but just a great bar spreading out below the right bank.

Jays, killdeers, wrens, cardinals, woodpeckers . . . With minute and amateurish interest, I found atop a scoop in the base of a big, drifted, scorched tree trunk five little piles of fox dung, a big owl's puke ball full of hair and rat skulls, and three fresher piles of what had to be coon droppings, brown and small, shaped like a dog's or a human's.

Why, intrigued ignorance asked, did wild things so often choose to stool on rocks, stumps, and other elevations?

Commonsense replied: Maybe for the view.

On the flat beach at the head of the island the night's geese had laid down a texture of crisscrossed toe-prints. Elsewhere, in dry sand, I found little pointed diggings an inch in diameter and four to five inches deep, much like those an armadillo makes in grassland but with no tracks beside them. A bird? A land-foraging crawfish? Another puzzle for my ignorance, underlined now by the clear note of the unknown sad-whistling bird from a willow a few steps from me. He wouldn't show himself, and when I eased closer said irascibly: *Heap, heap!* and fluttered out the other side. . . .

The trouble was, I *was* ignorant. Even in that country where I belonged, my ken of natural things didn't include a little bird that went *heap-heap* and

——

— — —, — — —,

——

and a few moronic holes in the sand. Or a million other matters worth the kenning.

I grew up in a city near there—more or less a city, anyhow, a kind of spreading imposition on the prairies—that was waked from a dozing cow-town background by a standard boom after the First World War and is still, civic-souled friends tell me, bowling right along. It was a good enough place, not too big then, and a mile or so away from where I lived, along a few side streets and across a boulevard and a golf course, lay woods and pastures and a blessed river valley where the stagnant Trinity writhed beneath big oaks. In retrospect, it seems we spent more time there than we did on pavements, though maybe it's merely that remembrance of that part is sharper. There were rabbits and squirrels to hunt, and doves and quail and armadillos and foxes and skunks. A few deer ran the woods, and one year, during a drouth to the west, big wolves. Now it's mostly subdivisions, and even then it lay fallow because it was someone's real-estate investment. The fact that caretakers were likely to converge on us blaspheming at the sound of a shot or a shout, scattering us to brush, only made the hunting and the fishing a bit saltier. I knew one fellow who kept a permanent camp there in a sumac thicket, with a log squat-down hut and a fireplace and all kinds of food and utensils hidden in tin-lined holes in the ground, and none of the caretakers ever found it. Probably they worried less than we thought; there weren't many of us.

I had the Brazos, too, and South Texas, where relatives lived, and my adults for the most part were good people who took me along on country expeditions when they could. In terms of the outdoors, I and the others like me weren't badly cheated as such cheatings go nowadays, but we were cheated nevertheless. We learned quite a lot, but not enough. Instead of learning to move into country, as I think underneath we wanted, we learned mostly how to move onto it in the old crass Anglo-Saxon way, in search of edible or sometimes mortal quarry. We did a lot of killing, as kids will, and without ever being told that it was our flat duty, if duty exists, to know all there was to know about the creatures we killed.

Hunting and fishing are the old old entry points into nature for men, and not bad ones either, but as standardly practiced these days, for the climactic ejaculation of city tensions, they don't go very deep. They aren't thoughtful; they hold themselves too straitly to their purpose. Even for my quail-hunting uncles in South Texas, good men, good friends to me, all smaller birds of hedge and grass were "chee-chees," vermin, confusers of dogs' noses. . . . And if, with kids' instinctive thrustingness, we picked up a store of knowledge about small things that lived under logs and how the oriole builds its nest, there was no one around to consolidate it for us. Our knowledge, if considerable, remained random.

This age, of course, is unlikely to start breeding people who have the organic kinship to nature that the Comanches had, or even someone like Mr. Charlie Goodnight. For them every bush, every bird's cheep, every cloud bank had not only utilitarian but mystical meaning; it was all an extension of their sensory systems, an antenna as rawly receptive as a snail's. Even if their natural world still existed, which it doesn't, you'd have to snub the whole world of present men to get into it that way.

Nor does it help to be born in the country. As often as not these days, countrymen know as little as we others do about those things. They come principally of the old hard-headed tradition that moved onto the country instead of into it. For every Charles Goodnight there were several dozen Ezra Shermans, a disproportion that had bred itself down through the generations. Your standard country lore about animals—about the nasal love life of the possum, or the fabled hoop snake—is picturesque rather than accurate, anthropocentric rather than understanding.

But Charlie Goodnight and the Ezra Shermans and their children and grandchildren all combined have burned out and chopped out and plowed out and grazed out and killed out a good part of that natural world they knew, or didn't know, and we occupy ourselves mainly, it sometimes seems, in finishing the job. The rosy preindustrial time is past when the humanism of a man like Thoreau (*was* it humanism?) could still theorize in terms of natural harmony. Humanism has to speak in the terms of extant human beings. The terms of today's human beings are air conditioners and suburbs and water impoundments overlaying whole countrysides, and the hell with nature except maybe in a cross-sectional park here and there. In our time quietness and sun and leaves and bird song and all the multitudinous lore of the natural world have to come second or third, because whether we wanted to be born there or not, we were all born into the prickly machine-humming place that man has hung for himself above that natural world.

Where, tell me, is the terror and wonder of an elephant, now that they can be studied placid in every zoo, and any office-dwelling sport with a recent lucky break on the market can buy himself one to shoot through telescopic sights with a cartridge whose ballistics hold a good fileful of recorded science's findings. With a box gushing refrigerated air (or warmed, seasonally depending) into a sealed house and another box flashing loud bright images into jaded heads, who gives a rat's damn for things that go bump in the night? With possible death by blast or radiation staring at us like a buzzard, why should we sweat ourselves over where the Eskimo curlew went?

The wonder is that a few people do still sweat themselves, that the tracks of short varmints on a beach still have an audience. A few among the audience still know something, too. If they didn't, one wouldn't have to feel so cheated, not knowing as much. . . . Really knowing, I mean—from childhood up and continuously, with all of it a flavor in you . . . Not just being able to make a little seem a lot; there is enough of that around. I can give you as much book data about the home life of the yellow-breasted chat as the next man can. Nor do I mean vague mystic feelings of unity with Comanche and Neanderthal as one wanders the depleted land, gun at the ready, a part of the long flow of man's hunting compulsion. I mean *knowing*.

So that what one does in time, arriving a bit late at an awareness of the swindling he got—from no one, from the times—is to make up the shortage as best he may, to try to tie it all together for himself by reading and adult poking.

But adult poking is never worth a quarter as much as kid poking, not in those real terms. There's never the time for that whole interest later, or ever quite the pure and subcutaneous receptiveness, either.

I mean, too—obviously—if you care. I know that the whicker of a plover in the September sky doesn't touch all other men in their bowels as it touches me, and that men whom it doesn't touch at all can be good men. But it touches me. And I care about knowing what it is, and—if I can—why.

Disgruntled from caring, I went to run my throwline. Coons' fresh tracks along the beach overlaid my own of the evening before; one had played with the end of the line and had rolled the jar of blood bait around on the sand trying to get inside it. The passenger followed some of the tracks into a drift tangle but lost interest, not knowing what he was trailing, robbed by long generations of show-breeding of the push that would have made him care. . . . In my fingers the line tugged with more than the pulse of the current, but when I started softly hand-over-handing it in, it gave a couple of stiff jerks and went slacker, and I knew that something on it in a final frenzy had finished the job of twisting loose. They roll and roll and roll, and despite swivels at last work the staging into a tight snarl against whose solidity they can tear themselves free. Whatever it had been, channel or yellow or blue, it had left a chunk of its lip on the second hook, and two hooks beyond that was a one-pounder which I removed, respectful toward the sharp septic fin spines.

In the old days we'd taken the better ones before they rolled loose by running the lines every hour or so during the night, a sleepless process and in summer a mosquito-chewed one. Once in Hood County, Hale and I and black Bill Briggs had gotten a twenty-five-pounder, and after an argument with Bill, who wanted to try to eat it, we sold it to a bridgeside café for a dime a pound. Another time on the Guadalupe to the south—but this is supposed to be about the Brazos. . . .

Tethering the little catfish to the chain stringer by the canoe, I got a rod and went down to the sharp tail of the island to cast a plug into green deep eddies I'd seen there while exploring. Without wind, the sun was almost hot now. From a willow a jay resented me with a two-note muted rasp like a boy blowing in and out on a harmonica with stuck reeds, and in an almost bare tree on the high river bank a flock of bobolinks fed and bubbled and called, resting on their way south.

Cast and retrieve, shallow and deep, across current and down and up, and no sign of bass . . . The sun's laziness got into me and I wandered up the lesser channel, casting only occasionally into holes without the expectation of fish. Then, on a long flow-dimpled bar, something came down over my consciousness like black pain, and I dropped the rod and squatted, shaking my head to drive the blackness back. It receded a little. I waddled without rising to the bar's edge and scooped cold water over my head. After four or five big throbs it went away, and I sat down half in the water and thought about it. It didn't take much study. My stomach was giving a lecture about it, loud. What it amounted to was that I was about half starved.

I picked up the rod, went back to camp, stirred the fire, and put on a pot of water into which I dumped enough dried lima beans for four men, salt, an onion, and a big chunk of bacon. Considering, I went down to the stringer and skinned and gutted the little catfish and carried him up and threw him in the pot, too. While it boiled, I bathed in the river, frigid in contrast to the air, sloshed out the canoe and sponged it down, and washed underclothes and socks. In shorts, feeling fine now but so hungry it hurt, I sat by the fire and sharpened knives and the ax for the additional hour the beans needed to cook soft in the middle. Fishing out the skeleton of the disintegrated catfish, and using the biggest spoon I had, I ate the whole mess from the pot almost without stopping, and mopped up its juices with cold biscuit bread.

Then I wiped my chin and lay back against the cotton-wood log with my elbows hanging over it behind and my toes digging into the sand, and considered that asceticism, most certainly, was for those who were built for it. Some were. Some weren't. I hadn't seen God in the black headache on the sand bar and I didn't want to try to any more, that way. . . . Starving myself hadn't had much to do with spir-ituality, anyhow, but only with the absence of company.

Philosophically equilibrated, I rolled down into the sand and went to sleep for two or three hours, waking into a perfect blue-and-yellow afternoon loud with the full-throat chant of the redbird.

Wood . . . I went roaming with the honed ax among the piles of drift, searching out solid timber. Bleached and un-barked as much of it is, you have a hard time seeing what it may be, but a two-lick notch with the ax usually bares its grain enough to name it. Cottonwood and willow slice soft and white before the first blow, and unless you're hard up you move on to try your luck on another piece; they're not serious fuel:

> The fire devoureth both the ends of it, and the midst of
> it is burnt. Is it meet for any work?

But the river is prodigal of its trees, and better stuff is usually near.

If food is to sit in the fire's smoke as it cooks, any of the elms will give it a bad taste, though they last and give good heat. Cedar's oil eats up its wood in no time, and stinks food, too, but the tinge of it on the air after supper is worth smelling if you want to cut a stick or so of it just for that. Rock-hard bodark—Osage orange if you want; bois d'arc if you're etymological—sears a savory crust on meat and burns a long time, if you don't mind losing a flake out of your ax's edge when you hit it wrong. For that matter, not much of it grows close enough to the river to become drift. Nor does much mesquite—a pasture tree and the only thing a conscientious Mexican cook will barbecue kid over. Ash is all right but, as dry drift anyhow, burns fast. The white oaks are prime, the red oaks less so, and one of the finest of aromatic fuels is a twisted, wave-grained branch of live oak, common in the limestone country farther down the river.

Maybe, though, the nutwoods are best and sweetest, kind to food and long in their burning. In the third tangle I nicked a huge branch of walnut, purple-brown an inch inside its sapwood's whitened skin. It rots slowly; this piece was sound enough for furniture making—straight-grained enough, too, for that matter. I chopped it into long pieces. The swing and the chocking bite of the ax were pleasant; the pup chased chips as they flew, and I kept cutting until I had twice as many billets as I would need. Then I stacked them for later hauling and went to camp to use up the afternoon puttering with broken tent loops and ripped tarps and sprung hinges on boxes, throwing sticks for the passenger, looking in a book for the differences among small streaked finches, airing my bed, sweeping with a willow branch the sandy gravel all through a camp I'd leave the next day. . . .

I lack much zeal for camping, these years. I can still read old Kephart with pleasure: nearly half a century later hardly anyone else has come anywhere near him for information and good sense. But there's detachment in my pleasure now. I no longer see myself choosing a shingle tree and felling it and splitting out the shakes for my own roof, though if I did want to he would tell me how. . . . Nor have I passion for canoeing, as such; both it and the camping are just ways to get somewhere I want to be, and to stay there for a time. I can't describe the cross-bow rudder stroke or stay serene in crashing rapids. I carry unconcentrated food in uncompact boxes. I forget to grease my boots and suffer from clammy feet. I slight hygiene, and will finger a boiled minnow from the coffee with equanimity, and sleep with my dog. My tent in comparison to the aluminum-framed, tight-snapping ones available is a ragged parallelogrammatic disaster.

Nevertheless, when camping for a time is the way of one's life, one tries to improve his style. One resolves on changes for future trips—a tiny and exactly fitted cook box; a contour-cut tarp over the canoe hooking to catches beneath the gunwales; no peaches in the mixed dried fruit. . . . One experiments and invents, and ends up, for instance, with a perfect aluminum-foil reflector for baking that agreeable, lumpy, biscuit-mixed bread that the Mexicans call *"pan ranchero"* and the northwoods writers "bannock" and other people undoubtedly other names.

One way or the other, it all generally turns out to be work. Late that afternoon, carrying abrasive armloads of the walnut from where I'd chopped it to camp, I got as though from the air the answer to a question that used to come into my mind in libraries, reading about the old ones and the Indians. I used to wonder why, knowing Indians were around, the old ones would let themselves be surprised so often and so easily. Nearly all the ancient massacres resulted from such surprise.

The answer, simple on the island, was that the old ones were laboring their tails off at the manifold tasks of the primitive life, hewing and hauling and planting and plowing and breaking and fixing. They didn't have time to be wary. Piped water and steam heat and tractors might have let them be alert, just as I'd been among the stacked tomes of the Southwest Collection.

It was a good day, work and all. At evening I sat astraddle the bow of the canoe on the beach, putting new line on the spinning reel, when three big honkers came flying up the river slowly, low searchers like the first ones of the evening before. The gun was at hand. Even though they veered, separating, as I reached for it, they still passed close, and it needed only a three-foot lead on the front one's head to bring him splashing solidly, relaxed, dead, into the channel. I trotted downstream abreast of him as he drifted and finally teased him ashore with a long crooked piece of cottonwood.

Till then I'd had the visceral bite of the old excitement in me, the gladness of clean shooting, the fulfillment of quarry sought and taken. But when I got him ashore and hefted the warm, handsome eight or nine pounds of him, and ran my fingers against the grain up through the hot thick down of his neck, the just-as-old balancing regret came into it. A goose is a lot of bird to kill. Maybe size shouldn't matter, but it seems to. With something that big and that trimly perfect and, somehow, that meaningful, you wonder about the right of the thing. . . .

For a while after the war I did no shooting at all, and thought I probably wouldn't do any more. I even chiseled out a little niche for that idea, half Hindu and tangled with the kind of reverence for life that Schweitzer preaches. But then one day in fall beside a stock tank in a mesquite pasture a friend wanted me to try the heft of a little engraved L.C.

Smith, and when I'd finished trying it I'd dropped ten doves with sixteen shots and the niche didn't exist any longer.

Reverence for life in that sense seems to me to be like asceticism or celibacy: you need to be built for it. I no longer kill anything inedible that doesn't threaten me or mine, and I never cared anything about big-game hunting. Possibly I'll give up shooting again and for good one of these years, but I believe the killing itself can be reverent. To see and kill and pluck and gut and cook and eat a wild creature, all with some knowledge and the pleasure that knowledge gives, implies a closeness to the creature that is to me more honorable than the candle-lit consumption of rare prime steaks from a steer bludgeoned to death in a packing-house chute while tranquilizers course his veins. And if there's a difference in nobility between a Canada goose and a fat white-faced ox (there is), how does one work out the quantities?

Though I threw the skin and head and guts into the river to keep them away from the pup, an eddy drifted them into shore and he found them and ate a good bit before I caught him at it. The two big slabs of breast hissed beautifully in foil on the fire after dark. When they were done I hung them up for a time uncovered in the sweet walnut smoke and then ate nearly all of one of them. The other would make sandwiches at noon for two or three days, tucked inside chunks of biscuit bread. Despite his harsh appetizers, the passenger gobbled the drumsticks and organs I'd half roasted for him, and when I unrolled the sleeping bag inside the tent he fought to be first into it.

Later, in half-sleep, I heard a rattle of dirty metal dishes beside the fire. I shot the flashlight's beam out there and a sage, masked face stared at me, indignant. Foreseeing sport, I hauled the pup up for a look. He blinked, warm and full, and dug in his toes against ejection into the cold air, and when I let him go he burrowed all the way down beside my feet, not a practical dog and not ashamed of it, either. The coon went away.

Later still, the goosefeathers began their emetic work and I woke to the rhythmic *wump, wump, wump* that in dogs precedes a heave. Though the account of it may lack wide interest, later it seemed to me that there had been heroic co-ordination in the way I came out of sleep and grabbed him, holding his jaws shut with one hand while I fought to find the bag's zipper with the other, then fought to find and loose the zipper of the tent, too, and hurled him out into the night by his nose. He stayed there for a while, and when I was sure he'd finished I let him back in, low-eared and shivering, but I preferred his unhappiness to what might have been.

It came to me then who it was that had slept with a dog for his health. Leopold Bloom's father. The dog's name had been . . . Athos! Old Man Bloom had slept with Athos to cure his aches and pains.

One can get pretty literary on islands.

COLIN FLETCHER

(1922–   )

Apparently Colin Fletcher has read and enjoyed other *Words for the Wild* authors, for his own works begin with epigraphs taken from theirs. Two of his five books even display a transcendentalist's words on the first page: Walt Whitman signals *The Winds of Mara*, Ralph Waldo Emerson, *The Man Who Walked Through Time*.

The latter's lines are noteworthy because they synthesize the meaningful intuition of Fletcher's solitary hike from one end of the Grand Canyon to the other. "There is a relation between the hours of our life and the centuries of time," Emerson wrote. "The hours should be instructed by the ages, and the ages explained by the hours." So Fletcher understands. After he has successfully managed his precipitous journey, a trip accomplished rather casually by boat but not so easily on foot, he realizes: "I had moved around on my own to

Emerson's conclusion. . . . I had seen the ages; now it was time to come back to the hours.'' Meanwhile, by sharing his canyon hours in a book of memorable highlights and hardships, he puts his accomplishment in genuine perspective.

He worried about water—too much, too fast, when he set himself adrift on the river—too little, at potholes too far apart, when he ventured across the Esplanade. He treasured the wildlife, from the pink snake who became too friendly to the beaver who built nearby to the intelligent-looking deer mouse who peered curiously around. He pondered the people, too—those who have lived in the canyon, those who merely glance over the edge. Describing what could be seen or heard or extrapolated from physical evidence, in each case he lets the reader do the interpreting.

This pattern replicates the sense of the epigraph that heads Fletcher's widely read *Thousand-Mile Summer*. ''It is better for the emissaries returning from the wilderness to record their marvel, not to record its meaning.'' The words are Loren Eiseley's, but the idea behind them echoes Fletcher's philosophy of composition. Neither in this narration of a California hike from the Mexican border to the Oregon line, nor in *The Man Who Walked Through Time*, does the author pontificate about his experiences. Rather, he describes the visual and psychological changes that took place by telling of the people he saw, the creatures encountered, the physical hazards overcome, the emotional needs met. Simply by recording the marvel of all he saw and felt, he invites the reader to draw the necessary conclusion.

This is not to say that he resists all opportunities to sound Emersonian. Obviously no *Words for the Wild* author can deny those flashes of insight that come in the natural world. But instead of dwelling on the abstractions of his experiences, Colin Fletcher focuses on an articulation of the concrete. No one who has read *The Thousand-Mile Summer* will forget the fury with which he killed the first rattlers he saw, or the way he finally learned to step around them. No one who has read *The Man Who Walked Through Time* will forget his fear of the river or the fact that at the end of his trip he swam across. The marvels of wilderness travel are there, period.

From "Beyond the Panamints" in *The Thousand-Mile Summer*

High in a rock crevice, a gleam of red. I scrambled up the steep gully. A cluster of prickly little brown shapes clung to the rock. And from their center, lifted to the sky like red-hot trumpets, sprang a battery of scarlet flowers.

As I photographed them, I found myself considering the cactus's role in the desert.

When the poet says

> *This is the dead land*
> *This is cactus land*

we feel his desolation. Yet for five hundred miles I had been walking past cacti and they had left no positive impression. They had not been a source of wonder like the flowers. They had not dragged at my feet like the sand or lifted my heart like the sunsets. Somehow they had hardly touched my life.

I had certainly noticed each new species. First there had been the striking sahuaros, towering up twenty feet and more. Sometimes their fluted spires rose straight and simple, with little thumbs nubbing off. Sometimes they forked, and stood with arms raised in stiff and stylized supplication. Then, along the Colorado, there had been the untidy candelabra that looked as though a bunch of prickly green sausages had been stuck haphazardly by their ends into an invisible core. In the Mojave I had found comic little brown porcupine-footballs that often sprouted puffs of white cotton. But as the novelty of each new species wore off they became an almost unnoticed item in the desert landscape.

There had been exceptions of course. Ever since Mexico I had been passing 'beavertails.' Their pimply green 'paddles' made them the dullest cacti of all. Until they flowered. Then their cup-shaped blooms, porcelain-fine, blazed out in glorious splashes of vivid magenta. One radiant cluster, alone in deathliest Death Valley, had stopped me in my tracks. Then there had been the evening and morning at a Mojave night camp when the low sun, setting and rising, had turned the prickles of a mixed cactus grove into a galaxy of contorted halos. But, by and large, cacti had been something so inert that after five hundred miles they had left no impression positive enough to justify the poet's desolation. Until they flowered, they were there—and that was about all.

As I put my camera away after photographing the red trumpets in the rock gully, I felt vaguely uneasy. It seemed wrong—almost sinful—that such symbols of the desert had become somthing hardly more likely to catch my eye than the drainage gratings in a city gutter.

Sometimes the new faces that the desert showed me were variations on old themes.

It lay at the edge of the road, almost invisible in the fading light. I am still not sure what stopped me treading on it. Perhaps I saw a slight movement. Perhaps I heard the faint buzz. In any case, I pulled up short, a pace and a half from trouble.

The snake was barely a foot long and no thicker than my little finger. It lay in tensed curves, its fingernail of a rattle raised and vibrant. Even when I bent down I could hear only the same faint fly-buzz that had come from the pile of timber at Saratoga Spring. I peered closer, wondering if it really was a sidewinder. I had been hoping for a chance to see their distinctive, half-sideways movement.

And suddenly I realized that even in the first shock I had not been afraid. Only curious. I knew the bootlace at my feet was just as dangerous as the diabolical creature that two months earlier had straddled the Wetback Trail; but would I be feeling so calm if it had been as big? I wasn't sure. I could only hope it was familiarity and not mere diminutiveness that had removed the fear.

This was the third rattlesnake I had met since Death Valley. Twice in the Panamints I had almost trodden on small specimens. Each time I had experienced only a little fear. Each time I had allowed the snake to crawl away unharmed.

"Why kill them?" Matt Ryan had said at Emigrant Ranger Station when I told him about the four rattlers along the Colorado and the one at Saratoga Spring. "If you leave them alone they won't do you any harm. They were one of America's earliest national symbols, you know. Not attackers, but venomous in defence. They're gentlemen: they'll give you warning if you give them half a chance. And they have their part to play in the balance of nature. Kill them off, and you disturb all sorts of things. Our policy in the Monument is to let them be. Out in the blue, I mean. Around buildings it's different of course, or where there's kids. But the dangers are exaggerated, you know."

"Yes, I gather not too many people are actually killed by rattlers?" I said.

"I'm not sure about the exact figure, but I think the total of recorded deaths in California history adds up to somewhere around five. Even then, there's almost always been some contributory factor—extreme youth or age, heart trouble, or something. So we don't kill them. After all, we're trying to preserve a corner of America as the white man found it. The men at the top of the Park System always have that aim in mind. And the white man found rattlesnakes. People try to tell us it's not worth the risk. But hell, since the Monument was created in 1933 we haven't had a single case of snakebite. There've been close shaves of course, but nobody's been bitten, let alone died. And if we don't kill them inside the Monument, why outside? Away from people, I mean.''

Matt's argument made sense. So I had allowed the next two rattlesnakes I met to escape. And I had felt good.

Now, as I stood looking down at the little bootlace with its vibrating rattle, I realized that early in The Walk rattlesnakes had worried me more than I had cared to admit. In the first month or so, rustling branches under my sleeping bag had given me several uneasy moments. But now I accepted rattlers as part of the desert. I would never collect them, as some people do, pushing ten or twenty into a sack and carrying the prize slung over one shoulder. But at least I could more or less live with them.

The snake still stood its ground. I flicked some sand and it began to retreat. Its body moved in wide, exaggerated curves that carried it forward with a peculiar semi-crabwise motion, as if an invisible force was diverting it at an angle from the path it wanted to travel. I watched it go, knowing that at last I had been lucky enough to see a sidewinder.

The snake disappeared into a bush and I walked on up the road, oddly pleased with myself. Stage by stage, as was its way, the desert had taught me something. When I killed those early rattlesnakes I could have justified myself with a score of reasons. But the 'reasons' would have been excuses. I knew now that what drove me to kill was plain, ordinary, understandable fear.

Sometimes the desert's 'new' faces were old features seen from a fresh angle.

As I ate lunch one day I glimpsed, close up, the heedless cruelty that lies hidden behind nature's 'peacefulness.' A leopard-lizard emerged from a bush, chewing reflectively on a grasshopper. The grasshopper kicked and the lizard let go. The mangled insect jerked about on the sand. The lizard, taking its time, repossessed it. The performance was repeated once, twice, three times. Finally the grasshopper summoned dying reserves and with its one remaining leg leaped into a bush. The lizard moved forward five or six inches, closed its eyes—and fell asleep.

Another day, I sat beside the road, a little muddle-headed from the sun. Around me the desert stretched flat and empty.

And then, as I rested, I became conscious that it was not empty at all: it teemed with grasshoppers. They were small creatures, so small that they escaped the casual naked eye. I focused my binoculars on the stony road, as close up as I could. And like Alice stepping through the looking glass, I found myself in a different world.

It was a torrid, glaring, shadowless world. Across its 'boulder-strewn' landscape a steady pilgrimage moved uphill, upwind, and into the sun. No terrible urgency drove the pilgrims forward. There was just a general I'll-move-on-when-I-want-to, this-sun-is-so-hot, we'll-get-there-sometime sort of attitude. They came in an irregular but continuous stream, rarely jumping, just crawling and resting, crawling and resting. At rest, they lapsed into torpor, all facing the same way, like ships anchored in a tideway.

They came in a hundred shapes and sizes and colors and conformations. Some were small and some were very small.

Some had obvious wings and some did not. Some were tapered aft and some were blunt. But they all had stupid grasshopper heads, as stupid in their compressed way as a giraffe's.

There were undistinguished gray ones with pale blue movie-actress eyes. There were battleship-gray ones with tropical dazzle-paint finish. There were brown ones, bravely mottled with yellow and red and blue. And some were hot cinnamon all over.

Once, a blue-eye cut, woman-like, across the bows of a restling battleship-gray, brushing his foreleg as she passed. The battleship-gray dreamily raised the leg. He held it high for ten seconds, then lowered it part way. Twenty seconds later he lowered it almost to the ground. After a full minute, still with the detachment of a drug addict, he put it down.

I was wondering whether the afternoon sun accounted for his muzziness when I became conscious of its heat on my exposed neck. I tilted back my hat and lowered the binoculars.

Around me, the desert once more stretched flat and empty.

But the desert did not always give even a superficial appearance of emptiness.

I was walking northward along the dirt road. All around stretched sand and stones and creosote bushes. Apart from the road, there had been no sign of man for several hours. And then I came to a clearly distinguishable object. It stood alone and aloof, a dozen feet off the road. It was pitless and therefore useless. Its door stood open, revealing all. It was, exactly as large as life, an ordinary old-fashioned wooden privy.

Sometimes the desert's new faces were new in every way, though I could not always say what it was that created the newness.

The last morning I would be following the road, I woke at sunrise to find the air cool, almost cold. I had camped at dusk on a high plateau. Now, in the first sunlight, I saw snow-filled gullies less than a mile away. It was the closest I had been to snow since Mexico, closer even than above Death Valley. And again the snow kindled that odd excitement.

I got up and shook my sleeping bag. And there on the road, six feet from my bed, so freshly imprinted in thick dust that I half expected to find the cause still strolling down the road, I saw a perfect set of bobcat tracks. The low sun flood-lit their indentations in sharp relief. As in a coarse-grained photograph, each speck of dust had value. I could almost hear the animal padding past while I slept.

After breakfast I walked on northward along the road. The bobcat tracks preceded me. The plateau that the road cut across was not a particularly beautiful place: just a rolling tableland with dark, buttony junipers dotting the pale green sagebrush. But some special quality in the light gave it a quickening vividness.

I turned a corner. A pair of junipers, one on each side of the road, framed a perfect picture. There was nothing very special about it, I suppose. Nothing that will quite go into words. There was no bobcat, no glorious splash of color, no sweeping panorama. Just the dark needles of the trees standing out in silhouette against the pale dust of the road. And a narrow view beyond. The view had a subtle, indefinite balance that was intensified by the vivid light. And away to the left, closer than ever, hung the snow-filled gullies. That was all.

I was standing still, devouring every detail of the scene, when for some reason I remembered it was Monday. Back in San Francisco another weekend was over. All around the world people were pouring back into their squirrel cages.

And all at once I understood how lucky I was. For the first time I saw quite clearly that what mattered in The Walk were the simple things—snow and vivid light and sharp-grained bobcat tracks. My exhilaration swelled up and over-flowed. And when at last I walked on past the two juniper trees toward the far side of the plateau I found I was feeling sorry for any man who was not free to abandon whatever futility detained him and to walk away into the desert morning with a pack on his back.

"Rock" in *The Man Who Walked Through Time*

I walked on down Bass Trail. It hairpinned through the brown sandstone, just as the trail had done below Hualpai Hilltop. And all at once I found myself standing in front of a little grotto. It was no more, really, than a hollow eroded back into the rock; a roofed-over shelf, ten feet long, four feet deep, and perhaps two feet high. But in the very center of its entrance, seeming to support the roof, stood a buttress. The buttress was, I knew, merely the chance result of erosion, a relic of rock that would in the slow and inexorable course of time dwindle beneath the wind and water that had carved it until at last it crumbled and vanished. But now, at this particular point in time, it was a beautiful thing.

The buttress merged with roof and floor in flowing and perfectly proportioned curves. And on its face was superimposed a small, delicately sculptured column, so oddly weathered that it seemed almost a decorative afterthought. The surface of this column was rounded and smooth, as if it had been sandpapered by a patient carpenter, and its fine-drawn strata stood out sharp and clear, like the grain on unstained, highly polished wood. The column's irregular outline flowed quite independently of the buttress's: it meandered upward, narrowed to a neck, then merged into a massive, curving

superstructure of heavily bedded rockbands. And these bands,
slanting down at a slight angle to the strata of both column
and buttress, dominated the grotto and fused each element
of it into a single harmony of curve and crosscut, grain and
color, light and enigmatic shade.

For a long time I stood and looked at the grotto, feeling
for something I knew was there but could not quite reach.
At last I turned and walked on down the trail. But now, as
I walked, I found myself looking at the rock more closely,
thinking it more closely, feeling it more closely. It seemed
as if all at once I could recognize, in some new and more
thorough way—without any sense of revelation, just with
an easy acceptance—how time, sandpapering rock, had created harmony and beauty. (But, after all, what was beauty
but some kind of harmony between the rock and my senses?)
And as I walked on down the trail I found that now at last
I could comprehend the reality of what had happened to
build the sandstone from which time had carved the grotto.
I could comprehend it more than intellectually now, so that
I could almost feel the dust stinging my bare legs. For the
sandstone had been built by the same kind of wind and the
same kind of dust that had blown at Hualpai Hilltop. The
wind had whipped the dust along and then had dropped it,
grain after grain, layer after layer, foot after foot—and had
gone on doing so day after year after decade after century
after millennium for perhaps ten million years, until at last
it had built a layer of sand more than three hundred feet
thick. Then the slow cementing action of water and colossal
pressure had converted sand into rock. Into rock that preserved the outlines of rolling dunes as tilted strata. As strata
that might stand out, where chance and time created a cliff
face, as the crosscut grain on a decorative column or the
slanting line of a massive rockband. A band that might, given

the right random erosion, help fuse the harmonies of an exquisite little grotto. It was very simple, really. The only thing the wind and the dust needed was time.

And now I found that I was ready to grant them the time. For at last I could look, steadily, beyond today and tomorrow. And beyond yesterday. I could accept the day after century after millennium after millennium after slow millennium during which the wind had blown the dust in pale clouds across rolling sand dunes. I knew now how it had been. The dust had filled up a hollow here and a hollow there, built new dunes beside them, filled the new hollows—on and on and on, layer upon layer, until the sand lay three hundred feet thick. Then some slow, chance movement of the earth's crust happened to submerge the dunes beneath a shallow sea and tiny white-shelled creatures began their task of living and dying, living and dying, living and dying, until they had built above the sand the four-hundred-foot layer of limestone that now formed the Canyon's Rim. Yes, it was very simple, really. And now I could accept it all, without effort and as a part of my natural range of thought. As a part of my natural range of thought, that was the important thing.

I came down out of the sandstone onto familiar red rock and walked across Darwin Plateau. And as the light failed I camped close under the white dome of Mount Huethawali, quite near Huxley Terrace and only just around the corner from Evolution Amphitheater.

I camped, for nostalgia's sake, beside a big juniper tree. The juniper grew on the brink of the Redwall, and beyond it there opened up, as there had opened up on other evenings, a gray, shape-filled pit. But this time, because I knew that in the morning I would go down into the pit, its shapes held new meaning. As darkness fell they seemed to challenge me; even, at first, to menace.

But in the morning it was different. There was an interval of superb synchronization when, at exactly the moment the moon sank behind the Rim and the pit's blue-black shadows eased over into black, a paleness began to invade the eastern sky. The shadows faded. Vague shapes crystallized, as they always did, into butte and cliff and mesa. Soon daylight had filled the pit with its colossal, solid sculpture. But when, after breakfast, I walked on down Bass Trail—acutely aware once more of the pages of the earth's autobiography—I no longer looked at the sculpture. Instead, my eyes sought out the strata that gave the sculpture meaning.

Below my nightcamp the trail swung around to the right and angled down across the face of the Redwall in a man-made cutting. Here the story of earth was no longer written in grains of sand. The smooth red rock under my feet had been built—much as the white upper limestone had been built—by the shells of minute organisms that had lived and died by the millions upon millions in an ancient sea and had gone on living and dying and sinking to the sea bed until their corpses had built a layer of blue-gray rock six hundred feet deep. A rock whose surface has been stained red by water seeping down from the red, iron-bearing strata above. Yes, it was all very simple still, and very easy to accept.

I moved down deeper into the Canyon.

Soon I was walking over interleaved layers, purple and green, of shale that had once been mud swirling down an ancient river that flowed long before the Colorado existed. Mud that had come to rest at last, thick and soft, off some primordial shore. Had come to rest in the same way that thick, soft mud is coming to rest today off the mouth of the Colorado and forming mud flats that will probably, in due time, become new layers of shale or slate.

I moved down yet deeper.

On the brink of the Inner Gorge I passed through a band of dark brown sandstone. (This time, it was sand from a beach.) And then, below the sandstone, I stepped down into a different world.

All at once, black and twisted rocks pressed in on me— rocks that had been so altered by time and heat and pressure that no one can tell for sure what their original form was. And as I walked down between them, sinking deeper into a narrow cleft that forms one of the rare major breaks in the wall of the Inner Gorge, I felt again, as I had not felt since my reconnaissance, the oppression of insignificance.

I walked on down. The cleft deepened. The black rock pressed closer, almost shutting out the sky. And then, quite suddenly, I had stepped out onto a broad rock platform. A hundred feet below me the river was sparkling blue-green and white. And the sky had opened up again.

I sat and rested on the rock platform, looking over and beyond the river at the strata on strata that mounted one on the other to the North Rim. I could see them all, every layer. They were replicas of those I had just moved down through. And after I had sat and looked at them for a while I saw that now, from a distance, I could see with eye and intellect what I had all day been understanding through instinct. Now, as my eye traveled downward from the Rim, it watched the rocks grow older.

It watched them grow older in a way that would have been impossible when I was living, day after day, surrounded and cushioned and segregated by the accouterments of the man-ruled world—by chairs and electricity and money-thrust and the rest of the tinsel. I knew that when I returned to that world I would probably remember what I saw as a flight of fancy, as airy symbolism. But at the time, as I sat there on the rock platform above the sparkling river, the pageant I saw spread out before me shone with a reality as rich as any I have ever caught in the beam of logic.

I saw, when I looked up at the Rim, that the uppermost layers of rock were bright and bold and youthful. Their unseamed faces shone pink or white or suntan-brown, untouched by the upheavals that time brings to all of us. But below the Redwall they began to show their age. There, in staid maturity, they wore dark greens and subdued browns. And their faces had begun to wrinkle. Then, as my eye reached the lip of the Inner Gorge, the rocks plunged into old age. Now they wore gray and sober black. The wrinkles had deepened. And their features had twisted beneath the terrible weight of the years. Old age had come to them, just as it comes in the end to all of us who live long enough.

I rested on the rock platform for an hour. Then I clambered down to the river through the darkest and most twisted rock of all. Once more, as on the Inner Gorge reconnaissance, every boulder and hanging fragment of the rock around me looked ready to come crashing down at any minute. But now I needed no tight and determined thinking to ward off fear. During my three weeks among crumbling rockfaces and loose talus, all apparently waiting to crash headlong at any minute, I had heard just once—a long way off—the sound of a small stone falling a very short distance. And now I understood why.

The poised boulders and fragments were indeed waiting to crash down at any minute. But there was not really too much danger that one would hit me during that particular hiccup of time we humans call May 1963. For our human clocks and the geologic clock kept different times. "Any minute now," geologic time, meant only that several fragments of rock might fall before May 2063, and that quite an appreciable number would probably do so by May 11963. I knew this now, through and through. I might not yet understand the explicit, absolute meaning of two hundred million years. But I had come to grips with the kind of geology I had hoped to find. I had begun at last to hear the rhythm of the rock.

EDWARD ABBEY

(1927–   )

Anyone who knows me well knows that Edward Abbey is one of my favorite *Words for the Wild* writers. I like the sound of his prose, the way the words come together in fresh and rhythmic ways. I like the places he talks about, perhaps because I've been there myself, and I enjoy his observations of what I was too blind to see. Most of all, I like his point of view. His tongue-in-cheek irreverence amuses me, even as his respect for the land touches me deeply. His books are still the ones I reread most often because they speak so directly to my own wilderness values.

Unlike many other nature essayists, Abbey writes good novels, too. His *Monkey-Wrench Gang* remains the funniest tale of Southwest shenanigans I've ever picked up, while *Black Sun* better reveals the plight of modern man than most textbooks on philosophy. *The Brave Cowboy* and *Fire on the Mountain* are provocative, too, questioning, as they do, the individual's ability to withstand the forces of society;

Good News projects a future should such forces prevail.

More popular than his novels, though, are Abbey's essays about the environment. His reputation began with the 1968 publication of *Desert Solitaire: A Season in the Wilderness* as the solitary ranger at what was then Arches National Monument. In its pages, Abbey describes everything he found significant—the plant and animal life, the rocks, the people he met, the escapades, the implications of both thought and action. Later essay collections have followed the same pattern. Abbey centers each one around personal responses to a particular set of surroundings, attempting meanwhile to make some sense of how an individual feels when so-called progress impinges on his natural world.

He dislikes conventional tags, so it is difficult to label the philosophic constant that threads through his writing. One word, however, comes close to characterizing his real point of view—*Eartheism*. "I suppose you could call it a basic loyalty to our planet," he explained in a 1984 interview, "a reverence for our lives and the lives of our families and friends, and a respect for the lives of the animals and plants that exist around us. Those are the only things that we can know well enough to revere, I think. So Eartheism is a love for and a faithfulness to the earth, to the real everyday life that we know, to all living things, and even to the rock that we stand on and the air that supports us and makes our lives possible."

Each of Abbey's wilderness essays explores his own faithfulness, or else it exposes some mechanistic desecration. From the mountains of Colorado to the rivers of Alaska, from the coral of the Great Barrier Reef to the black sands of Mexico's Pinacate country, Abbey eyes the landscape with love while fretting about its future. For comfort, then, he always returns to the Slickrock country of southern Utah and northern Arizona. There he finds the space and freedom, the images, the colors, the imaginative input he needs to express the Eartheism that dominates his prose.

"Come On In" in
The Journey Home: Some Words in Defense of the American West

The canyon country of southern Utah and northern Arizona—the Colorado Plateau—is something special. Something strange, marvelous, full of wonders. As far as I know there is no other region on earth much like it, or even remotely like it. Nowhere else have we had this lucky combination of vast sedimentary rock formations exposed to a desert climate, a great plateau carved by major rivers—the Green, the San Juan, the Colorado—into such a surreal land of form and color. Add a few volcanoes, the standing necks of which can still be seen, and cinder cones and lava flows, and at least four separate laccolithic mountain ranges nicely distributed about the region, and more hills, holes, humps and hollows, reefs, folds, salt domes, swells and grabens, buttes, benches, and mesas, synclines, monoclines, and anticlines than you can ever hope to see and explore in one lifetime, and you begin to arrive at an approximate picture of the plateau's surface appearance.

An approximate beginning. A picture framed by sky and time in the world of natural appearances. Despite the best efforts of a small army of writers, painters, photographers, scientists, explorers, Indians, cowboys, and wilderness guides, the landscape of the Colorado Plateau lies still beyond the reach of reasonable words. Or unreasonable representation. This is a landscape that has to be seen to be believed, and even then, confronted directly by the senses, it strains credulity.

Comprehensible, yes. Perhaps nowhere is the basic structure of the earth's surface so clearly, because so nakedly, revealed. And yet—when all we know about it is said and measured and tabulated, there remains something in the soul of the place, the spirit of the whole, that cannot be fully assimilated by the human imagination.

My terminology is far from exact; certainly not scientific. Words like "soul" and "spirit" make vague substitutes for a hard effort toward understanding. But I can offer no better. The land here is like a great book or a great symphony; it invites approaches toward comprehension on many levels, from all directions.

The geologic approach is certainly primary and fundamental, underlying the attitude and outlook that best support all others, including the insights of poetry and the wisdom of religion. Just as the earth itself forms the indispensable ground for the only kind of life we know, providing the sole sustenance of our minds and bodies, so does empirical truth constitute the foundation of higher truths. (If there is such a thing as higher truth.) It seems to me that Keats was wrong when he asked, rhetorically, "Do not all charms fly . . . at the mere touch of cold philosophy?" The word "philosophy" standing, in his day, for what we now call "physical science." But Keats was wrong, I say, because there is more charm in one "mere" fact, confirmed by test and observation, linked to other facts through coherent theory into a rational system, than in a whole brainful of fancy and fantasy. I see more poetry in a chunk of quartzite than in a make-believe wood nymph, more beauty in the revelations of a verifiable intellectual construction than in whole misty empires of obsolete mythology.

The moral I labor toward is that a landscape as splendid as

that of the Colorado Plateau can best be understood and given human significance by poets who have their feet planted in concrete—concrete data—and by scientists whose heads and hearts have not lost the capacity for wonder. Any good poet, in our age at least, must begin with the scientific view of the world; and any scientist worth listening to must be something of a poet, must possess the ability to communicate to the rest of us his sense of love and wonder at what his work discovers.

The canyon country does not always inspire love. To many it appears barren, hostile, repellent—a fearsome land of rock and heat, sand dunes and quicksand, cactus, thornbush, scorpion, rattlesnake, and agoraphobic distances. To those who see our land in that manner, the best reply is, yes, you are right, it is a dangerous and terrible place. Enter at your own risk. Carry water. Avoid the noonday sun. Try to ignore the vultures. Pray frequently.

For a few others the canyon country is worth only what they can dig out of it and haul away—to the mills, to the power plants, to the bank.

For more and more of those who now live here, however, the great plateau and its canyon wilderness is a treasure best enjoyed through the body and spirit, *in situ* as the archeologists say, not through commercial plunder. It is a regional, national and international treasure too valuable to be sacrificed for temporary gain, too rare to be withheld from our children. For us the wilderness and human emptiness of this land is not a source of fear but the greatest of its attractions. We would guard and defend and save it as a place for all who wish to rediscover the nearly lost pleasures of adventure, adventure not only in the physical sense, but also mental, spiritual, moral, aesthetic and intellectual adventure. A place for the free.

Here you may yet find the elemental freedom to breathe deep of unpoisoned air, to experiment with solitude and stillness, to gaze through a hundred miles of untrammeled atmosphere, across redrock canyons, beyond blue mesas, toward the snow-covered peaks of the most distant mountains—to make the discovery of the self in its proud sufficiency which is not isolation but an irreplaceable part of the mystery of the whole.

Come on in. The earth, like the sun, like the air, belongs to everyone—and to no one.

From "Fun and Games on the Escalante" in *Slickrock*

The Escalante is a small river which flows from the plateaus of south-central Utah into what was the Colorado River near its junction with the San Juan River. By any but desert standards it would be called a creek. Or crick. During most of the year it runs shallow, not more than a foot deep, but in the spring and late summer, swollen with snow-melt or cloudbursts, it looks more like a real river and bears a heavy load of silt and sand.

Armed with these abrasives and aided by a liberal allowance of time, the little Escalante River has carved a deep, winding and dramatic canyon through the massive and monolithic sandstone formations. Toward its deeper end, near the currently submerged channel of the Colorado, the walls of the Escalante's main canyon are more than 1,500 feet high—and sheer, vertical or overhanging, slick as the wall of your living room, with only the smallest of niches for such things as cliff swallows, canyon wrens, owls, hawks and bats.

In the flat sunlight of midday the mighty cliffs appear

buff-colored, a pale auburn, but at morning and evening when the sun's rays come slanting in at a low angle the rock takes on an amber tone, with a glow like the bead of good bourbon. At sundown the coloring deepens still more and smolders—you can feel the heat—through the twilight in all the hues of hot iron cooling off.

There is much more to the Escalante and its surrounding 500,000 acres of de facto wilderness than the central gorge. The Escalante is a system of canyons, dozens of canyons, all feeding into the river, each of them rich in marvels: intricate detail in water and stone, plants and animals, light and shade and color, solitude and stillness. Most of the tributary canyons contain seeps, springs, perennial streams. There are waterfalls and pools, and in some of the canyons great natural stone arches and bridges, such as Gregory Bridge (presently submerged by Lake Powell, but waiting), Stevens Arch, Broken Bow Arch, Hamblin Arch.

Above and beyond the canyons is the slickrock benchland, that weird world of hills, holes, humps and hollows where, they say, the wind always blows and nothing ever grows. But even here, in what looks at first sight like nothing but naked rock, there are pockets of life. In the wind-drilled potholes you will see, after a rain, the resurgence of living things: tadpoles, mosquito larvae, fairy shrimp, threadworms and water beetles. Between rains these natural waterholes go dry but the life is still there, buried under the sediment in the form of eggs, spores and seeds, and sometimes even adult, estivating toads. Dove feathers and coyote scat offer evidence that the water is known to more than insect and amphibian.

A variety of desert plants grow in the sandy basins among the knobs and pinnacles, despite the local mythology. Plants such as juniper, yucca, prickly pear, sand sage and chamiso may not be transmutable, through the stomachs of cows, into money in the bank but they are things of interest and beauty and therefore of value all the same.

Except for the sixty-mile dirt road from the town of Escalante to the dead-end point called Hole-in-the-Rock, there are no permanent roads within the Escalante area. Some older maps show a jeep trail crossing the Escalante at Harris Wash but this is seldom used. The last time I went down there, in the spring of 1970, some stockmen had strung a fence across it. Oil companies have also bulldozed a few temporary roads on the benchlands above the canyons but these are soon made impassable by erosion, although they leave scars on the land which will take a long time to heal. Except from the air, however, they are not noticeable. There are no roads of any kind down in the Escalante and its side canyons nor even any man-made trails. A few old corrals and cabins on the benches above the canyons add a pictur- esque note to the scene; they do not detract from its primitive character. The Escalante may not be a *completely untouched* wilderness—where on earth is there any such thing any more?—but it is the closest thing to it that still remains in southeast Utah.

Best of all, the Escalante country belongs to *us*. It lies entirely within the public domain, and is therefore the prop- erty not of land and cattle companies, not of oil and mining corporations, not of the Utah State Highway Department or any Utah Chamber of Commerce, but of *all* Americans. It's *our* country.

Or should be. It's supposed to be. . . .

The trail begins in Hurricane Wash. Hurricane Wash *is* the trail. The way is well trodden by the hooves of cattle, the boots of hikers. If you're out of luck you might even find the track of some clown on a motorbike going down into the canyons before you. But he won't get far: as in Buckskin Gulch and the Paria, the main canyon of the Escalante is much too rocky, rugged and quick for such contraptions. I passed a slab of sandstone on which a troop of boy scouts had petroglyphed their presence only a year before. That takes care of the argument that hiking in the Escalante is a pastime for the idle rich.

Gradually the wash deepens, becomes a little canyon. There is some plant life, not much: the canyon floor is nothing but dry sand and rock. The walls close in, forming a channel of sand and sandstone, then widen again as the canyon sinks deeper. The first signs of water appear: wet sand, alluvial mud banks, pickleweed, wire grass and clumps of willow. Cow dung and flies, of course. Deer prints and cliff rose. Dried algae on the rocks, then tiny stagnant pools with water-skippers, dragonflies and swarms of wriggling larvae.

In a deep-shaded undercurve of the wall I came to the first seep and a perceptively flowing rill of water. One could drink here, if necessary, although the stink of cattle discourages the thought. I trudged on without pausing; although hot and thirsty I had a gallon of water in my pack, untouched. Besides, I wanted to see how far I could go in tolerable comfort without a drink. In that way I'd find out how much water I'd need for the hike out, back to the car.

Hurricane Wash cuts deeper and deeper into the rock and the walls become much higher than the canyon is wide. The little pools are joined to one another now by a trickling rivulet which oozes out of the mud and sand and slides, barely moving, over the slick rock. I passed some cottonwoods growing tall and slender in this deep shadowy canyon. More thickets of willow and tamarisk, many tracks of deer, cattle, smaller beasts.

From somewhere ahead, around the next bend, I could hear the alluring sound of rushing water. I hurried on and found that the wash now joined a much bigger canyon. Here were sand beaches, groves of giant cottonwoods and a clear-flowing creek—not a stream but a creek—which issues, brisk as a bee, from a gap in the walls.

I sat down in the shade and studied my map. I'd come about five miles and had now reached Coyote Gulch, one of the major side canyons of the Escalante. The Escalante itself was still seven or eight miles away, as nearly as I could judge from the elaborately meandering course of Coyote Gulch. I rewarded myself with a good drink of water, switched from boots to tennis shoes and went on down the gulch, slogging through the water when necessary. The stream-bed itself makes the best trail, most of the way.

Rock and water, huge cliffs and delicate details. On my right I first heard, then saw, a thread of water falling from a seep in the undercut wall of the canyon. I stepped over to it, held out my cup and listened to water tinkling into tin—most musical of desert sounds. Over my head, moist and dripping with a fine spray, was another rock-wall garden of ferns and orchids, ivy and columbine. Here would be a good place to tank up, fill a canteen or two, before beginning the walk out.

I went on.

The canyon curves deeply to the left and right, sinuous as a snake, no more willing to follow a straight line than is anything else true and beautiful and good in this world. The walls curve not only laterally, with the winding of the stream-bed, but also vertically, parallelling each other like the surfaces of a ball and socket. Where a wall is deeply undercut it forms something like the inside of a half-dome. Standing inside one of these alcoves, which may be hundreds of feet high, you will not be able to see the sky at all; the light is reflected and refracted from the opposite canyon wall, creating a strange golden ambience within the chamber.

Because of the looping course of the canyon, with high walls which often shut out the sun, you can never determine with any precision what direction you're following. In fact your points of orientation are reduced to a simple pair: upstream and downstream. Which is really all you need anyway.

I came to Jacob Hamblin Arch. Weathered through the neck of a sandstone fin that juts out into a bow of the canyon, this arch will someday become a natural bridge, when the creek below completes the work of chiseling a shortcut through its own meander.

The way up through the arch looked rough and rocky; with the heavy pack on my back I preferred not to try it. Instead I followed the creek on its way around the gooseneck, passing beneath one of the largest half-domes I had ever seen. Imagine the Hollywood Bowl expanded to ten times its present size. The apex of this structure must be at least 500 feet above the stream-bed.

The last of the afternoon sunlight had long since vanished from the upper walls. I walked through lavender twilight, through the sounds of flowing water, rasping toads, swaying willows, the papery rustle of cottonwood leaves. It was time to make camp if I wanted to cook before dark, but the charm and magic of this canyon were so great I didn't want to stop. Each turn in the walls promised some new delight; exploring such a place is like exploring the personality of a new friend, a new love.

But, since I would not stop for dark, the dark stopped for me, surrounded me. On a shore of sand well away from the cattle paths I made my bed and prepared supper in the starlight. Cottonwood makes poor fuel, burns too fast and smoky; I scrambled up the talus under the cliff where I had earlier noticed scrub oak and brought back an armload of *real* wood. Over the red coals of oak I hydrated my dehydrated meat and vegetables, stirred up a quick goulash. Well seasoned with salt and pepper and blow-sand, nothing could have tasted better.

In the morning I went on down the gulch, leaving my pack behind, carrying only enough raisins and jerky for lunch. I was now below the seep-line in the overlying Navajo sandstone and the stream grew larger, fed by the many springs. I climbed around a gap in the rock that had once been a natural bridge, passed several small waterfalls, and came to a natural bridge that was still standing.

This is a young bridge, geologically speaking, about big enough to drive a school bus through, with plenty of room for enlargement. There were the mud homes of cliff swallows on the inside, and under the base of the outer buttress I saw the gray smudge of an old campfire. Some hobo might have camped here once (having wandered far from the steel trail)—I probably knew the man. Or maybe it was Everett Ruess.

I walked under the bridge, feeling the sensuous pleasure of moving through a wall of stone, wading the stream that made the opening, standing in shadow and looking back at the upstream canyon bathed in morning light, the sparkling water, the varnished slickrock walls, the fresh cool green of the cottonwoods, the pink and violet plumes of tamarisk.

From the cliffs far above I could hear the clear falling notes of a canyon wren—characteristic song in this land of stone and stillness.

What would it be like to *live* in this place? Could a man ever grow weary of such a home? Someday, I thought, I shall make the experiment, become an ancient baldheaded troglodyte with a dirty white beard tucked in my belt, be a shaman, a wizard, a witch doctor crazy with solitude, starving on locusts and lizards, feasting from time to time upon lost straggler boy scout.

Madness: of course a man would go mad from the beauty and the loneliness, both equally mysterious. But perhaps it would be—who can say?—a kind of *blessed* insanity, like the bliss of a snake in the winter sun, a buzzard on the summer air.

The canyon grows bigger, wider, wilder as it descends by jumpoff and cataract toward the Escalante. At one place a vast section of the north wall has collapsed quite recently, perhaps within the past century, and tumbled in blocks the size of boxcars to the canyon bottom. The rock-fall is clean, sharp-edged, free of all plant life, even lichens, and the floods have not yet had time enough to round off and polish the broken slabs that obstruct the creek. Here the footing is tricky, impossible for cattle and horses; I found steps chipped in the sandstone above the fall where somebody—Indian? Mormon cowboy? Ken Sleight?—had made a by-pass for his horse.

More cascades, some of them fifteen to twenty feet high. At one point the only route is down a log leaning against a shelf of stone on the canyon wall. Here the walls must be close to 1,000 feet high on either side and the sky no more than a narrow strip of blue.

Around one more bend, hearing the soft steady roar of floodwater, and I came to the master stream, the Escalante River.

The water was reddish-brown that day, about fifty feet wide, knee-deep in the main channel as I discovered when I waded in. The current strong and swift. Since the river at this point filled its bed from wall to wall I had no choice but to wade through if I wanted to go on. I headed *up* the river; at least that way I'd have a good chance to make it back to the mouth of Coyote Gulch if the river should suddenly rise.

The going was hard against the current. I could feel the sand giving way beneath my feet at every step. I went only far enough up the river to see Stevens Arch and to reach the mouth of Stevens Canyon beyond. I had hoped to explore Stevens but the day was already more than half over; we were running short of light. I walked a mile or so up Stevens Canyon—a rare, secret, lovely place it seemed— and then, most reluctantly, turned back, waded the river, and trudged the long and winding rock-and-mud sand-and-water trail up the meanders of Coyote Gulch. A second time I cooked my supper in the dark but it didn't matter. I was tired, hungry, happy.

The next day, before returning up Hurricane Wash to my car, I decided to have a look at the world that lay above and between the canyons. Upstream from the confluence of the wash and Coyote Gulch I found an egress from the canyon by scaling a rounded hummock of sandstone.

I kept climbing until I topped out on a bare ridge about halfway between Coyote Gulch and Escalante Canyon. From there I could see a great deal of the world: not only the dark gashes of the canyons below but also a stretch of the Waterpocket Fold, the snowy dome of Navajo Mountain, the Straight Cliffs of Kaiparowits, and other mesas and plateaus east of the Colorado River, some of them I suppose fifty miles away by line of sight.

Nearby was the equally interesting terrain of the slickrock boondocks—naked sandstone shaped by ages of weathering and erosion into the science-fiction landscape of fins and pinnacles, knobs, nodes and knolls, potholes and hollows. Some of the potholes contained old rain water which I sampled, along with a sampling of the bugs, beetles, dead flies, worms and smaller things, some dead, some alive, which flourished in the water. Spring flowers were blooming in the sandy basins: cactus, cliff rose, paintbrush, verbena, princess plume, purple penstemon, globemallow, scarlet penstemon, purple beeplant (also known as Cowboy's Delight) and others.

I'd neglected to mark my trail and so spent a couple of hours searching for the way back down into Coyote Gulch. All of the sandstone hills look dismayingly alike, at least when you're lost, and my first two approaches to the canyon ended at rimrock. I was rimmed up. Nor could I simply follow the rim until I hit my spoor, for it—the rim—is broken at numerous points by precipitous "hanging canyons" too wide to jump, too deep and sheer to descend into. I had to backtrack and circle, once, twice, a third time, until I chanced upon the one and only route down. If I were the John Muir I'd like to be I would have spent the night up there.

Down in the canyon I returned to my pack, filled my belly with seep water, had something to eat. Little hog-nosed bats with translucent wings flickered over my head in the evening light, making clicking sonar noises. A swarm of gnats performed their ritual molecular dance in the air before my face. A bat swept through the swarm, scooping dozens away forever. The gnats closed ranks and carried on the dance, indifferent to disaster. Should one despise their passive fatalism—or envy their nonchalance?

In dusk and desert music I walked up peaceful Hurricane Wash toward my wheels and that road which leads—to where? not back home: who can speak of home anymore? who can say he had not forsaken home?—but back to where we all are now.

JOHN McPHEE

(1931–   )

Since each of John McPhee's books differs radically from all the others, it is nearly impossible to generalize about the content of his prose. He chooses topics as diverse as oranges, an isolated Scottish island, the Pine Barrens of New Jersey, plate tectontics, the "deltoid pumpkin seed." Most of his essays first appeared in the *New Yorker*, and their breadth seems to match the eclecticism of that magazine's readership.

Despite the variousness of his subject matter, however, McPhee's approach remains relatively constant. He usually accompanies someone somewhere, reporting the trip or the trek in a nonjudgmental way. He avoids taking sides, even when controversial issues are in question, and he personally stays in the background, even when the situation is a dramatic one. Two of his best-known volumes (ones that might appropriately be included in *Words for the Wild* if more space were available) illustrate the pattern.

Encounters with the Archdruid joins three developers with McPhee and the Sierra Club's David Brower. Author and archdruid go to the North Cascades with a mining engineer from Kennecott Copper, to a Georgia sea island with the man who built Hilton Head, to Lake Powell and the Colorado River with the United States Commissioner of Reclamation. In each locale the men walk and talk, experiencing what the landscape has to offer while simultaneously debating its fate. McPhee listens, dramatizes the encounters, reports what he hears; but he never injects his personal opinions into the text. In spite of the conflicting values and occasional feistiness of his companions, he maintains a rational objectivity. It is up to the reader to decide who is right and who, if anyone, is wrong.

Coming into the Country follows a similar format, yoking McPhee with natives and nesters and politicians and preservationists in Alaska's boom towns and backcountry, but never advocating one point of view at the expense of any other. A respect for the bush pilots appears only a few pages after a reverence for grizzly bears is acknowledged, and an enjoyment of the wilderness itself is interspersed with pleasant descriptions of habitations in its midst. While the choice of subject matter in this book or in *Conversations* may suggest where his sympathies lie, nothing in either narrative directly reveals McPhee's own attitudes toward the environment.

So McPhee's essays are rather unlike those written by other *Words for the Wild* authors. His tone is low-key, his vision unromantic. His prose is relatively unencumbered with rhetorical or metaphysical analogies, and it is wholly free from polemical effusions. Nonetheless, I perceive in McPhee's words a deep concern for man's relationship with the land

and an interest in the land's delicate future, especially when he finds himself floating down the Salmon River in the far north or topping the final rise to Cloudy Pass. That view of Glacier Peak elicits a sincere, if untranscendental, response. "I said slowly, the words just involuntarily falling out, 'My God, look at that.'"

The following excerpt from *Basin and Range*, describing a drive with geologist Kenneth Deffeyes across some lonely stretch of Nevada couples a journalistic reserve with an enthusiasm McPhee simply can't hide. Even though he maintains a reporter's distance, he instinctively selects language that exposes his attitude toward what he sees. It's what I see, too, from my house on the edge of a range above a basin.

From *Basin and Range*

Basin. Fault. Range. Basin. Fault. Range. A mile of relief between basin and range. Stillwater Range. Pleasant Valley. Tobin Range. Jersey Valley. Sonoma Range. Pumpernickel Valley. Shoshone Range. Reese River Valley. Pequop Mountains. Steptoe Valley. Ondographic rhythms of the Basin and Range. We are maybe forty miles off the interstate, in the Pleasant Valley basin, looking up at the Tobin Range. At the nine-thousand-foot level, there is a stratum of cloud against the shoulders of the mountains, hanging like a ring of Saturn. The summit of Mt. Tobin stands clear, above the cloud. When we crossed the range, we came through a ranch on the ridgeline where sheep were fenced around a running brook and bales of hay were bright green. Junipers in the mountains were thickly hung with berries, and the air was unadulterated gin. This country from afar is synopsized and dismissed as "desert"—the home of the coyote and the pocket mouse, the side-blotched lizard and the vagrant shrew, the MX rocket and the pallid bat. There are minks and river otters in the Basin and Range. There are deer and antelope, porcupines and cougars, pelicans, cormorants, and common loons. There are Bonaparte's gulls and marbled godwits, American coots and Virginia rails. Pheasants. Grouse. Sandhill cranes. Ferruginous hawks and flammulated owls. Snow geese. This Nevada terrain is not corrugated, like the folded Appalachians, like a tubal air mattress, like a rippled potato chip. This is not—in that compressive manner—a ridge-and-valley situation. Each range here is like a warship standing on its own, and the Great Basin is an ocean of loose sediment with these mountain ranges standing in it as if they were members of a fleet without precedent, assembled at Guam to assault Japan. Some of the ranges are forty miles long, others a hundred, a hundred and fifty. They point generally north. The basins that separate them—ten and fifteen miles wide—will run on for fifty, a hundred, two hundred and fifty miles with lone, daisy-petalled windmills standing over sage and wild rye. Animals tend to be content with their home ranges and not to venture out across the big dry valleys. "Imagine a chipmunk hiking across one of these basins," Deffeyes remarks. "The faunas in the high ranges here are quite distinct from one to another. Animals are isolated like Darwin's finches in the Galápagos. These ranges are truly islands."

Supreme over all is silence. Discounting the cry of the occasional bird, the wailing of a pack of coyotes, silence—a great spatial silence—is pure in the Basin and Range. It is a soundless immensity with mountains in it. You stand, as we do now, and look up at a high mountain front, and turn your head and look fifty miles down the valley, and there is utter silence. It is the silence of the winter forests of the Yukon, here carried high to the ridgelines of the ranges.

318 Words for the Wild

As the physicist Freeman Dyson has written in *Disturbing the Universe*, "It is a soul-shattering silence. You hold your breath and hear absolutely nothing. No rustling of leaves in the wind, no rumbling of distant traffic, no chatter of birds or insects or children. You are alone with God in that silence. There in the white flat silence I began for the first time to feel a slight sense of shame for what we were proposing to do. Did we really intend to invade this silence with our trucks and bulldozers and after a few years leave it a radioactive junkyard?"

What Deffeyes finds pleasant here in Pleasant Valley is the aromatic sage. Deffeyes grew up all over the West, his father a pertroleum engineer, and he says without apparent irony that the smell of sagebrush is one of two odors that will unfailingly bring upon him an attack of nostalgia, the other being the scent of an oil refinery. Flash floods have caused boulders the size of human heads to come tumbling off the range. With alluvial materials of finer size, they have piled up in fans at the edge of the basin. ("The cloudburst is the dominant sculptor here.") The fans are unconsolidated. In time to come, they will pile up to such enormous thicknesses that they will sink deep and be heated and compressed to form conglomerate. Erosion, which provides the material to build the fans, is tearing down the mountains even as they rise. Mountains are not somehow created whole and subsequently worn away. They wear down as they come up, and these mountains have been rising and eroding in fairly even ratio for millions of years—rising and shedding sediment steadily through time, always the same, never the same, like row upon row of fountains. In the southern part of the province, in the Mojave, the ranges have stopped rising and are gradually wearing away. The Shadow Mountains. The Dead Mountains, Old Dad Mountains, Cowhole Mountains, Bullion, Mule, and Chocolate Mountains. They are inselberge now, buried ever deeper in their own waste. For the most part, though, the ranges are rising, and there can be no doubt of it here, hundreds of miles north of the Mojave, for we are looking at a new seismic scar that runs as far as we can see. It runs along the foot of the mountains, along the fault where the basin meets the range. From out in the valley, it looks like a long, buff-painted, essentially horizontal stripe. Up close, it is a gap in the vegetation, where plants growing side by side were suddenly separated by several metres, where, one October evening, the basin and the range—Pleasant Valley, Tobin Range—moved, all in an instant, apart. They jumped sixteen feet. The erosion rate at which the mountains were coming down was an inch a century. So in the mountains' contest with erosion they gained in one moment about twenty thousand years. These mountains do not rise like bread. They sit still for a long time and build up tension, and then suddenly jump. Passively, they are eroded for millennia, and then they jump again. They have been doing this for about eight million years. This fault, which jumped in 1915, opened like a zipper far up the valley, and, exploding into the silence, tore along the mountain base for upward of twenty miles with a sound that suggested a runaway locomotive.

"This is the sort of place where you really do not put a nuclear plant," says Deffeyes. "There was other action in the neighborhood at the same time—in the Stillwater Range, the Sonoma Range, Pumpernickel Valley. Actually, this is not a particularly spectacular scarp. The lesson is that the whole thing—the whole Basin and Range, or most of it—is alive. The earth is moving. The faults are moving. There are hot springs all over the province. There are young volcanic rocks. Fault scars everywhere. The world is splitting open and coming apart. You see a sudden break in the sage like this and it says to you that a fault is there and a fault block is coming up. This is a gorgeous, fresh, young, active fault scarp. It's growing. The range is lifting up. This Nevada topography is what you see *during* mountain building. There are no foothills. It is all too young. It is live country. This is the tectonic, active, spreading, mountain-building world. To a nongeologist, it's just ranges, ranges, ranges.''

Most mountain ranges around the world are the result of compression, of segments of the earth's crust being brought together, bent, mashed, thrust and folded, squeezed up into the sky—the Himalaya, the Appalachians, the Alps, the Urals, the Andes. The ranges of the Basin and Range came up another way. The crust—in this region between the Rockies and the Sierra—is spreading out, being stretched, being thinned, being literally pulled to pieces. The sites of Reno and Salt Lake City, on opposite sides of the province, have moved apart fifty miles. The crust of the Great Basin has broken into blocks. The blocks are not, except for simplicity's sake, analogous to dominoes. They are irregular in shape. They more truly suggest stretch marks. Which they are. They trend north-south because the direction of the stretching is east-west. The breaks, or faults, between them are not vertical but dive into the earth at roughly sixty-degree angles, and this, from the outset, affected the centers of gravity of the great blocks in a way that caused them to tilt. Classically, the high edge of one touched the low edge of another and formed a kind of trough, or basin. The high edge—sculpted, eroded, serrated by weather—turned into mountains. The detritus of the mountains rolled into the basin. The basin filled with water—at first, it was fresh blue water—and accepted layer upon layer of sediment from the mountains, accumulating weight, and thus unbalancing the block even further. Its tilt became more pronounced. In the manner of a seesaw, the high, mountain side of the block went higher and the low, basin side went lower until the block as a whole reached a state of precarious and temporary truce with God, physics, and mechanical and chemical erosion, not to mention, far below, the agitated mantle, which was running a temperature hotter than normal, and was, almost surely, controlling the action. Basin and range. Integral fault blocks: low side the basin, high side the range. For five hundred miles they nudged one another across the province of the Basin and Range. With extra faulting and whatnot, they took care of their own irregularities. Some had their high sides on the west, some on the east. The escarpment of the Wasatch Mountains—easternmost expression of this immense suite of mountains—faced west. The Sierra—the westernmost, the highest, the predominant range, with Donner Pass only halfway up it—presented its escarpment to the east. As the developing Sierra made its skyward climb—as it went on up past ten and twelve and fourteen thousand feet—it became so predominant that it cut off the incoming Pacific rain, cast a rain shadow (as the phenomenon is called) over lush, warm, Floridian and verdant Nevada. Cut it off and kept it dry.

We move on (we're in a pickup) into dusk—north up Pleasant Valley, with its single telephone line on sticks too skinny to qualify as poles. The big flanking ranges are in alpenglow. Into the cold clear sky come the ranking stars. Jackrabbits appear, and crisscross the road. We pass the darkening shapes of cattle. An eerie trail of vapor traverses the basin, sent up by a clear, hot stream. It is only a couple of feet wide, but it is running swiftly and has multiple sets of hot white rapids. In the source springs, there is a thumping sound of boiling and rage. Beside the springs are lucid green pools, rimmed with accumulated travertine, like the travertine walls of Lincoln Center, the travertine pools of Havasu Canyon, but these pools are too hot to touch. Fall in there and you are Brunswick stew. "This is a direct result of the crustal spreading," Deffeyes says. "It brings hot mantle up near the surface. There is probably a fracture here, through which the water is coming up to this row of springs. The water is rich in dissolved minerals. Hot springs like these are the source of vein-type ore deposits. It's the same story that I told you about the hydrothermal transport of gold. When rainwater gets down into hot rock, it brings up what it happens to find there—silver, tungsten, copper, gold. An ore-deposit map and a hot-springs map will look much the same. Seismic waves move slowly through hot rock. The hotter the rock, the slower the waves. Nowhere in the continental United States do seismic waves move more slowly than they do beneath the Basin and Range. So we're not woofing when we say there's hot mantle down there. We've measured the heat."

The basin-range fault blocks in a sense are floating on the mantle. In fact, the earth's crust everywhere in a sense is floating on the mantle. Add weight to the crust and it rides deeper, remove cargo and it rides higher, exactly like a vessel at a pier. Slowly disassemble the Rocky Mountains and carry the material in small fragments to the Mississippi Delta. The delta builds down. It presses ever deeper on the mantle. Its depth at the moment exceeds twenty-five thousand feet. The heat and the pressure are so great down there that the silt is turning into siltstone, the sand into sandstone, the mud into shale. For another example, the last Pleistocene ice sheet loaded two miles of ice onto Scotland, and that dunked Scotland in the mantle. After the ice melted, Scotland came up again, lifting its beaches high into the air. Isostatic adjust-

ment. Let go a block of wood that you hold underwater and
it adjusts itself to the surface isostatically. A frog sits on the
wood. It goes down. He vomits. It goes up a little. He jumps.
It adjusts. Wherever landscape is eroded away, what remains
will rise in adjustment. Older rock is lifted to view. When,
for whatever reason, crust becomes thicker, it adjusts downward. All of this—with the central image of the basin-range
fault blocks floating in the mantle—may suggest that the
mantle is molten, which it is not. The mantle is solid. Only
in certain pockets near the surface does it turn into magma
and squirt upward. The temperature of the mantle varies
widely, as would the temperature of anything that is two
thousand miles thick. Under the craton, it is described as
chilled. By surface standards, though, it is generally white
hot, everywhere around the world—white hot and solid but
magisterially viscous, permitting the crust above it to "float."
Deffeyes was in his bathtub one Saturday afternoon thinking about the viscosity of the mantle. Suddenly he stood up
and reached for a towel. "Piano wire!" he said to himself,
and he dressed quickly and went to the library to look up
a book on piano tuning and to calculate the viscosity of the
wire. Just what he guessed—10^{22} poises. Piano wire. Look
under the hood of a well-tuned Steinway and you are looking at strings that could float a small continent. They are
rigid, but ever so slowly they will sag, will slacken, will de-
form and give way, with the exact viscosity of the earth's
mantle. "And that," says Deffeyes, "is what keeps the piano
tuner in business." More miles, and there appears ahead of
us something like a Christmas tree alone in the night. It is
Winnemucca, there being no other possibility. Neon looks
good in Nevada. The tawdriness is refined out of it in so
much wide black space. We drive on and on toward the glow
of colors. It is still far away and it has not increased in size.

We pass nothing. Deffeyes says, "On these roads, it's ten to the minus five that anyone will come along." The better part of an hour later, we come to the beginnings of the casino-flashing town. The news this year is that dollar slot machines are outdrawing nickel slot machines for the first time, ever.

ANNIE DILLARD

(1945–   )

Pulitzer Prize-winning Annie Dillard is best known for her 1974 vision of a stream and a valley in Virginia's Blue Ridge country, *Pilgrim at Tinker Creek*. In that book she details precisely what can be seen when walking along the water's edge at various times of year. With a microscopic eye, she watches the mating process of the praying mantis (in mid-act, the female chews off the male's head), the dining habits of a giant water bug (after reducing its victim to juice, it sucks the innards out of the skin), the migratory death of a monarch butterfly (and its delicate scent of honeysuckle). Her world often is violent, but her scope always expands beyond apparently cruel confines to insist on some broader metaphysical design.

As Dillard explains, she discovers "the uncertainty of vision, the horror of the fixed, the dissolution of the present, the intricacy of beauty, the pressure of fecundity, the elusiveness of the free, and the flawed nature of perfection." Beyond that, she knows there is an unfathomable secret power that has made the universe not in jest but in "solemn earnest." Such a power cannot be defined, but its infinitude may be explored. The process continues in her later narratives, *Holy the Firm* and *Teaching a Stone to Talk*.

Although she prefers to be called mystical, Annie Dillard, of all our contemporaries who write about the natural world, is the most transcendental. She quotes Emerson, she quotes Thoreau. She describes Tinker Creek in language reminiscent of Walden Pond, transforming the stream's banks and riffles into metaphors for her own creative process. She makes disturbing analogies as well as exemplary ones, calling "this deciduous business," for example, "the brainchild of a deranged manic-depressive with limitless capital." Much of her imagery, though, is drawn directly from the four elements—fire, air, earth, and water. Into that milieu, she adds creatures small and minute, plus a recurrent linguistic flirtation with words that connote seeing and envisioning.

She does not concern herself with many other people. Dillard's tends to be a solitary existence, one which touches other lives on occasion but one which primarily is introspective and self-contained. She explains what she has in mind when, in her latest collection of essays, she paraphrases the Thoreauvian process of self-knowledge. "I would like to learn, or remember, how to live," she concedes. "I come to Hollins Pond not so much to learn how to live as, frankly, to forget about it. That is, I don't think I can learn from a wild animal how to live in particular—shall I suck warm blood, hold my tail high, walk with my footprints precisely over the prints of my hands?—but I might learn something of mindlessness, something of the purity of living in the physical sense and the dignity of living without bias or motive."

What we can learn from Annie Dillard is something equally

important. We can learn to look closely; we can learn to sit silently; we can learn to think deeply. We can learn to be, as she describes herself, "a sojourner seeking signs."

From "Stalking" in
Pilgrim at Tinker Creek

Learning to stalk muskrats took me several years.

I've always known there were muskrats in the creek. Sometimes when I drove late at night my headlights' beam on the water would catch the broad lines of ripples made by a swimming muskrat, a bow wave, converging across the water at the raised dark vee of its head. I would stop the car and get out: nothing. They eat corn and tomatoes from my neighbors' gardens, too, by night, so that my neighbors were always telling me that the creek was full of them. Around here, people call them "mushrats"; Thoreau called them "Musquashes." They are not of course rats at all (let alone squashes). They are more like diminutive beavers, and, like beavers, they exude a scented oil from musk glands under the base of the tail— hence the name. I had read in several respectable sources that muskrats are so wary they are almost impossible to observe. One expert who made a full-time study of large populations, mainly by examining "sign" and performing autopsies on corpses, said he often went for weeks at a time without seeing a single living muskrat.

One hot evening three years ago, I was standing more or less *in* a bush. I was stock-still, looking deep into Tinker Creek from a spot on the bank opposite the house, watching a group of bluegills stare and hang motionless near the bottom of a deep, sunlit pool. I was focused for depth. I had long since lost myself, lost the creek, the day, lost everything but still amber depth. All at once I couldn't see. And then I could: a young muskrat had appeared on top of the water, floating on its back. Its forelegs were folded langorously across its chest; the sun shone on its upturned belly. Its youthfulness and rodent grin, coupled with its ridiculous method of locomotion, which consisted of a lazy wag of the tail assisted by an occasional dabble of a webbed hind foot, made it an enchanting picture of decadence, dissipation, and summer sloth. I forgot all about the fish.

But in my surprise at having the light come on so suddenly, and at having my consciousness returned to me all at once and bearing an inverted muskrat, I must have moved and betrayed myself. The kit—for I know now it was just a young kit—righted itself so that only its head was visible above water, and swam downstream, away from me. I extricated myself from the bush and foolishly pursued it. It dove sleekly, reemerged, and glided for the opposite bank. I ran along the bankside brush, trying to keep it in sight. It kept casting an alarmed look over its shoulder at me. Once again it dove, under a floating mat of brush lodged in the bank, and disappeared. I never saw it again. (Nor have I ever, despite all the muskrats I have seen, again seen a muskrat floating on its back.) But I did not know muskrats then; I waited panting, and watched the shadowed bank. Now I know that I cannot outwait a muskrat who knows I am there. The most I can do is get "there" quietly, while it is still in its hole, so that it never knows, and wait there until it emerges. But then all I knew was that I wanted to see more muskrats.

I began to look for them day and night. Sometimes I would see ripples suddenly start beating from the creek's side, but as I crouched to watch, the ripples would die. Now I know what this means, and have learned to stand perfectly still to make out the muskrat's small, pointed face hidden under overhanging bank vegetation, watching me. That summer I haunted the bridges, I walked up creeks and down, but no muskrats ever appeared. You must just have to be there, I thought. You must have to spend the rest of your life standing in bushes. It was a once-in-a-lifetime thing, and you've had your once.

Then one night I saw another, and my life changed. After that I knew where they were in numbers, and I knew when to look. It was late dusk; I was driving home from a visit with friends. Just on the off chance I parked quietly by the creek, walked out on the narrow bridge over the shallows, and looked upstream. Someday, I had been telling myself for weeks, someday a muskrat is going to swim right through that channel in the cattails, and I am going to see it. That is precisely what happened. I looked up into the channel for a muskrat, and there it came, swimming right toward me. Knock; seek; ask. It seemed to swim with a side-to-side, sculling motion of its vertically flattened tail. It looked bigger than the upside-down muskrat, and its face more reddish. In its mouth it clasped a twig of tulip tree. One thing amazed me: it swam right down the middle of the creek. I thought it would hide in the brush along the edge; instead, it plied the waters as obviously as an aquaplane. I could just look and look.

But I was standing on the bridge, not sitting, and it saw me. It changed its course, veered towards the bank, and disappeared behind an indentation in the rushy shoreline. I felt a rush of such pure energy I thought I would not need to breathe for days.

That innocence of mine is mostly gone now, although I felt almost the same pure rush last night. I have seen many muskrats since I learned to look for them in that part of the creek. But still I seek them out in the cool of the evening, and still I hold my breath when rising ripples surge from under the creek's bank. The great hurrah about wild animals is that they exist at all, and the greater hurrah is the actual moment of seeing them. Because they have a nice dignity, and prefer to have nothing to do with me, not even as the simple objects of my vision. They show me by their very wariness what a prize it is simply to open my eyes and behold.

Muskrats are the bread and butter of the carnivorous food chain. They are like rabbits and mice: if you are big enough to eat mammals, you eat them. Hawks and owls prey on them, and foxes; so do otters. Minks are their special enemies; minks live near large muskrat populations, slinking in and out of their dens and generally hanging around like mantises outside a beehive. Muskrats are also subject to a contagious blood disease that wipes out whole colonies. Sometimes, however, their whole populations explode, just like lemmings', which are their near kin; and they either die by the hundreds or fan out across the land migrating to new creeks and ponds.

Men kill them, too. One Eskimo who hunted muskrats for a few weeks each year strictly as a sideline says that in fourteen years he killed 30,739 muskrats. The pelts sell, and the price is rising. Muskrats are the most important fur animal on the North American continent. I don't know what they bring on the Mackenzie River delta these days, but around here, fur dealers, who paid $2.90 in 1971, now pay $5.00 a pelt. They make the pelts into coats, calling the fur anything but muskrat: "Hudson seal" is typical. In the old days, after they had sold the skins, trappers would sell the meat, too, calling it "marsh rabbit." Many people still stew muskrat.

Keeping ahead of all this slaughter, a female might have

as many as five litters a year, and each litter contains six or seven or more muskrats. The nest is high and dry under the bank; only the entrance is under water, usually by several feet, to foil enemies. Here the nests are marked by simple holes in a creek's clay bank; in other parts of the country muskrats build floating, conical winter lodges which are not only watertight, but edible to muskrats.

The very young have a risky life. For one thing, even snakes and raccoons eat them. For another, their mother is easily confused, and may abandon one or two of a big litter here or there, forgetting as it were to count noses. The newborn hanging on their mother's teats may drop off if the mother has to make a sudden dive into the water, and sometimes these drown. The just-weaned young have a rough time, too, because new litters are coming along so hard and fast that they have to be weaned before they really know how to survive. And if the just-weaned young are near starving, they might eat the newborn—if they can get to them. Adult muskrats, including their own mothers, often kill them if they approach too closely. But if they live through all these hazards, they can begin a life of swimming at twilight and munching cattail roots, clover, and an occasional crayfish. Paul Errington, a usually solemn authority, writes, "The muskrat nearing the end of its first month may be thought of as an independent enterprise in a very modest way."

The wonderful thing about muskrats in my book is that they cannot see very well, and are rather dim, to boot. They are extremely wary if they know I am there, and will outwait me every time. But with a modicum of skill and minimum loss of human dignity, such as it is, I can be right "there," and the breathing fact of my presence will never penetrate their narrow skulls.

What happened last night was not only the ultimate in muskrat dimness, it was also the ultimate in human intrusion, the limit beyond which I am certain I cannot go. I would never have imagined I could go that far, actually to sit beside a feeding muskrat as beside a dinner partner at a crowded table.

What happened was this. Just in the past week I have been frequenting a different place, one of the creek's nameless feeder streams. It is mostly a shallow trickle joining several pools up to three feet deep. Over one of these pools is a tiny pedestrian bridge known locally, if at all, as the troll bridge. I was sitting on the troll bridge about an hour before sunset, looking upstream about eight feet to my right where I know the muskrats have a den. I had just lighted a cigarette when a pulse of ripples appeared at the mouth of the den, and a muskrat emerged. He swam straight toward me and headed under the bridge.

Now the moment a muskrat's eyes disappear from view under a bridge, I go into action. I have about five seconds to switch myself around so that I will be able to see him very well when he emerges on the other side of the bridge. I can easily hang my head over the other side of the bridge, so that when he appears from under me, I will be able to count his eyelashes if I want. The trouble with this maneuver is that, once his beady eyes appear again on the other side, I am stuck. If I move again, the show is over for the evening. I have to remain in whatever insane position I happen to be caught, for as long as I am in his sight, so that I stiffen all my muscles, bruise my ankles on the concrete, and burn my fingers on the cigarette. And if the muskrat goes out on a bank to feed, there I am with my face hanging a foot over the water unable to see anything but crayfish. So I have learned to take it easy on these five-second flings.

When the muskrat went under the bridge, I moved so I could face downstream comfortably. He reappeared, and I had a good look at him. He was eight inches long in the body, and another six in the tail. Muskrat tails are black and scaled, flattened not horizontally, like beavers' tails, but vertically, like a belt stood on edge. In the winter, muskrats' tails sometimes freeze solid, and the animals chew off the frozen parts up to about an inch of the body. They must swim entirely with their hind feet, and have a terrible time steering. This one used his tail as a rudder and only occasionally as a propeller; mostly he swam with a pedaling motion of his hind feet, held very straight and moving down and around, "toeing down" like a bicycle racer. The soles of his hind feet were strangely pale; his toenails were pointed in long cones. He kept his forelegs still, tucked up to his chest.

The muskrat clambered out on the bank across the stream from me, and began feeding. He chomped down on a ten-inch weed, pushing it into his mouth steadily with both forepaws as a carpenter feeds a saw. I could hear his chewing; it sounded like somebody eating celery sticks. Then he slid back into the water with the weed still in his mouth, crossed under the bridge, and, instead of returning to his den, rose erect on a submerged rock and calmly polished off the rest of the weed. He was about four feet away from me. Immediately he swam under the bridge again, hauled himself out on the bank, and unerringly found the same spot on the grass, where he devoured the weed's stump.

All this time I was not only doing a elaborate about-face every time his eyes disappeared under the bridge, but I was also smoking a cigarette. He never noticed that the configuration of the bridge metamorphosed utterly every time he went under it. Many animals are the same way: they can't see a thing unless it's moving. Similarly, every time he turned his head away, I was free to smoke the cigarette, although of course I never knew when he would suddenly turn again and leave me caught in some wretched position. The galling thing was, he was downwind of me and my cigarette: was I really going through all this for a creature without any sense whatsoever?

After the weed stump was gone, the muskrat began ranging over the grass with a nervous motion, chewing off mouthfuls of grass and clover near the base. Soon he had gathered a huge, bushy mouthful; he pushed into the water, crossed under the bridge, swam towards his den, and dove.

When he launched himself again shortly, having apparently cached the grass, he repeated the same routine in a businesslike fashion, and returned with another shock of grass.

Out he came again. I lost him for a minute when he went under the bridge; he did not come out where I expected him. Suddenly to my utter disbelief he appeared on the bank next to me. The troll bridge itself is on a level with the low bank; there I was, and there he was, at my side. I could have touched him with the palm of my hand without straightening my elbow. He was ready to hand.

Foraging beside me he walked very humped up, maybe to save heat loss through evaporation. Generally, whenever he was out of water he assumed the shape of a shmoo; his shoulders were as slender as a kitten's. He used his forepaws to part clumps of grass extremely tidily; I could see the flex in his narrow wrists. He gathered mouthfuls of grass and clover less by actually gnawing than by biting hard near the ground, locking his neck muscles, and pushing up jerkily with his forelegs.

His jaw was underslung, his black eyes close set and

glistening, his small ears pointed and furred. I will have to try and see if he can cock them. I could see the water-slicked long hairs of his coat, which gathered in rich brown strands that emphasized the smooth contours of his body, and which parted to reveal the paler, softer hair like rabbit fur underneath. Despite his closeness, I never saw his teeth or belly.

After several minutes of rummaging about in the grass at my side, he eased into the water under the bridge and paddled to his den with the jawful of grass held high, and that was the last I saw of him.

In the forty minutes I watched him, he never saw me, smelled me, or heard me at all. When he was in full view of course I never moved except to breathe. My eyes would move, too, following his, but he never noticed. I even swallowed a couple of times: nothing. The swallowing thing interested me because I had read that, when you are trying to hand-tame wild birds, if you inadvertently swallow, you ruin everything. The bird, according to this theory, thinks you are swallowing in anticipation, and off it goes. The muskrat never twitched. Only once, when he was feeding from the opposite bank about eight feet away from me, did he suddenly rise upright, all alert—and then he immediately resumed foraging. But he never knew I was there.

I never knew I was there, either. For that forty minutes last night I was as purely sensitive and mute as a photographic plate; I received impressions, but I did not print out captions. My own self-awareness had disappeared; it seems now almost as though, had I been wired with electrodes, my EEG would have been flat. I have done this sort of thing so often that I have lost self-consciousness about moving slowly and halting suddenly; it is second nature to me now. And I have often noticed that even a few minutes of this self-forgetfulness is tremendously invigorating. I wonder if we do not waste most of our energy just by spending every waking minute saying hello to ourselves. Martin Buber quotes an old Hasid master who said, "When you walk across the fields with your mind pure and holy, then from all the stones, and all growing things, and all animals, the sparks of their soul come out and cling to you, and then they are purified and become a holy fire in you." This is one way of describing the energy that comes, using the specialized Kabbalistic vocabulary of Hasidism.

I have tried to show muskrats to other people, but it rarely works. No matter how quiet we are, the muskrats stay hidden. Maybe they sense the tense hum of consciousness, the buzz from two human beings who in the silence cannot help but be aware of each other, and so of themselves. Then too, the other people invariably suffer from a self-consciousness that prevents their stalking well. It used to bother me, too: I just could not bear to lose so much dignity that I would completely alter my whole way of being for a muskrat. So I would move or look around or scratch my nose, and no muskrats would show, leaving me alone with my dignity for days on end, until I decided that it was worth my while to learn—from the muskrats themselves—how to stalk.

The old, classic rule for stalking is, "Stop often 'n' set frequent." The rule cannot be improved upon, but muskrats will permit a little more. If a muskrat's eyes are out of sight, I can practically do a buck-and-wing on his tail, and he'll never notice. A few days ago I approached a muskrat feeding on a bank by the troll bridge simply by taking as many gliding steps towards him as possible while his head was turned. I spread my weight as evenly as I could, so that he wouldn't feel my coming through the ground, and so that no matter when I became visible to him, I could pause motionless until he turned away again without having to balance too awkwardly on one leg.

When I got within ten feet of him, I was sure he would flee, but he continued to browse nearsightedly among the mown clovers and grass. Since I had seen just about everything I was ever going to see, I continued approaching just to see when he would break. To my utter bafflement, he never broke. I broke first. When one of my feet was six inches from his back, I refused to press on. He could see me perfectly well, of course, but I was stock-still except when he lowered his head. There was nothing left to do but kick him. Finally he returned to the water, dove, and vanished. I do not know to this day if he would have permitted me to keep on walking right up his back.

It is not always so easy. Other times I have learned that the only way to approach a feeding muskrat for a good look is to commit myself to a procedure so ridiculous that only a total unself-consciousness will permit me to live with myself. I have to ditch my hat, line up behind a low boulder, and lay on my belly to inch snake-fashion across twenty feet of bare field until I am behind the boulder itself and able to hazard a slow peek around it. If my head moves from around the boulder when the muskrat's head happens to be turned, then all is well. I can be fixed into position and still by the time he looks around. But if he sees me move my head, then he dives into the water, and the whole belly-crawl routine was in vain. There is no way to tell ahead of time; I just have to chance it and see.

I have read that in the unlikely event that you are caught in a stare-down with a grizzly bear, the best thing to do is talk to him softly and pleasantly. Your voice is supposed to have a soothing effect. I have not yet had occasion to test this on grizzly bears, but I can attest that it does not work on muskrats. It scares them witless. I have tried time and again. Once I watched a muskrat feeding on a bank ten feet away from me; after I had looked my fill I had nothing to lose, so I offered a convivial greeting. Boom. The terrified muskrat flipped a hundred and eighty degrees in the air, nose-dived into the grass at this feet, and disappeared. The earth swallowed him; his tail shot straight up in the air and then vanished into the ground without a sound. Muskrats make several emergency escape holes along a bank for just this very purpose, and they don't like to feed too far away from them. The entire event was most impressive, and illustrates the relative power in nature of the word and the sneak.

Stalking is a pure form of skill, like pitching or playing chess. Rarely is luck involved. I do it right or I do it wrong; the muskrat will tell me, and that right early. Even more than baseball, stalking is a game played in the actual present. At every second, the muskrat comes, or stays, or goes, depending on my skill.

Can I stay still? How still? It is astonishing how many people cannot, or will not, hold still. I could not, or would not, hold still for thirty minutes inside, but at the creek I slow down, center down, empty. I am not excited; my breathing is slow and regular. In my brain I am not saying, Muskrat! Muskrat! There! I am saying nothing. If I must hold a position, I do not "freeze." If I freeze, locking my muscles, I will tire and break. Instead of going rigid, I go calm. I center down wherever I am; I find a balance and repose. I retreat—not inside myself, but outside myself, so that I am a tissue of senses. Whatever I see is plenty, abundance. I am the skin of water the wind plays over; I am petal, feather, stone.

BARRY HOLSTUN LOPEZ
(1945–   )

I know it is paradoxical to conclude a nonfiction collection
with two fictional excerpts, but in the case of Barry
Holstun Lopez's prose, it is appropriate. Three of his books—
Desert Notes, River Notes, and *Winter Count*—delicately
bridge that almost undefinable borderland between the wilderness worlds of what is real and what is imagined. An
uninitiated reader can hardly tell the difference, although
anyone can perceive the environmental communion in everything he writes.

Lopez's fictional narratives describe abstract encounters
with the more tangible realities of the land. In their pages,
the reader shares shorelines and riverbeds, hawks and herons,

desert dust, human eccentricities, and a gathering of skies. What is most striking about each of these encounters is the intense intimacy with the earth itself. The reader not only sees its riches, but feels and smells and touches them as well. "The wind had a quality of wild refinement about it," one discovers in the upper Sonoran country near Tucson, "like horses turning around suddenly in the air by your ear." Far away, a Caribbean noon is "fired with a white belligerence" and "shells draw July heat from the languid air." Back in the desert, "The last thing you notice will be the stones, small bits of volcanic ash, black glass, blue tourmaline, sapphires, narrow slabs of grey feldspar, rose quartz, sheets of mica and blood agate . . . the last things to give up the light."

Ostensibly Lopez's nonfiction is quite different. *Of Wolves and Men* examines the historical and psychological range of man's actual and imagined meetings with *Canis lupus*. *Arctic Dreams* joins the writer with Eskimos, marine biologists, oil men, sea men, and seal hunters, with history, with geography, and with the landscape of the Arctic Circle. In both books some chapters end in mystical vagaries, but more often they close with a perceptive sense of man's relationship to his environment and with an appreciation for what man can learn from that experience. Like the fiction, then, the nonfiction descriptions continue emphasizing that crucial ingredient of intimacy with the natural world.

Words for the Wild could have ended conventionally enough, with a passage or two from either of Lopez's nonfiction works. Instead, I decided to stretch the borders a little, to track ever so briefly into a different imaginative landscape. "The Search for the Heron" and "Perimeter" belong in that other place, wherever it is. But I don't believe it's very far away from Oregon and Arizona after all.

"The Search for the Heron" in *River Notes*

I see you on the far side of the river, standing at the edge of familiar shadows, before a terrified chorus of young alders on the bank. I do not think you know it is raining. You are oblivious to the *thuck* of drops rolling off the tube of your neck and the slope of your back. (Above, in the sweepy cedars, drops pool at the tips of leather needles, break away, are sheered by the breeze and, *thuck*, hit the hollow-boned, crimson-colored shoulders of the bird and fall swooning into the river.)

Perhaps you know it is raining. The intensity of your stare is then not oblivion, only an effort to spot between the rain splashes in the river (past your feet, so well-known, there beneath the hammered surface like twigs in the pebbles) the movement of trout.

I know: your way is to be inscrutable. When pressed you leave. This is no more unexpected or mysterious than that you give birth to shadows. Or silence. I watch from a distance. With respect. I think of standing beside you when you have died of your own brooding over the water—as shaken as I would be at the collapse of a cathedral, wincing deep inside as at the screech of an overloaded cart.

You carry attribution well, refusing to speak. With your warrior's feathers downsloped at the back of your head, those white sheaves formed like a shield overlaying your breast, your gray-blue cast, the dark tail feathers—do you wear wolves' tails about your ankles and dance in clearings in the woods when your blood is running? I wonder where you have fought warrior. Where!

You retreat beneath your cowl, spread wings, rise, drift upriver as silent as winter trees.

I follow you. You have caught me with your reticence. I will listen to whatever they say about you, what anyone who has seen you wishes to offer—and I will return to call across the river to you, to confirm or deny. If you will not speak I will have to consider making you up.

Your sigh, I am told, is like the sound of rain driven against tower bells. You smell like wild ginger. When you lift your foot from the river, water doesn't run off it to spoil the transparent surface of the shallows. The water hesitates to offend you. You stare down with that great yellow eye, I am told, like some prehistoric rattlesnake: that dangerous, that blinding in your strike, that hate-ridden. But (someone else has insisted) you really do smell like wild ginger, and snakes smell like cucumber. A false lead.

Cottonwoods along the river, stained with your white excrement, are young enough to volunteer complaint about you. They have grown so fast and so high with such little effort that they can understand neither failure nor triumph. So they will say anything they think might be to their advantage. I, after a somewhat more difficult life, am aware that they will lie, and that lies serve in their way.

(It was one of these who told me you were without mercy and snakelike.) One of them said something about your fishy breath—vulgar talk, I know. But I heard it out. It is, after all, in their branches where you have dreamed at night, as immobile as a piece of lumber left in their limbs, and considered your interior life. This idea attracts me. I know: this is not something to inquire into with impunity, but I did not start out on this to please you. And in spite of my impatience I am respectful.

One dream alone reveals your grief. The trees said you dreamed most often of the wind. You dreamed that you lived somewhere with the wind, with the wind rippling your feathers; and that children were born of this, that they are the movement of water in all the rivers. You wade, it is suggested, among your children, staring hard, pecking in that lightning way your life from the water that is your child; and sleeping in trees that do not hold you sacred.

I know why you appear so fierce and self-contained. I can imagine fear in the form of a frog in your beak screaming and you, undisturbed, cool. When you finally speak up, feigning ignorance with me won't do; enigmatic locutions, distracting stories of the origin of the universe—these will not do. I expect the wisdom of the desert out of you.

The cottonwoods also told me of a dance, that you dreamed of a dance: more than a hundred great blue herons riveted by the light of dawn, standing with wind-riffled feathers on broad slabs of speckled gray granite, river-washed bedrock, in that sharp, etching backlight, their sleek bills glinting, beginning to lift their feet from the thin sheet of water and to put them back down. The sound of the rhythmic splash, the delicate *kersplash* of hundreds of feet, came up in the sound of the river and so at first was lost; but the shards of water, caught blinding in the cutting light (now the voices, rising, a keening) began to form a mist in which appeared rainbows against the white soft breasts; and where drops of water dolloped like beads of mercury on the blue-gray feathers, small rainbows of light here, and in the eyes (as the voices, louder, gathering on one, high, trembling note) rainbows—the birds cradled in light shattered in rainbows everywhere, and with your great blue wings fanning that brilliant mist, open, utterly vulnerable and stunning, you urged them to begin to revolve in the light, stretching their wings, and you lay back your head and closed the steely eyes and from deep within your belly came the roar of a cataract, like the howling of wolves—that long moment of your mournful voice. The birds quieted, their voices quieted. The water quieted, it quieted, until there was only your quivering voice, the sound of the birth of rivers, tapering finally to silence, to the sound of dawn, the birds standing there full of grace. One or two feathers floating on the water.

I understand it is insensitive to inquire further, but you see now your silence becomes even more haunting.

I believe we will dance together someday. Before then will I have to have been a trout, bear scars from your stabbing misses and so have some deeper knowledge? Then will we dance? I cannot believe it is so far between knowing what must be done and doing it.

The cottonwoods, these too-young trees, said once, long ago, you had a premonition in a nightmare. An enormous owl arrived while you slept and took your daughter away, pinioned in his gray fists. You woke, bolt upright, in the middle of the night to find her there, undisturbed beside you. You aired your feathers, glared into the moon-stilled space over the water and went uneasily back to sleep. In the morning—your first glance—the limb was empty. You were young, you had also lost a wife, and you went down to the river and tore out your feathers and wept. The soundlessness of it was what you could not get over.

The cottonwoods said there was more, but I put my hand, tired, on edge at the sound of my own voice asking questions. I went into the trees, wishing to cry, I thought, for what had been lost, feeling how little I knew, how anxious I was, how young.

The big maples, where you have slept since then—I resolved to ask them about your dreams. No; they refused. I climbed up in their limbs, imploring. They were silent. I was angered and made a fool of myself beating on the trunks with my fists screaming, "Tell me about the bird! It is only a bird!"

Learning your dreams unnerved me. What unholy trespass I had made.

When I regained my composure I apologized, touching the maple trunks gently with my fingers. As I departed a wind moved the leaves of a low branch against my face and I was embarrassed, for I was waiting for some sign of understanding. I walked on, alert now to the wind showing here and there in the grass. The wind suddenly spoke of you as of a father. The thoughts were incomplete, hinting at something incomprehensible, ungraspable, but I learned this: you are able to stand in the river in such a way that the wind makes no sound against you. You arrange yourself so that you cast no shadow and you stop breathing for half an hour. The only sound is the faint movement of your blood. You are quiet enough to hear fish swimming toward you.

When I asked, discretely, whether long ago you might have fought someone, some enemy whose name I might recognize, the wind was suddenly no longer there. From such strength as is in you I suspect an enemy. I have inquired of the stones at the bottom of the river; I have inquired of your other enemy, the pine marten; I have waded silently with your relatives, the bitterns, alert for any remarks, all to no avail.

I have been crippled by my age, by what I have known, as well as by my youth, by what I have yet to learn, in all these inquiries. It has taken me years, which might have been spent (by someone else) seeking something greater, in some other place. I have sought only you. Enough. I wish to know you, and you will not speak. . . .

· · ·

It is not easy to tell the rest, but I know you have heard it from others. Now I wish you to hear it from me. I took bits of bone from fish you had eaten and pierced my fingers, letting the blood trail away in the current. I slept on what feathers of yours I could find. From a tree felled in a storm I took your nest, climbed with it to a clearing above the river where there was a good view, as much sky as I could comprehend. Bear grass, pentstemon, blue gilia, wild strawberries, Indian paintbrush growing there. Each night for four nights I made a small fire with sticks from the old nest and looked out toward the edge of the shadows it threw. On the last night I had a great dream. You were standing on a desert plain. You were painted blue and you wore a necklace of white salmon vertebrae. Your eyes huge, red. Before you on the dry, gray earth a snake coiled, slowly weaving the air with his head. You spoke about the beginning of the world, that there was going to be no fear in the world, that everything that was afraid would live poorly.

The snake said coldly, weaving, yes, there would be fear, that fear would make everything strong, and lashed out, opening a wound in your shoulder. As fast, you pinned his head to the ground and said—the calmness in your voice— fear might come, and it could make people strong, but it would be worth nothing without compassion. And you released the snake.

I awoke sprawled in bear grass. It was darker than I could ever remember a night being. I felt the spot on the planet where I lay, turned away from the sun. My legs ached. I knew how old I was lying there on the top of the mountain, a fist of cold air against my breast as some animal, a mouse perhaps, moved suddenly under my back.

An unpronounceable forgiveness swept over me. I knew

how much had to be given away, how little could ever be asked. The sound of geese overhead in the darkness just then, and all that it meant, was enough.

I leap into the jade color of the winter river. I fight the current to reach the rocks, climb up on them and listen for the sound of your voice. I stand dripping, shivering in my white nakedness, in the thin dawn light. Waiting. Silent. You begin to appear at a downriver bend.

"Perimeter" in *Desert Notes*

I.

In the west, in the blue mountains, there are creeks of grey water. They angle out of the canyons, come across the brown scratched earth to the edge of the desert and run into nothing. When these creeks are running they make a terrific noise.

No one to my knowledge has ever counted the number, but I think there are more than twenty; it is difficult to be precise. For example, some of the creeks have been given names that, over the years, have had to be given up because a creek has run three or four times and then the channel has been abandoned.

You can easily find the old beds, where the dust has been washed out to reveal a level of rock rubble—cinnabar laced with mercury, fool's gold, clear quartz powder, and fire opal; but it is another thing to find one of the creeks, even when they are full. I have had some success by going at night and listening for the noise.

There is some vegetation in this area; it does not seem to depend on water. The rattlesnakes live here along with the rabbits. When there is any thunder it is coming from this direction. During the day the wind is here. The smells include the hellebore, vallo weed and punchen; each plant puts out its own smell and together they make a sort of pillow that floats a few feet off the ground where they are not as likely to be torn up by the wind.

II.

To the north the blue mountains go white and the creeks become more dependable though there are fewer of them. There is a sort of swamp here at the edge of the desert where the creeks pool and where grasses and sedges grow and the water takes a considerable time to evaporate and seep into the earth. There are some ducks here, but I do not know where they come from or where they go when the swamp dries up in the summer. I have never seen them flying. They are always hiding, slipping away; you will see their tail feathers disappearing in the screens of wire grass. They never quack.

There are four cottonwood trees here and two black locusts. The cottonwoods smell of balsam, send out seeds airborne in a mesh of exceedingly fine white hair, and produce a glue which the bees use to cement their honeycombs. Only one of the cottonwoods, the oldest one, is a female. The leaf stem meets the leaf at right angles and this allows the leaves to twitter and flash in the slightest breeze. The underside of the leaf is a silver green. I enjoy watching this windflash of leaves in strong moonlight.

The black locusts are smaller, younger trees and grow off by themselves a little. They were planted by immigrants and bear sweet smelling pea-like flowers with short, rose-like thorns at the leaf nodes. There are a few chokecherry bushes and also a juniper tree. You can get out of the sun here at noon and sleep. The wind runs down the sides of the cottonwoods like water and cools you.

An old tawny long-haired dog lives here. Sometimes you will see him, walking along and always leaning to one side. There is also part of a cabin made with finished lumber lying on its back; the dark brown boards are dotted with red and yellow lichen and dry as sun-baked, long forgotten shoes.

III.

To the east the white mountains drop off and there is a flat place on the horizon and then the red mountains start. There is almost nothing growing in these mountains, just a little sagebrush. At the base, where they come to the desert, there are dunes, white like gypsum.

Inside the mountains are old creeks that run in circles over the floors of low-ceilinged caves. The fish in these waters are white and translucent; you can see a pink haze of organs beneath the skin. Where there should be eyes there are grey bulges that do not move. On the walls are white spiders like tight buttons of surgical cotton suspended on long hairy legs. There are white beetles, too, scurrying through the hills of black bat dung.

I have always been suspicious of these caves because the walls crumble easily under your fingertips; there is no moisture in the air and it smells like balloons. The water smells like oranges but has no taste. Nothing you do here makes any sound.

You have to squeeze through these red mountains to get around them; you can't walk over them. You have to wedge yourself in somewhere at the base and go in. There is always a moment of panic before you slip in when you are stuck. Your eyes are pinched shut and the heels of your shoes wedge and make you feel foolish.

At night the wind lies in a trough at the base of the red mountains, sprawled asleep over the white sand dunes like a caterpillar. The edge of the desert is most indistinct in this place where the white sand and the alkaline dust blow back and forth in eddies of the wind's breath while it sleeps.

IV.

In the south the red mountains fall away and yellow mountains rise up, full of silver and turquoise rock. There are plenty of rabbits here, a little rain in the middle of the summer, fine clouds tethered on the highest peaks. If you are out in the middle of the desert, this is the way you always end up facing.

In the south twelve buckskin horses are living along the edge of the yellow mountains. The creeks here are weak; the horses have to go off somewhere for water but they always come back. There is a little grass but the horses do not seem to eat it. They seem to be waiting, or finished. Ten miles away you can hear the clack of their hooves against the rocks. In the afternoon they are motionless, with their heads staring down at the ground, at the little stones.

At night they go into the canyons to sleep standing up.

From the middle of the desert even on a dark night you can look out at the mountains and perceive the differences in direction. From the middle of the desert you can see everything well, even in the black dark of a new moon. You know where everything is coming from.

Afterword

Whenever I've written about a Western writer, I've tried to follow his or her trail. Zane Grey led me along the Mogollon Rim for miles, Edward Abbey drew me to Organ Pipe and the Superstitions and the Sonoran desert and a lot of other Southwest country, a cluster of pioneer women taught me about Tonopah, Nevada, and the list goes on. I think a reader knows Western writers better after tracking them awhile, and I think the same holds true for nature writers too. To really hear them, each of us ought to walk with them.

Obviously, though, trailing twenty-three authors across a continent in a single year (while putting this book together and holding down a full-time job) would be impossible. So I had to find another way to share the worlds of the writers in *Words for the Wild*.

My answer was simple—two week-long backpacking trips, one to the desert, another to the mountains. Along the way I would follow my own path, but I also would try to see the land as others did. Birds I would view through Audubon's eyes, bugs through Annie Dillard's. Desert plants I'd see as Joseph Wood Krutch saw them, the Sierras in the light of Muir. Even a drive to the trailhead would be part of the experience, for I couldn't cross Nevada's sagebrush expanses in any direction without thinking of Fremont's slow explorations back and forth across the West.

The first venture took me to the nearest available red rock. Not only is southern Utah just a day's drive from Reno, but its high canyon country yields more suitable June temperatures than lower desert terrain. I found a spot on the map I'd never seen, and headed east. I guess I'm still a purist at heart. Since we met only one other hiker in eight days, I hesitate to say exactly where we went.

By contrast, the second trip passed through Tent City. Because the Hoover Wilderness provides relatively easy access to the eastern Sierras and to a corner of Yosemite Park, and because it contains a myriad of trout-filled lakes, its trails are immensely popular. Californians and non-Californians alike camp side by side. A little cross-country travel, though, coupled with a little extra effort, took us well away from the hoards. In keeping with my philosophy of wilderness, we never spent a night in sight of another human being.

I like to think I always have my priorities straight. Before we started along the Utah trail, we drank the last two beers in the truck because otherwise they might spoil and because Edward Abbey would approve. Before we trudged into the Sierras, we did the same.

The Utah way led along a sandy creek bed and down a ridge to a stream that ran red with particled silt. That stream became our guide, as we splashed back and forth three or four dozen times a day up its rocky gorge and down again. Calf-deep and about fifteen feet wide, it felt deliciously cool. The side canyons were special treats, some steep-walled and forbidding, others sunny and flower-filled, still others squishy with quicksand and stagnant pools. Red rock was everywhere, but so were cottonwoods, oak, red blossoms, pink cactus, and creatures enjoying the shade.

Equally luxuriant were the mountain meadows a month later, as July flowers literally crowded the Sierra Nevada hillsides. I couldn't begin to count the kinds or even to catalogue the colors, but I know a botanist would have been delighted. The trip reversed a route I'd followed twelve years before, with conventionally beautiful mountain vistas and an excess of stream crossings, willow tangles, rock slides, snow patches, lake shores, and granite peaks. Not so very different from a hundred other jaunts in California's high country, it nontheless was fun.

As I think about the two hikes now, in retrospect, I find my imagination stretched in two quite different directions. The canyon drew my eyes to what was near at hand. More intimate—perhaps because red walls, standing high on either side, block out a longer view—it was a place to examine pale golden butterflies, delicate seeps, hanging moss, the mottled colors of a baby rattler. This is not to say that I wasn't impressed by the big picture, for one side canyon led to an arch as high as I've ever seen and another to a waterfall as lovely as I could imagine. but on the whole I recall details rather than drama, specifics rather than spectacle.

The same is not true of my week in the Sierras. There a hiker crosses ten-thousand-foot passes and stares out over a landscape punctuated by peaks and clouds. One looks at one's feet only to keep from stumbling, as shapes and shades change on the horizon. John Muir coined a perfectly characteristic phrase, saying of the Sierras, "after ten years of wandering and wondering in the heart of it, rejoicing in its glorious floods of light, the white beams of the morning streaming through the passes, the noonday radiance on the crystal rocks, the flush of the alpenglow, and the irised spray of countless waterfalls, it still seems above all others the Range of Light." I agree.

I woke with a start in the Hoover Wilderness, the smell of smoke sharp in my nostrils. My watch told me it was nearly 5:30, but daylight was barely visible and a pall completely blocked my view. Since I know a modern forest fire brings an armada of planes and helicopters and since I could hear nothing but the riffle of a tiny stream, I knew we were in no danger. Nonetheless, the dim light cast an eerie shroud everywhere (even at noon, we couldn't see more than a couple of hundred feet in any direction), and we were conscious of filtered shadows all day long. Several uneasy parties left the area. We did the opposite, heading west into the smoke and the subtleties of light and dark, the ragged edges of just-glimpsed peaks, the blinking ray of sun that appeared and then was gone.

Friday's wind brought Saturday's fresh air, along with Saturday's storm. This time a light patter of rain on tent woke me. A downpour might soak through eventually, but this shower appeared short-lived. To my left Virginia Peak glowed orange in the morning sunrise while elsewhere, against the horizon, puffy clouds reflected the same amber tint. The black cloud directly overhead swept west, then east again, grew darkly ominous, then faded into a watery blue. For almost an hour the sky pulsed with shades of light, as John Muir's very words came true. I've read *The Mountains of California* perhaps a dozen times; I've never understood it as well as I did that morning while I watched the sunrise through the rain.

I think I understand Edward Abbey's writing better, too, every time I go into red-rock country. A description like my favorite one in *Desert Solitaire*—"great curving cliffs with their tapestries of water stains, the golden alcoves, the hanging gardens, the seeps, the springs where no man will ever drink, the royal arches in high relief and the amphitheatres shaped like seashells. A sculptured landscape mostly bare of vegetation—earth in the nude"—means more when I, myself, thread my way beneath a shadowed canyon wall. One Utah side canyon, called Beartrap, brought Abbey's words freshly to mind.

It swung sharply east from our mainstream route, a deep cut so narrow that the sky appeared a sliver overhead. An inch or two of water lapped from side to side—"No place to be caught in a flash flood," I remarked, craning my head in anticipation of nonexistent thunderheads. Obviously the creek ran deeper than a few inches a good many times each year. Dark caves scalloped the cliffs both high and low, polished boulders lay helter skelter in the way, clusters of ferns grew rampant. But even the ferns couldn't disguise the nudity of Beartrap Canyon, a stark cavern slashing a third of a mile into flesh-colored rock. "No place to escape," I kept my thoughts to myself while I eyed the slick steepness and listened to a growing undertone of sound.

Then I was reminded not so much of Abbey's words, but of John Wesley Powell's. "Down in these grand, gloomy depths we glide, ever listening, for the mad waters keep up their roar; . . . so we listen for falls and watch for rocks, stopping now and then in the bay of a recess to admire the gigantic scenery." A pool ten feet deep filled the dead end of Beartrap Canyon, a waterfall thirty feet high filled the silhouetting pool. It wasn't mysterious or frightening after all, this incredibly picturesque surprise, yet it was awesome. I could close my eyes and listen to the sullen crash of the falls; I could open them and see a royal amphitheater carved in high relief. In short, I could listen with Powell's ears, pretend to write with Abbey's pen.

Now, at home, I can read the words of either man and see not only the canyons of the Colorado but Beartrap Canyon, too. Their *Words for the Wild* mean more to me than they did three months ago, their voices speak more directly.

Other voices speak more directly also. I had selected most of the excerpts in *Words for the Wild* before setting out on my summer adventures, so I had my writers' visions well in mind. I intended to heed their cautions, to honestly attempt to see the wilderness from their points of view. This meant that I had to look at some new things in some startlingly new ways. After reading Joseph Wood Krutch's essays about the desert and then studying Annie Dillard's depictions of her creek, I was more than ready to view the wilderness kingdom with an open eye, to lie quietly, to look and listen, to watch the creatures lead their daily lives.

Every night at sundown, the Utah chorus—a cacophony of desert frog noise—began. Incredible tenors and bass emitted from voice boxes no bigger than thimbles. One evening I watched for an hour, as one lonely soul blasted the still air with an anthem of praise. The next day I took my lunch break alongside a snoozing rattlesnake—two and a half feet long, ten buttons proud. He was digesting a meal, gently burping a bulge down the length of his body. The state of inactivity suited me fine. I settled myself nearby, then tried to guess what animal had let itself get caught and how. When a second rattler prowled into view, I realized that, compared to the reality of reptile hunting, my imagination was feeble. Head high, tongue darting, it slid noiselessly through fallen oak leaves and disappeared. So did I.

Then, on Saturday morning, Darwin's world came closer still. We stepped onto a dusty battlefield just as the war had been decided. A striped whipsnake, clasping a flailing lizard in its mouth, wriggled victorious. We watched, then, as the snake delivered the final indignity. Carefully turning the unhappy victim lengthwise, the conqueror unhinged its jaw, gulped twice, and swallowed the lizard whole. We watched the little arms thrash, saw the lizard's body elongate to match the snake's shape, felt a sympathetic twinge when headfirst it disappeared.

On the spot I decided I should have majored in biology. Now I could understand long hours spent beside Tinker Creek waiting for the swift appearance of a muskrat's head or hoping to spy a water bug sucking his dinner meal. I could feel the clammy wrench of life and death enacted, the uneasy juxtaposition of pleasure and pain. Nothing in the Sierras matched the experience. A mother ptarmigan scolding her young was fun to watch—and I must admit I watched more closely than in my pre-Dillard days—but the interlude was benign. Four fluff balls skidding down a snowbank are hardly comparable to a striped whipsnake triumphantly lashing its tail.

As a matter of fact, I found the geographical and geological formations in my overpopulated part of the Sierras more fascinating than the few animals scattered here and there. Several *Words for the Wild* authors—John Muir, Clarence King, Joseph LeConte—first viewed these mountains in terms of available minerals, of volcanic activity, of glacial designs. While I can replicate neither a scientific purview nor a technical vocabulary, I can (and did) pay close attention to the rocks. The Hoover Wilderness exudes color—peaks of reddish orange, others of dull brown, dark walls of gray-black rock, occasional striations of green.

Past Summit Lake all that changes. Ahead lie granite domes rising from deep-cut valleys—Yosemite National Park. Even a neophyte can see the difference, but a neophyte who has just read about the California Geological Survey can appreciate it a little more. In the early morning, it still looks like this: "slant sunlight streamed in among gilded pinnacles along the slope, . . . touching here and there, in broad dashes of yellow, the gray walls, which rose sweeping up on either hand like the sides of a ship.''

I could go on describing my two brief outings, canyon and clouds, for a good many more pages. Indeed, the longer I sit staring at my idle pen, the more details I remember. Some aren't wonderful, like the gnat attack that sent me into a personal-best sprint with thirty-five pounds on my back, or the day-long enforced march past an armada of cows placidly guarding the available springs. Most, though, are the sort that keep me going all winter—a mossy seep marked by tiny white petals, a battered yellow fungus clasping a fallen pine, a happy weasel with a mole in her mouth, a less happy chipmunk objecting to my tent, a shared shot of whiskey cut with unchlorinated water, a sunset (there's always a sunset).

"We need the tonic of wilderness," Thoreau wrote more than a century ago. He was absolutely right.

For Further Reading

Abbey, Edward. *Abbey's Road.* New York: E.P. Dutton, 1979.
———. *Desert Solitaire.* New York: Ballantine, 1968.
———. *Down the River.* New York: E.P. Dutton, 1982.
———. *The Journey Home.* New York: E.P. Dutton, 1977.
Audubon, John James. *Audubon's Wildlife.* Edited by Edwin Way Teale. New York: Viking, 1964.
Austin, Mary. *The Land of Journeys' Ending.* 1924. Tucson: University of Arizona Press, 1983.
———. *The Land of Little Rain.* 1903. Albuquerque: University of New Mexico Press, 1974.
Beebe, William. *The Log of the Sun: A Chronicle of Nature's Year.* 1906. Norwood, PA: Telegraph Books, 1982.
Berry, Wendell. *The Long-Legged House.* New York: Ballantine, 1971.
———. *The Unsettling of America.* New York: Avon, 1978.
Beston, Henry. *The Outermost House.* 1928. New York: Ballantine, 1976.
Bird, Isabella. *A Lady's Life in the Rocky Mountains.* 1879. Norman: University of Oklahoma Press, 1969.
Brautigan, Richard. *Trout Fishing in America.* New York: Dell, 1967.

Brewer, William. *Up and Down the Mountains of California, 1860–1874*. Edited by Francis P. Farquhar. Berkeley: University of California Press, 1974.

Brewster, William. *October Farm*. Cambridge: Harvard University Press, 1936.

———. *Concord River*. Cambridge: Harvard University Press, 1937.

Brooks, Paul. *The Pursuit of Wilderness*. Boston: Houghton Mifflin, 1971.

———. *Roadless Area*. New York: Ballantine, 1971.

Brower, David. *Only a Little Planet*. New York: Ballantine, 1975.

Burroughs, John. *John Burroughs' America*. Edited by Farida A. Wiley. New York: Devin-Adair, 1967.

Carr, Archie. *The Windward Road*. Gainesville: University Press of Florida, 1979.

Carrighar, Sally. *Home to the Wilderness*. New York: Penguin, 1974.

———. *One Day at Teton Marsh*. Lincoln: University of Nebraska Press, 1979.

———. *One Day on Beetle Rock*. Lincoln: University of Nebraska Press, 1978.

Carson, Rachel. *The Edge of the Sea*. Boston: Houghton Mifflin, 1979.

———. *The Sea Around Us*. 1950. New York: Signet, 1961.

———. *Silent Spring*. New York: Fawcett Crest, 1962.

———. *Under the Sea Wind*. 1941. New York: Signet, 1956.

Davis, H.L. *Kettle of Fire*. New York: William Morrow, 1957.

Devoto, Bernard, ed. *The Journals of Lewis and Clark*. Boston: Houghton Mifflin, 1953.

Dillard, Annie. *Pilgrim at Tinker Creek*. New York: Bantam, 1975.

———. *Teaching a Stone to Talk*. New York: Harper & Row, 1983.

Dutton, Clarence Edward. *Tertiary History of the Grand Canyon District*. 2 vols. 1882. Layton, UT: Gibbs M. Smith, 1985.

Eckhart, Allan W. *Wild Season*. Dayton, OH: Landfall Press, 1981.

Eiseley, Loren. *The Immense Journey*. New York: Vintage, 1953.

———. *Invisible Pyramid*. New York: Scribner's, 1972.

———. *The Night Country*. New York: Scribner's, 1971.

Emerson, Ralph Waldo. *The Portable Emerson*. Edited by Carl Bode and Malcolm Cowley. New York: Penguin, 1981.

Finch, Robert. *The Primal Place*. New York: Norton, 1983.

Fremont, John C. *Narratives of Exploration and Adventure*. Edited by Allan Nevins. New York: Longmans, Green & Co., 1956.

Graves, John. *From a Limestone Ledge*. 1980. Austin: Texas Monthly Press, 1984.

———. *Hardscrabble*. Austin: Texas Monthly Press, 1984.

———. *Goodbye to a River*. 1960. Austin: Texas Monthly Press, 1984.

Halle, Louis J. *Spring in Washington*. New York: Athenaeum, 1963.

Hay, John. *The Great Beach*. New York: Norton, 1980.

———. *The Run*. New York: Norton, 1979.

———. *The Undiscovered Country*. New York: Norton, 1984.

Hoagland, Edward. *Red Wolves and Black Bears*. 1976. New York: Penguin, 1983.

Hornaday, William Temple. *Camp-Fires on Desert and Lava*. 1908. Tucson: University of Arizona Press, 1983.

———. *Our Vanishing Wildlife*. 1913. Salem, NH: Ayer, 1970.

Janovy, John, Jr. *Back in Keith County*. Lincoln: University of Nebraska Press, 1983.

———. *Keith County Journal*. New York: St. Martin's, 1980.

Kappel-Smith, Diana. *Wintering*. New York: McGraw-Hill, 1984.

King, Clarence. *Mountaineering in the Sierra Nevada*. 1872. Lincoln: University of Nebraska Press, 1970.

Krutch, Joseph Wood. *The Desert Year*. 1951. New York: Viking, 1964.

———. *Grand Canyon*. 1958. New York: Doubleday, 1962.

LaBastille, Anne. *Women and Wilderness*. San Francisco: Sierra Club Books, 1980.

———. *Woodswoman*. New York: E.P. Dutton, 1976.

LeConte, Joseph. *A Journal of Ramblings Through the High Sierra of California*. 1875. New York: Ballantine, 1971.

Lopez, Barry. *Arctic Dreams*. New York: Scribner's, 1986.

McPhee, John. *Basin and Range*. New York: Farrar, Straus and Giroux, 1981.

———. *Coming into the Country*. New York: Bantam, 1979.

———. *Encounters with the Archdruid*. New York: Farrar, Straus and Giroux, 1971.

Madson, John. *Where the Sky Began*. San Francisco: Sierra Club Books, 1985.

Marsh, George Perkins. *Man and Nature*. 1864. Cambridge, MA: Belknap Press, 1965.

Marshall, Robert. *Alaska Wilderness*. 2nd ed. Edited and Introduction by George Marshall. Berkeley: University of California Press, 1970.

———. *Arctic Village*. New York: The Literary Guild, 1933.

Marx, Wesley. *The Frail Ocean*. New York: Ballantine, 1967.

Matthiessen, Peter. *The Snow Leopard.* New York: Bantam, 1979.

———. *The Tree Where Man Was Born.* London: Picador, 1972.

Mills, Enos. *The Grizzly.* 1919. Sausalito, CA: Comstock Editions, 1976.

Moon, William Least Heat. *Blue Highways.* New York: Fawcett Crest, 1982.

Mowat, Farley. *Never Cry Wolf.* New York: Bantam, 1975.

———. *A Whale for the Killing.* New York: Bantam, 1981.

Muir, John. *Mountaineering Essays.* Layton, UT: Gibbs M. Smith, 1980.

———. *The Mountains of California.* 1911. Berkeley, CA: Ten Speed Press, 1977.

———. *Wilderness Essays.* Layton, UT: Gibbs M. Smith, 1980.

Murie, Margaret. *Island Between.* Fairbanks: University of Alaska Press, 1977.

———. *Two in the Far North.* 2nd ed. Edmonds, WA: Alaska Northwest, 1978.

———. *Wapiti Wilderness.* New York: Knopf, 1966.

Murie, Olaus J. *Elk of North America.* 1951. Jackson, WY: Teton Bookshop, 1979.

Ogburn, Charles, Jr. *The Winter Beach.* New York: Pocket Books, 1971.

Olson, Sigurd F. *Reflections from the North Country.* New York: Knopf, 1976.

Peattie, Donald C. *An Almanac for Moderns.* 1935. Boston: Godine, 1981.

Powell, John Wesley. *Canyons of the Colorado.* 1895. Golden, CO: Outbooks, 1980.

Roosevelt, Theodore. *Ranch Life and the Hunting Trail.* 1888. Lincoln: University of Nebraska Press, 1983.

Ruess, Everett. *On Desert Trails*. El Centro, CA: Desert Magazine Press, 1940.

Russell, Andy. *Trails of a Wilderness Wanderer*. New York: Knopf, 1970.

Russell, Terry, and Renny Russell. *On the Loose*. San Francisco: Sierra Club Books, 1979.

Ryback, Eric. *The High Adventure of Eric Ryback*. San Francisco: Chronicle Books, 1971.

Seton, Ernest Thompson. *Trail of an Artist-Naturalist*. 1940. Salem, NH: Ayer, 1978.

———. *Wild Animals I Have Known*. New York: Bantam, 1957.

Sharp, Dallas L. *The Face of the Fields*. 1911. Salem, NH: Ayer, 1985.

Stegner, Wallace. *The Sound of Mountain Water*. 1969. Lincoln: University of Nebraska Press, 1985.

———, ed. *This Is Dinosaur*. Boulder, CO: Rinehart, 1985.

———. *Wolf Willow*. 1962. Lincoln: University of Nebraska Press, 1980.

Teal, John, and Mildred Teal. *Life and Death of the Salt Marsh*. New York: Ballantine, 1969.

Thomas, Lewis. *Lives of a Cell: Notes of a Biology Watcher*. New York: Viking, 1974.

———. *The Medusa and the Snail: More Notes of a Biology Watcher*. New York: Viking, 1979.

Thoreau, Henry David. *The Maine Woods*. Boston: Houghton Mifflin, 1893.

———. *The Natural History Essays*. Edited by Robert Sattelmeyer. Layton, UT: Gibbs M. Smith, 1980.

———. *The Portable Thoreau*. Edited by Carl Bode. New York: Penguin, 1980.

Torrey, Bradford. *Birds in the Bush*. Boston: Houghton Mifflin, 1895.

———. *A Rambler's Lease.* Boston: Houghton Mifflin, 1899.

Van Dyke, John C. *The Desert.* 1901. Layton, UT: Gibbs M. Smith, 1980.

Wilson, Alexander. *American Ornithology.* 1840. Salem, NH: Ayer, 1970.

Woodin, Ann. *Home Is the Desert.* Tucson: University of Arizona Press, 1984.

Wright, Mabel Osgood. *Birdcraft.* New York: Macmillan, 1925.

———. *The Friendship of Nature.* 1895. New York: Macmillan, 1906.

Zwinger, Ann. *A Desert Counry Near the Sea.* New York: Harper & Row, 1983.

———. *Beyond the Aspen Grove.* New York: Harper & Row, 1970.

———. *Run, River, Run.* 1975. Tucson: University of Arizona Press, 1984.

———. *Wind in the Rock.* New York: Harper & Row, 1978.

———, and Edwin W. Teale. *A Conscious Stillness: Two Naturalists on Thoreau's Rivers.* Amherst: University of Massachusets Press, 1984.

———, and Beatrice E. Willard. *Land Above the Trees.* New York: Harper & Row, 1972.